"Matt Livigni's *Bread* is encou extraordinary g is hope in today can help you fin ... joy and peace that is in God's Word.

Earl Musick, Christian-Speaker/Comedian/Cartoonist

"Every now and then something gives you an Aha! moment—when Scripture's truth jumps off the page and lands in your real life situation. *Journey Bread* is filled with a-ha! moments. It's a rare combination of rich theology and street-level practicality. Watch what happens if you read this book daily. You'll find an uncanny recurrence, where God speaks directly to the very situation you're facing through the reading you encounter that day. It's filled with clarity, insight, and practical application of God's truth to where we're living right now. *Journey Bread* incorporates bite-sized doses of intensely practical truth that you can carry with you and apply instantly. It's *My Utmost for His Highest* for a twenty-first-century generation."

Dr. Tom Bennardo, Senior Pastor,
Life Community Church, Hilliard, Ohio

"*Journey Bread* has helped each day of my life with a unique mix of spiritual depth and simplicity. Each day I've read it I'm snapped into a reality that (1) causes me to appreciate God's amazing Word and (2) helps me to live it in my 'real world'. 'The Bread', as I like to call it, will head you out the door with an eye on what really matters in your busy world. It has this captivating ability to peer into my complacent heart. As I read God's Word and then apply it through Matt's keen observations of life I'm always challenged to live on a higher plane that honors God."

Brian Early, Lead Pastor,
Journey Church, Huntersville, North Carolina

"*Journey Bread* has given me a way to share with others because the message is usually a one-minute read with a very useful teaching."

Debbie Keener, Arbonne International,
Independent Consultant, District Manager

"*Journey Bread* is an outstanding spiritual food for those that want to know how to follow God. God is using *Journey Bread* as a vessel for my family. It has helped feed us for the purpose of reaching souls for Christ and building a business to support the ministry."

Carole A. Turso, Founder,
www.DigiKeepsakes.com, Charlotte, North Carolina

"*Journey Bread* is real-life, curent-day scriptural encouragement that cuts to the chase and challenges the reader to lead the full Christian life of spiritual abundance through being totally sold out to Jesus. I look forwardto reading it every day."

Don Krom, Southeastern NationaLease,
General Manager

"*Journey Bread* gives me a start to each day and makes me feel complete. It has also influenced my relationship with my wife. If I see a verse that the two of us can relate to in our daily inter actions, I pass it on. We have discussed how she enjoy reading these on a regular basis. The benefits are endless."

Quinton Brantley, Continental Tire North America, Inc.,
Manager, Fleet Sales Operations and Programs

"*Journey Bread* has become my daily devotional. Thanks and may God continue to bless you and your ministry Matt!

Rick Swartz, Fleet Manager,
DH Griffin Companies, Greensboro, North Carolina

"*Journey Bread* has been the start of my day for over a year now. Matt's writings always seem to touch right where God is comforting, encouraging, or stretching me. These devotionals guide me to the realness of God's Word in my everyday life."

Sylvia Price Life Group Leader,
Journey Church, Huntersville, North Carolina

"Journey Bread has been an inspiration for me. It seems like every day the message lifts me up and really lets me see others and myself as real people with real hope for our future."

Dave Flowers, Maintenance Manager,
Carolina Tank Lines, Inc.

"I have loved your beautiful style of writing since the first time I read Journey Bread. The writings are so full of truth, and the Holy Spirit can be seen speaking through you urging all readers to continue to follow Christ and to lift Him up and experience his wonderful blessings and deep love he has for us all. Very, very well done."

Julie Lancaster

"I look forward each day to reading Journey Bread. It has been a source of encouragement for me each day and some days it was just what I needed for encouragement during an experience I was having at that particular time."

Janet Kirkman, Women's Bible Study Leader,
Charlotte, North Carolina

"Journey Bread has been my daily reminder to connect with God. Matt Livigni gives insightful and honest teachings that challenge you daily to stay connected."

Joel McNelly,
Journey Church Elder, Huntersville, North Carolina

"The insight and wisdom that Matt brings to light through the Bible versesthat he highlights has never failed to make me think and learn and want to be a better person. I love the Journey Bread!"

Donna Early, Director, Worship and Creative Arts, Journey Church Member, Huntersville, North Carolina

"Journey Bread is a great way to start my day, focusing on what truly is important: life with Christ. Matt has a natural talent of relating the Scripture of the day into what is really happening in the world today. Very inspirational and motivating to live a better life with our Savior Jesus."

Tom Gavin, Sales Account Executive

"Journey Bread devotions are such a spiritual highlight for my day. Not only are they an encouragement, but a wonderful teaching lesson of the Scripture for the day explained so well in Matt's message."

Nancy Straw, Guest Relations, The Chapel–Akron Campus

"Matt Livigni has a very unique way of spreading life's jams over slices of the Word. This daily Journey Bread reminds me that there is no better way then to start your day in God's Word. I wake up each morning with the Journey Bread."

Earl Musick, Cartoonist-Speaker/Comedian

JOURNEY
BREAD

JOURNEY
BREAD

FIVE-MINUTE MEALS
FOR THE SOUL

MATT **LIVIGNI**

TATE PUBLISHING & Enterprises

Published by Tate Publishing & Enterprises, LLC
127 E. Trade Center Terrace | Mustang, Oklahoma 73064 USA
1.888.361.9473 | www.tatepublishing.com

Tate Publishing is committed to excellence in the publishing industry. The company reflects the philosophy established by the founders, based on Psalm 68:11,
"The Lord gave the word and great was the company of those who published it."

Book design copyright © 2008 by Tate Publishing, LLC. All rights reserved.
Cover Design by Lynly Taylor
Interior design by Kandi Evans

Published in the United States of America
ISBN: 978-1-60462-974-3
1. Christian Living: Spiritual Growth: General
08.05.27

DEDICATION

This book is dedicated to my loving wife, Paula, who is truly my most treasured gift from God outside of his saving grace. The patience, self-sacrifice, and unconditional love that she shows in support of me pursuing my dreams has been the fuel that keeps me pressing on each day in my own journey of knowing God, becoming more like him, and using my gifts for his glory. She is my best friend, the only one who truly understands me, and a treasure that I will enjoy and give all of my love to forever!

ACKNOWLEDGMENTS

First and foremost, I would like to thank my Lord and Savior, Jesus Christ, who for the last two and a half years since I started writing these devotions has never failed to place a word on my heart while studying his Word, which was destined to be shared with his people to encourage and challenge and inspire in his awesome love! Second, my deepest thanks goes out to Brian and Donna Early, the founders of Journey Church in Huntersville, North Carolina, whose commitment and faith to reach out and share the love of Christ to the people of greater Charlotte inspired me to start utilizing my own God-given talents and gifts through writing these daily devotions for their congregation. Last but certainly not least, I would like to thank all of the other saints, both near and afar, that have encouraged me in my own personal journey and through their godly example have been the encouragement and inspiration that I have needed to surrender completely to God in order that he could use these daily writings to encourage and touch the hearts of many.

FOREWORD

I've heard it said that the greatest gift we can bring to ministry is a healthy, joyful, loving, vital self. Matt does just that.

He loves God, loves the church, loves people, and lives every day seeking to make God's words relevant to his own life. In an effort to help himself stay on track with God, he decided to start journaling his journey through the Word. When he realized how much this encouraged him to apply what he learned in his everyday life, he offered to share his thoughts with others. Two years later he's still helping to make God's Word relevant to all of us. This book flows out of Matt's unshakable conviction that Jesus is the answer!

Matt has been my friend for the past few years. I've watched him walk through personal struggles and celebrate personal and professional victories. I've seen him live out his walk with God in his marriage, in his work, and even through struggles with sin. He doesn't pretend to be something he's not. He's the real deal and his writing bears that out. Matt has never met a stranger, so journey with him as a friend through these daily devotions and nourish your soul.

Donna Early
Director, Worship and Creative Arts
Journey Church–Huntersville, North Carolina

UNCHARTERED GROUND

He told them this parable: "No one tears a patch from a new garment, and sows it on an old one. If he does, he will have torn the new garment, and the patch from the new will not match the old. And no one pours new wine into old wineskins. If he does, the new wine will burst the skins, the wine will run out and the wineskins will be ruined. No, new wine must be poured into new wineskins. And no one after drinking old wine wants the new, for he says, 'the old is better.'"

Luke 5:36–39

Much can be learned through this awesome parable by Jesus where he is trying to illustrate how a life that has been transformed through a relationship with him should look and act differently than the old self that was apart from Christ. You see, Jesus is trying to explain in this parable that you can't give your life to him and then try to adapt his ways to your old lifestyle; he says that if you try to do this then your new life that you have found in him will be "torn" and that you will no longer fit in to the lifestyle that you once had since your life is different now that you have received this free gift of salvation and relationship with God Almighty. I experienced this firsthand at a New Year's Eve celebration. As I watched the crowd bringing in the New Year with festive attire (that was far too revealing, I might add) and drinking themselves into oblivion, I felt just a little out of place—like a new patch that had been sewn on an old garment. There was a time in my life when I really enjoyed this kind of thing, but over the years God has shown me how keeping a clean and sober mind and heart that is fully devoted to him can be so indescribably rewarding and full of blessings.

I had an attitude that evening that a person who has never experienced that peace and joy that I am speaking of would not understand. You see, being a Christ follower and living your life for him means that you will enter unchartered ground, and things that may have been fun and fulfilling for you in the past will no longer satisfy you since your heart is now thirsty for new experiences that draw you closer to the Lord and make you more like him! So today, don't get drawn back in to your old patterns of life that will only leave you with feelings of disappointment and regret, but instead seek the Lord for direction and guidance on living your new life for him. Seek God with all of your heart and let his love transform and mold your heart and life into the masterpiece that he is making with you.

LORD OF ALL

One Sabbath, Jesus was going through the grain fields, and His Disciples began to pick some heads of grain, rub them in their hands and eat the kernels. Some of the Pharisees asked, "Why are you doing what is unlawful on the Sabbath?"

Jesus answered them, "Have you never read what David did when he and his companions were hungry? He entered the house of God, and taking the consecrated bread, he ate what is lawful only for priests to eat. And he also gave some to his companions." Then Jesus said to them, "The Son of Man is Lord of the Sabbath."

Luke 6: 1–5

The Pharisees here just didn't get it! They continued all throughout the New Testament to follow the rules that God laid down for them instead of getting to know the Maker of the rules and learning from Jesus who ultimately is Lord of everything including the Law that was written down by Moses so many years ago. You see, Jesus was not interested in someone who just followed the rules; what he was interested in was someone that followed him and made him the Lord of his or her life through a deepening, interactive relationship with the Son of God. And let me tell you that Jesus is still the same today; he never changes! Even today he is not interested in a legalistic Christian that tries to follow the rules and be perfectly holy in everyone's sight, but what he is looking for is someone who admits she can't live this life on her own—someone who surrenders control of her heart and mind to his lordship and enters into a relationship with him where he is the most important thing in her life. The rules and boundaries that God has put into place are not the most important things; what other people think of them is not the most important thing. What is important is a living, breathing relationship with God Almighty, where he knows and shares your deepest needs, desires, longings, successes, and failures, all because you have taken time out of the busyness of this life to get to know him and spend time communicating and committing all of the issues of your life to his faithful and loving hands to do with as he pleases. God is looking for your heart, not your works. Works do come eventually, but they come as a result of a heart that has surrendered to the lordship of Jesus Christ!

My wife and I were recently having a discussion about how much wine is too much wine. What God has shown me since that discussion is that I was missing the point and that sometimes I act just like the Pharisees did and pay too much attention to the rules and my focus gets distorted from where it should be—on the Maker of the rules and my own relationship with him! For this I must apologize, but thanks be to God for his amazing grace and the work that he is doing in all of our lives to make us more like him!

LOVE YOUR ENEMIES

"But I tell you who hear me: Love your enemies, do good to those who curse you, pray for those who mistreat you. If someone strikes you on one cheek, turn to him the other also. If someone takes your cloak, do not stop him from taking your tunic. Give to everyone who asks you, and if anyone takes what belongs to you, do not demand it back. Do to others as you would have them do to you.

If you love those who love you, what credit is that to you? Even sinners love those who love them. And if you do good to those who are good to you, what credit is that to you? Even 'sinners' do that. And if you lend to those from whom you expect repayment, what credit is that to you? Even 'sinners' lend to 'sinners' expecting to be repaid in full. But love your enemies, do good to them, and lend to them without expecting to get anything back. Then your reward will be great, and you will be sons of the Most High, because He is kind to the ungrateful and wicked. Be merciful, just as your Father is merciful."

Luke 6:27–36

How hard is this command from our heavenly Father? It definitely does not come naturally for me, as I am sure it doesn't for you either. But see, that is the whole point, isn't it? It takes the power of the Holy Spirit to actually love people around you that hate you and hurl insults and throw backstabbing blows and betray your confidence and maybe even steal, lie, and cheat, their efforts aimed directly at you. But if you are connected to the power source of this world—Jesus Christ—then you do have the power to love these people unconditionally and show them and others who are watching that the power of God is a very real part of your life. In order for the lost people of this world to believe in God and have a relationship with him as you do, they need to see Jesus Christ for who he really is, living in and through your very life. If you love your enemies out of a sincere heart like we are commanded here by Jesus, then they will see him and believe that he is real and as a result, your life will be blessed beyond belief because of your obedience to him! Draw near to him today and ask him for the power to make a difference in this world in which we live!

HEART PROBLEM

No good tree bears bad fruit, nor does a bad tree bear good fruit. Each tree is recognized by its own fruit. People do not pick figs from thorn bushes, or grapes from briers. The good man brings good things out of the good stored up in his heart, and the evil man brings evil things out of the evil stored up in his heart. For out of the overflow of his heart his mouth speaks.

Luke 6:43–45

I saw a documentary on the new CEO of Sony. The one thing that this gentleman said that stuck out the most to me was the fact that he only got to spend a few days a month with his wife and kids as a result of his rigorous travel schedule. Hearing this broke my heart as I thought about how lonely and fleeting that kind of life can be, running up the corporate ladder. You see, a few years ago that was me—racing up the corporate ladder, wanting more money, more respect, taking up roots, and moving from state to state in order to achieve what? The pride and power of being in senior management? More responsibility that would keep me from my wife, friends, family, and church? Now don't get me wrong, I see nothing wrong with trying to achieve success in the business world, but for me, it had become my primary focus and was distracting my attention away from many more blessings that God had for me—blessings that would far outweigh any title or position, blessings like having the time and mind-set to write this book, or like living in the same place for more than two years that enabled my wife and I to build solid friendships and get firmly rooted in a wonderful church where God is doing amazing things, blessings like having an indescribable peace about my life that enables me to enjoy each and every day and to soak in all that God has to reveal to my heart throughout the day.

For many years of my life I had a heart problem in that God did not have control of my whole heart. I was keeping part of it back, thinking foolishly that I knew what would make me happy in this life and I was going to race through this life trying to make that happen, when what I was really doing was racing farther from the only one who could fulfill me and bring me the happiness, joy, and fulfillment that I was looking for! God knows exactly what you need! He designed you and put you here on this earth for a reason and he wants to start using you right now for that very purpose for which he created you—that purpose that is found in him that will bring you more joy in this life than you can ever imagine. The key to staring this amazing journey in him is that you must first surrender your whole heart to his loving hands; you must put aside your own selfish motives and selfish desires that this world would make you believe are going to fulfill you and make you happy, and you must start trusting and getting to know the God of this world who loves you and wants the very best for your life! Surrender everything to him and he will give you a heart that bears good fruit and will last for all eternity.

A RESPONSIVE HEART

Because your heart was responsive and you humbled yourself before the Lord when you heard what I have spoken against this place and its people, that they would become accursed and laid waste, and because you tore your robes and wept in my presence, I have heard you, declares the Lord.

2 Kings 22:19

Here in the Old Testament we read about King Josiah, who happened to find the book of God's Law that had been written many years before his reign as King. He read the book, which foretold of God's anger against his people for disobedience and that God was going to destroy the Israelites because of their lack of faith in him. Not an encouraging read, I am sure, but we see here how King Josiah responded to the Word of God by humbling himself before him and inquiring as to how he could make things right, even with tears in his eyes and a torn robe. Because of his humbling response to God, God hears his prayer and saves him from the terrible disasters that were about to happen. For some of you, as you delve into God's Word and are convicted by the Holy Spirit of actions that God wants you take in order to have a closer relationship with him, that might not be an encouraging read for you either as you are challenged by God to make a change in your life.

But look at the reward: the God of this world hears King Josiah's prayer and saves him from the wrath of God's anger and all of the destruction that was about to take place, all because he had a responsive heart and humbled himself before the Lord, seeking his direction. All that God asks of you and me is to listen for his voice and direction through studying his Word and then to respond in obedience to what we have read by humbling ourselves and obeying what he commands. He wants responsive hearts that love him so much that they take time out of their busy day for him and then act on what he has to tell them. And the act can be as simple as just humbling yourself before the Lord and letting his Spirit take control of your heart and life through setting your own personal agendas and selfish motives aside, letting go of the control of your life, and placing it in the hands of a loving God!

What kind of response do you have for whatever God's Spirit is convicting you of today? Maybe God is asking you to surrender your heart for the very first time to him; maybe his Spirit is convicting your heart to be obedient to him by being baptized in his name so that the world will see and know that you have truly surrendered your heart and life to Jesus Christ; maybe he is asking you to finally let go of that one thing that you have been hanging on to in this life, that one sin that has been separating you from all the great things that God wants to do with your life here on this earth. Whatever it is, I would encourage you to respond to him today by humbling yourself and surrendering your whole heart to his loving hands, and then you will see God move in and through your life like never before! Humbly respond in love and obedience to him today.

FLOODS OF LIFE

Why do you call me "Lord, Lord" and do not do what I say? I will show you what he is like who comes to me and hears my words and puts them into practice. He is like a man building a house, who dug down deep and laid the foundation on rock. When a flood came, the torrent struck that house but could not shake it, because it was well built. But the one who hears my words and does not put them into practice is like a man who built a house on the ground without a foundation. The moment the torrent struck that house, it collapsed and its destruction was complete.

Luke 6:46–49

One thing that I know for sure about the floods of life is that we live in a fallen world, and that means that you can be sure that trials and temptations will come your way many times throughout your life. The question that you need to answer is whether or not you are ready for what this world is about to throw at you. Have you built your house on solid ground? Do you have a relationship with Jesus Christ where you spend time with him in his Word and obey what he tells you to do? There have been times in my life when I have been disappointed, lonely, and defeated with seemingly no light at the end of the dark tunnel that I was in; in these times the only thing that I had to hold on to was the fact that I had a God who loved me and wanted the best for my life, and ultimately I knew deep down that eventually he would pull me out of the dark valley in which I found myself and turn everything around for good so that his glory could be revealed in my life.

Sometimes life will throw you a curve ball and things that happen to you just don't make sense and no matter how hard you try, you can't understand why things are as they are or even how to make them better. It is in these times that if you have entrusted your life into the hands of Almighty God and have built a solid foundation in him and been obedient to his direction and guidance for your life that you won't be shaken because God himself will be there to carry you through the storm and protect you in the shadow of his wings, comforting you with his peace, love, and forgiveness all the while. Be ready for the storm!

HEART OF GOD

Soon afterward, Jesus went to a town called Nain, and His disciples and a large crowd went along with Him. As he approached the town gate, a dead person was being carried out—the only son of his mother, and she was a widow. And a large crowd from the town was with her. When the Lord saw her, his heart went out to her and said, "Don't cry."

Luke 7:11–13

You know, sometimes in this fallen world you might feel all alone, battered and bruised, not unlike this poor woman from Nain that had lost her husband and now seemingly her only son. The good news this morning is that you are not alone! The God of this world knows exactly where you are, why you are hurting, and how to make you better! Luke tells us here that Jesus' heart went out to this lady so much that he tells her not to cry, and this same heart that hasn't changed is going out to you today—right were you are—and is saying, "Don't cry, I am here for you, I love you, and I will comfort you and make things better because you are so important to me that I gave my life to be with you so that I could carry you through this trial that you are in."

Later in the chapter, Jesus raised this widow's son from the dead. He might not change your circumstances in such a dramatic way, but today he offers to you something that is much more real and goes far deeper than what the eye can see. He offers you a relationship with him where his Spirit actually dwells inside of you and gives you an indescribable peace and joy that will follow you wherever you find yourself in this sinful world in which we live. God hears your cry this morning. You are not alone; he loves you more than you can imagine. Let his love and mercy heal your wounds and give you something to live for once again!

AT THE FEET OF JESUS

Now one of the Pharisees invited Jesus to have dinner with Him, so He went to the Pharisee's house and reclined at the table. When a woman who had lived a sinful life in that town learned that Jesus was eating at the Pharisee's house, she brought an alabaster jar of perfume, and she stood behind Him at His feet weeping, she began to wet His feet with her tears. Then she wiped them with her hair, kissed them and poured perfume on them. When the Pharisee who had invited Him saw this, he said to himself, "If this man were a prophet, he would know who is touching Him and what kind of woman she is—that she is a sinner."

Luke 7:36–39

There is something about Jesus that is so powerful—a love that is so genuine and forgiveness that is so real that it would cause a prostitute to go into the house of the most judgmental, legalistic people of that time—a Pharisee—with the faith that Jesus would indeed forgive her of her sins no matter how despicable they were. This is a great reminder of how we, as his temple here on earth, should be in regards to the ungodly and lost people that are all around us! When a lost person comes into contact with you, does he or she experience this same kind of love and forgiveness, or does he or she just experience some of the same judgmental attitudes that everyone else exhibits toward him or her? You see, it is going to take a supernatural act of love and forgiveness in order for that person to see and know that God is real, and you are the person that God wants to use today in order to reflect his love to those around you! Maybe today you need to spend some time at the feet of Jesus so that you will truly understand how much he has forgiven you in order that you can turn around and forgive others with the same unconditional love and grace that God has so freely offered to you. Don't blend into the crowd today; be a light to those around you, a safe harbor where people can feel accepted, loved, and truly forgiven! Share the love of Jesus today so that others may see and believe!

FAITH

Jesus said to the woman, "Your faith has saved you; go in peace."

Luke 7:50

Jesus is saying this to the sinful woman who came to kneel at Jesus' feet and ask forgiveness of her sins. Jesus says here that her faith has saved her. What does it mean to have faith? Many people miss the reality of what faith really is. Some people today confuse "faith" with "believe." To just believe in God is much different than putting your faith and trust in him. To believe that a parachute will save you when you jump out of a plane at 10,000 feet in the air is one thing, but to actually jump is something much bigger! Faith requires action: the action of being baptized after you have surrendered your heart and life to Jesus Christ; the action of getting to know your new savior by spending time in his Word; the action of obeying what he teaches you in his word; the action of resisting the temptations of the enemy and running the other direction from sin; the action of loving and forgiving those that have hurt you; the action of communicating with the God of this universe in prayer; the action of letting God be in control of everything that you say and do! God says in James 2:19: "You believe that there is one God. Good! Even the demons believe that—and shudder." True faith is indeed much more than just belief. Put your faith in him today!

SOIL OF YOUR HEART

A farmer went out to sow his seed. As he was scattering the seed, some fell the path; it was trampled on, and the birds of the air ate it up. Some fell on rock, and when it came up, the plants withered because they had no moisture. Other seed fell among thorns, which grew up with it and choked the plants. Still other seed fell on good soil. It came up and yielded a crop, a hundred times more than was sown. When He said this, He called out, "He who has ears to hear, let him hear." His disciples asked him what this parable meant. He said, "The knowledge of the secrets of the Kingdom of God has been given to you, but to others I speak in parables, so that, though seeing they may not see; though hearing, they may not understand."

This is the meaning of the parable: The seed is the word of God. Those along the path are the ones who hear, and then the devil comes and takes away the word from their hearts, so that they may not believe and be saved. Those on the rock are ones who receive the word with joy when they hear it, but they have no root. They believe for awhile, but in the time of testing they fall away. The seed that fell among thorns stands for those who hear, but as they go on their way they are choked by life's worries, riches and pleasures, and they do not mature. But the seed on good soil stands for those with a noble and good heart, who hear the word, retain it, and by persevering produce a crop.

Luke 8: 5–15

When we first got married, my wife and I planted a garden on the perimeter of a huge fence that enclosed the backyard of our house. This was a lot of fun at first, watching the plants grow and enjoying the beauty of them as we relaxed with friends and family admiring the results of all our hard work. This gardening thing, however, became a huge burden to us as we learned how dry it can get in the summertime in North Carolina and what these ugly green things called weeds were that grew up all around our once beautiful flowers surrounding our fence. The once enthusiastic task of gardening soon became way too time consuming and far too much of a burden to enjoy, so after about a year we moved into a condominium complex and have chosen to live the low-maintenance lifestyle of a condo or town home ever since.

Thank goodness that our heavenly Father never tires of removing the thorns and weeds that take root in the soil of our hearts so that they will not stunt our growth as believers in him! I am not sure about you, but I find thorns that appear around my heart on a daily basis that God is so gracious to make me aware of and then delicately remove as only the Master Gardener can! Just think what would happen if God chose the low-maintenance lifestyle and left us to ourselves to be choked out by the thorns and the weeds of this world that seem to separate us from him. Don't miss that last part of this passage that gives us the three keys to living a successful Christian life: "Hear the word, retain it, and persevere"! To persevere through times of weeding and pruning by our Lord and Savior may be the toughest one of the three, but the result of a beautiful crop (which is a heart that has matured in Christ and daily walks with God) is well worth the effort, both for us and even more so for him!

Guard your heart today! Let the seed of God's Word be firmly rooted in good soil so that he can create a beautiful crop for the rest of the world to see and then believe that he is God!

OVERCOME WITH FEAR

They sailed to the region of the Gerasenes, which is across the lake from Galilee. When Jesus stepped ashore, he was met by a demon-possessed man from the town. For a long time this man had not worn clothes or lived in a house, but had lived in tombs. When he saw Jesus, he cried out and fell at His feet, shouting at the top of His voice, "What do you want with me, Jesus, Son of the Most High God? I beg you, don't torture me!" For Jesus had commanded the evil spirit to come out of the man. Many times it had seized him, and though he was chained hand and foot and kept under guard, he had broken his chains and had been driven by the demon into solitary places.

Jesus asked him, "What is your name?"

"Legion," he replied, because many demons had gone into him. And they begged him repeatedly not to order them to go into the Abyss. A large herd of pigs was feeding there on the hillside. The demons begged Jesus to let them go into them, and he gave them permission. When the demons came out of the man, they went into the pigs, and the herd rushed down the steep bank into the lake and was drowned. When those tending the pigs saw what had happened, they ran off and reported this in the town and countryside, and the people went out to see what had happened. When they came to Jesus, they found the man from whom the demons had gone out, sitting at Jesus' feet, dressed and in his right mind; and they were afraid. Those who had seen it told the people how the demon-possessed man had been cured. Then all of the people of the region of the Gerasenes asked Jesus to leave them, because they were overcome with fear. So He got into the boat and left.

Luke 8:26–37

The spiritual reality of life can be very scary to people who do not understand what is happening and who don't have the key to being victorious in that third realm by having a relationship with

Jesus Christ. Like it or not, there are angels and demons that are all around you who are battling for control of your mind and heart, and decisions that you make today will have an effect on who will ultimately win the battle. I find it ironic that these people of Gerasenes sent away the only one who could save them from the very thing that frightened them—the evil and satanic forces that are present in this fallen world in which we live.

Jesus Christ has won the battle for your heart by giving his life for you on a Cross, and the only thing that needs to be done in order to be victorious in the battle for your heart is to draw near to him and to accept the free gift of salvation and freedom that is already there for the taking. It is done! The price has been paid in full for the sin in your life; God has already won the battle for your heart and he longs for you to accept the prize that he so lovingly gave his life for in order that he can once again have a relationship with you, his most prized possession that he loves with a love that goes so deep—a love that consumes, fulfills, and brings joy and peace! Seek Jesus today with all of your heart, surrender you heart and mind to his control, and discover a whole new world!

TRAPPED AND ALONE

He brought me out into a spacious place; He rescued me because He delighted in me.

Psalm 18:19

Living the Christian life in this fallen world can be very hard, and at times you will feel lonely and may even want to give up and give in to the evil and godlessness that is present all around you. At times you may feel like you are the only one who is trying to stay pure in the eyes of God, and you may even feel like your light for him is dimming, and you may wonder if anyone cares or notices, if your life even means anything or is worthwhile at all for the Kingdom of God. The good news today is that someone does care! Someone cares so much that he will indeed rescue you from this pit of sin and despair that you may find yourself trapped in for a short time on this earth! He cares so much that he died a terrible death on a Cross so that he could be a very real part of your life, all because he delights in you! The God of this world delights in your company and wants so much to have a relationship with you where he can bless you and love you and give you everything that you need, everything that you desire, everything that you could ever hope for or dream about in this life! He notices your struggles; he wants to deliver you and bring you out into a "spacious place" where you are delivered from the junk of this world and free to just love him back and live your life for him—a place where you are free to enjoy all of incredible blessings that he has for you.

Today, God loves you more than you can ever imagine! He delights in your company and wants to bless you in this life with his presence, and all that he asks of you in order to receive his blessings and his best for you life is to surrender control of your heart and mind to him in order that he can mold and shape them into the beautiful masterpiece that he has always intended for your life to be. God loves you. He delights in your company and is waiting for your love and devotion.

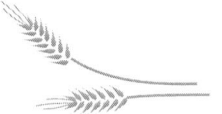

COMPLETE TRUST IN GOD

When Jesus had called the twelve together, he gave them power and authority to drive out all demons and to cure diseases, and he sent them out to preach the Kingdom of God and to heal the sick. He told them: "Take nothing for the journey—no staff, no bag, no bread, no money, no extra tunic."

Luke 9:1–3

I find it interesting here that as the twelve disciples are sent out by Jesus for the first time by themselves to spread the Good News that he deliberately told them to take absolutely nothing with them; they were completely dependent upon God for their provision along the journey.

Did you know that if you have accepted Jesus Christ as your personal Savior that Jesus calls you one of his disciples today? Did you know also that the same principle of having to trust completely in God for direction, power, and provision still holds true today as we go out into the world as his disciples and share with others what God has done in our lives? Nothing that we have to offer of ourselves can even begin to compare with the greatness of God and his Spirit as he works in and through the life of one of his children who does nothing more but make himself available to be used by God and then gives him the glory in the end! Now don't get me wrong, I believe that education and financial success are good and that God can use both of these to do great things for his Kingdom; however, the point that I am trying to make here is that you don't have to be a biblical scholar, a financial success, or even feel like you have this whole Christian-living thing figured out in order to be used by God in a great way. The only thing that needs to be done is to prayerfully commit your way to him each day and then to completely trust in him for power and direction on how you should live moment by moment—if you do this then you will see God move in and through you life like never before!

God is calling you today to be his disciple and to spread the Good News of how he has touched your life with other people that you come in contact with! Answer the call! Completely surrender your heart and mind to him today and then hang on for dear life as his Spirit will overwhelm you with power and love as you reach others in the world for him!

SACRIFICIAL SERVITUDE

Then He said to them all: "If anyone would come after me, he must deny himself and take up his cross daily and follow me. For whoever wants to save his life will lose it, but whoever loses his life for me will save it. What good is it for a man to gain the whole world, and yet lose or forfeit his very self?"

Luke 8:23–25

To be a Christian is much more than just praying a prayer one time asking for repentance and forgiveness in order to be saved. To be a Christian is to daily die to your own selfish desires and emotions in order to obey and live in obedience to our heavenly Father. It is a moment-by-moment relationship with our heavenly Father in which we focus all of our attention on him—so much so that it is impossible for the devil to deceive us or to entice our attention away since we are zeroed in on the only one who could give us the power to live in such a way: Jesus Christ! It is a mind-set that we take every morning and even at times throughout the day to live our life in a way that is pleasing to the Lord and in a way that will enable his Spirit to work through our lives to reach other people for him. It really is like taking up our own cross since we crucify our old self in order to live in him—to realize God's best for our lives by living the life that God had always planned for us to live! It is not giving in to emotions of bitterness and hatred, but to the contrary, it is forgiving unconditionally, no matter what the circumstance. It is wiping out that thought of lust from your mind instead of letting it take hold and ultimately steal your heart away from God. It is admitting that you are wrong when you so want to be right. It is seeing people around you with the eyes of your heart, not judging them but instead loving them so much that they might want to inquire about what makes you different and ultimately come to know our awesome Lord for themselves! It is a sacrificial lifestyle that can only be lived by one who has a daily relationship with Jesus Christ where he or she spends time getting to know him and is tuned in to his Spirit and direction moment by moment. It is everything that you will ever want or could ever hope to be. It really is an abundant life that is full of love and joy, purpose and meaning, happiness and laughter, ultimate fulfillment and eternal hope. I pray that you will find this life today!

RADICAL CHRISTIANITY

If anyone is ashamed of me and my words, the Son of Man will be ashamed of him when he comes in His glory and in the glory of the Father and of the Holy Angels. I tell you the truth, some who are standing here will not taste death before they see the Kingdom of God.

Luke 9:26–27

The Kingdom of God is as real today as it was back in the time of Jesus, and we are called as Christians to live a life of radical obedience to God, loving everyone around us with God's supernatural, unconditional love that draws people to him. There is no time to let the man-made religious correctness and tolerance get in the way of spreading the good news of how God has changed your life for the better and "how" he died so that all people could come to know him in a personal way.

So today, don't be ashamed, but let someone else know what God is doing in your life and how surrendering your life to him has made all the difference for you in this life on earth. Yes, the best testimony is to live out your life like Jesus Christ lived his; however, there are times when God calls us to use words and not to be ashamed to speak his name and tell of all the wonderful things that knowing him and having a relationship with him has done for you in your life. So pray now that God would give you an opportunity to share your faith with someone today and that he would give you the words to say and use your testimony to make a difference in someone else's life!

LIFE WITH GOD

And David became more and more powerful, because the Lord almighty was with him.

1 Chronicles 11:9

Just like King David had much success in governing the people of Israel as a direct result of his relationship with God, you too will have much success, peace, and happiness in this life if you walk with God. Life does not have to be as hard as we make it out to be; it gets hard when we separate ourselves from the power source, the one who gives us everything that we need, everything that we desire, and everything that we live for in this life. God has a perfect plan for your life. He has a perfect plan for you and for how he will use you to dramatically impact the world around you for him. He is waiting for you to connect with him so he can show you what this life is all about. He is waiting for you to walk with him each day so that he can fill you with more love, purpose, meaning, and joy than you could ever imagine! Don't be deceived by the enemy and think that your way of living will make you happy. Surrender your heart, your mind, and everything that you are to the God of this world today and start living life as it was meant to be lived—start living life with God.

SOMETHING BIG IS HAPPENING

About eight days after Jesus said this, he took Peter, John and James with Him as He went up onto a mountain to pray. As He was pray-ing, the appearance of His face changed, and His clothes became as bright as a flash of lightning. Two men, Moses and Elijah, appeared in glorious splendor, talking with Jesus. They spoke about His departure, which He was about to bring to fulfillment at Jerusalem. Peter and his companions were very sleepy, but when they became fully awake, they saw His glory and the two men standing with Him. As the men were leaving Jesus, Peter said to him, "Master, it is good for us to be here. Let us put up three shelters—one for you, one for Moses and one for Elijah." (He did not know what he was saying.) While he was still speaking, a cloud appeared and enveloped them, and they were afraid as they entered the cloud.

A voice came from the cloud, saying, "This is my son, whom I have chosen; listen to Him. When the voice had spoken, they found Jesus was alone. The disciples kept this to themselves, and told no one at the time what they had seen."

Luke 9:28–36

Moses, the Old Testament deliverer; Elijah, a prophet who would foretell of all the great miracles of God that were about to come; Jesus, the Son of God who paid the ultimate sacrifice in order to save the human race, and now, you, a son or daughter of the Most High with Jesus Christ living inside of you and using you and your talents in order to show the rest of the world who doesn't know him yet that he is indeed alive and that they too can live forever in him! This is the final act of a great epic that is playing out in your life here on earth!

As a Christian, you have an important role to play during your limited time here on earth. God wants to use you in a great way to reach other people in the world for him. Don't let the enemy distract you away from your mission to live your life for God and to share his love with other people around you. It is so easy to get wrapped up in your own little world and miss out on the great things that God wants to do in and through your very life. Even Jesus, the Son of God, had to spend time in prayer with God each day in order to maintain the right perspective and be victorious in his mission, which was to give his life in order that you could be saved and have eternal life in him. Now it is your turn to carry out your mission here on earth. Do you even know what that mission is or what gifts God has given you to use to make a difference in other people's lives for him? Spend some time in prayer with him today! Get connected to the power source, ask him to show you what your part is to play, and then relentlessly act it out, keeping your eyes straight ahead on him. Your time on earth is short and your role to play is huge. Spread the love of Jesus Christ today!

BECOMING GREAT IN GOD'S KINGDOM

An argument started among the disciples as to which of them would be the greatest. Jesus, knowing their thoughts, took a little child and had him stand beside him. Then He said to them, "Whoever welcomes this little child in my name welcomes me; and whoever welcomes me welcomes the one who sent me. For he who is least among you—he is the greatest."

Luke 9:46–48

The secret to becoming a great man or woman of God is to spend less time concerned about yourself and your own interests, desires, and ambitions and more time looking out for the interests of others because of your love and reverence for God Almighty! It is so easy in this world in which we live to get wrapped up in self and much harder to genuinely care about the needs of people around you. When was the last time that you called a friend for no other reason than to see how he or she is doing and to listen to everything that is happening in his or her life? When was the last time you smiled at the cashier in the grocery store and asked how he or she is doing, not just saying the words but genuinely listening and caring about what is going on in his or her life? When was the last time you gave money to a struggling family, prepared a meal for a family in need, spent time talking with a lonesome elderly person in a nursing home, took time away from your important duties to just "be there" for someone who needed a friend? All of these things are so easy to do if we as Christians will focus our eyes outside of ourselves to God Almighty and look for opportunities in which we can serve him and genuinely love others! I am as guilty as anyone for becoming self-consumed and wrapped up in my own little world, so I pray, God, change our hearts today to become more like you and more concerned about other people. Help us to deny ourselves and love others so that they too can enter in to a loving relationship with you!

CHOOSE TODAY WHOM YOU WILL SERVE

Jesus replied, "No one who puts his hand to the plow and looks back is fit for service in the Kingdom of God."

Luke 9:62

You cannot live a successful Christian life if you are still hanging on to parts of your old way of life and old fleshly desires. Were you serious when you prayed that prayer and asked Jesus to come into your heart? If so, then don't look back for even a minute to your old ways of life but keep your eyes focused straight ahead on Christ! Run to him with all of your might; relentlessly pursue this relationship with God that will bring you an abundant life that is full of meaning, purpose, joy, and peace. Don't for a second consider feeding your old fleshly desires that only lead to disappointment and despair, but instead let God's Spirit lead you into this amazing life in Christ that we all so undeservedly can have from now until the rest of eternity!

The Apostle Paul said it this way in Philippians 3:13: "But one thing I do: Forgetting what is behind and straining toward what is ahead, I press on toward the goal to win the prize for which God has called me heavenward in Christ Jesus." Surrender all to him today!

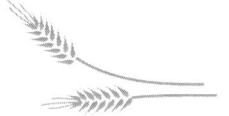

PLENTIFUL HARVEST

After this the Lord appointed seventy-two others and sent them two by two ahead of Him to every town and place where He was about to go. He told them, "The harvest is plentiful, but the workers are few. Ask the Lord of the harvest, therefore, to send out workers into His harvest field. Go! I am sending you out like lambs among wolves. Do not take a purse or bag or sandals; and do not greet anyone on the road."

Luke 10:1–4

We live in a world where people are lonely, hurting, unsatisfied, unfilled, heartbroken, and empty and in desperate need of a Savior. The harvest is plentiful! People everywhere have hearts that are ripe for the Gospel of Jesus Christ! There is a sense of urgency as Jesus sends out the seventy-two ahead of him that is obvious since Jesus tells them not to greet anyone on the road as they go. That same sense of urgency is present today as we as Christians live our lives in a way that reflects the love of Christ to everyone with whom we come into contact. Remember today that it is not about us—it is all about him and spreading his love so that other people may see and believe.

MY REFUGE; MY STRENGTH; MY EVERYTHING

Yet I am always with you; you hold me by my right hand.

You guide me with your counsel, and afterward you will take me into glory.

Whom have I in heaven but you? And earth has nothing I desire besides you.

My flesh and my heart may fail,

but God is the strength of my heart and my portion forever.

Those who are far from you will perish; you destroy all who are unfaithful to you.

But as for me, it is good to be near to God.

I have mad the Sovereign Lord my refuge; I will tell of all your deeds.

Psalm 73:23–28

How great is our God? He leads us and directs us in this life in order that we receive his very best. The blessings that he has planned as a result of our devotion to him are timeless, unending, and overabundant. Words cannot express the greatness and fullness of his love, peace, and joy that he gives to all those who call on his name. He is my refuge, my strength, and my everything. He is all that I am and everything that I ever hope to be! Seek him today with all of your heart; draw near to him and you will see and experience the greatness of our God that we serve!

STAYING AT THE MASTER'S FEET

As Jesus and His disciples were on their way, he came to a village where a woman named Martha opened her home to Him. She had a sister called Mary, who sat at The Lord's feet listening to what He said. But Martha was distracted by all the preparations that had to be made.

She came to Him and asked, "Lord, don't you care that my sister has left me to do the work myself? Tell her to help me!"

"Martha, Martha," the Lord answered, "you are worried and upset about many things, but only one thing is needed. Mary has chosen what is better, and it will not be taken away from her."

Luke 10:38–42

How easy it is do get distracted, even by good things that we as Christians do in this life. It is easy to get so wrapped up in service that we lose our perspective on why we are even putting forth the energy to serve in the first place. We serve because we love Jesus Christ and because we want to be more like him! The most important thing, then, as Jesus describes here in this parable, is to spend time with him. Then the works or service will come as a result of our relationship with him because of the time that we have spent worshipping and getting to know this most awesome God that we serve! If we don't know Christ and we don't have his love in our hearts as our motivation for serving and living the Christian life, then everything that we do, we will do in vain. To know him, to let him renew our minds and change our way of thinking and change the way that we see the world around us minute by minute, this is the most important as well as the most exciting thing that we will ever do as Christians here on earth! So spend some time getting to know Jesus Christ today and then be sure that you let him into every part of your life. He is there right by your side whether you choose to acknowledge him or not. Take his hand and let him guide and direct your thoughts and actions so that you too may discover a whole new world that is full of his love and blessing in your life!

BLACK OR WHITE

He who is not with me is against me, and he who does not gather with me, scatters.

Luke 11:23

To be a Christ follower is a choice that is black or white; that is, there is no gray area when it comes to either surrendering your heart to the power and control of Jesus or to continue on in this life calling your own shots and going your own way. Sure, the Christian life can be hard and there may be times of discipline and growing where the Lord shapes and molds your heart to be more like his, but at the end of the day, someone who calls himself a Christian makes a conscious choice to live life for him, no matter what the circumstances.

I heard a quote the other day that I thought was phenomenal: "Many people in this life are very good at starting things, but very few people are good at finishing what they have started." When it is all said and done, the Christ follower finishes the pursuit that he or she has started to become more like Christ! Where do you stand today? Are you for him or against him? Have you surrendered your heart and life? Are you pressing on in the midst of difficult times in order that you can come out on the other side with a changed heart and life that has been transformed by the love of God? Or are you still walking the line, so to speak, not making a choice one way or the other? God illustrates for us in Luke 11:23 that if you haven't made a choice to follow him, then you really have made one—you have made one to oppose him and all he stands for. Surrender your heart and life to Jesus Christ today!

HOW DO YOU SEE THE WORLD?

Your eye is the lamp of your body. When your eyes are good, your whole body is full of light. But when they are bad, your body is also full of darkness. See to it, then, that the light within you is not darkness.

Luke 11:34–35

How do you see the world around you? Do you see God working in you and in other people's lives all around you? Do you see the needs of others and how God can use you to meet those needs? Do you see lost souls that are desperate, lonely, hurting, and in dire need of a Savior? Do you see the beauty of God's creation all around you? Do you see the great blessing that he has given you in your spouse? Do you see God? Or are you letting your eyes be filled with things of this world that do nothing but hinder your relationship with God and fill your body with darkness—things like self-centeredness, envy, jealousy, lust, greed, bitterness, etc.? Today, let your body be filled with his most incredible light of love. Make a conscience effort to look at the world around you with the eyes of your heart; don't miss what God is doing and what God is about to do in your life! Look for God today in your world and don't let your eyes be filled with things that are not of God. Focus on him and open your eyes to a whole new world that is full of the light of God's love!

GIVE IT AWAY

Then the Lord said to him, "Now then, you Pharisees clean the outside of the cup and dish, but inside you are full of greed and wickedness. You foolish people! Did not the one who made the outside make the inside also? But give what is inside the dish to the poor, and everything will be clean for you."

Luke 11:39–41

A Pharisee was surprised at Jesus because he did not wash before the meal, and in this verse we hear Jesus' response to him. The Pharisees were so wrapped up in making sure their outward appearance of godliness was perfect that they neglected what really mattered to God—their heart! What God cares about the most is not how we look or act, but what condition our heart is in. The answer that we find here to having a heart that is acceptable to God Almighty is to have a heart that invests in the lives of other people by giving of itself. A heart the gives time, money, love, and attention to other people in this world and thus to God himself—this is a heart that is acceptable to God! So today, stop worrying about the external things of this life and start living the abundant life that God has called us all to live. Look for ways to give back this amazing gift of love that God has given you to people that you come into contact with today. Give back to those who are poor in spirit the good news of how God has changed your life; share with them all of the amazing things that God is doing for you! Be more concerned about others than yourself. Do this and God will wash you clean and make you whole and complete in him.

GOD LOVES YOU

I tell you, my friends, do not be afraid of those who kill the body and after that can do no more. But I will show you whom you should fear: Fear Him who, after the killing of the body, has the power to throw you into hell. Yes, I tell you, fear Him. Are not five sparrows sold for two pennies? Yet not one of them is forgotten by God. Indeed, the very hairs of your head are all numbered. Don't be afraid; you are worth more than many sparrows.

Luke 12:4–7

The NIV Study Bible says that to fear God is to "respect his authority; stand in awe of His majesty and to trust in Him." With the exception of a few countries abroad, we as Christians today fortunately do not have to fear people that are trying to kill us as a result of our faith in Jesus Christ. There are many things to fear, however, in this world. There is the fear of rejection, the fear of poverty, the fear of losing a loved one, the fear of getting old, the fear of failure, the fear of stepping out of your comfort zone in order to be obedient to God, the fear of loneliness, and many other fears that we face as we live our life as strangers here in a fallen world.

I have a fear of losing my hair, and if God has the hairs on my head numbered, then that number must be decreasing rapidly! In all seriousness though, isn't it great to know that know matter what happens in this life—no matter how our heads look or how many times we fail or how often we are disappointed by people that are friendly but will never be our friends—we have a God in heaven who loves us and who knows exactly what we are going through. A God who wants only the very best for us and who promises to follow through with his perfect plan for our lives. A God who will never let us down and who gives us everything that we need to enjoy life. A God who promises to always provide for us and to always love us no matter how we treat him or how many times we stubbornly take our own path in life. A God that is full of love and mercy.

God, you are awesome! Your love is so amazing and so incomprehensible. We do not even come close to deserving the sweet, fulfilling, unfailing love that you give! We love you and today, we give you our lives. Help us to share this amazing love with others.

GODLY TREASURE

For where your treasure is, there your heart will be also.

Luke 12:34

Where is your heart today? What do you treasure in this life? A good test is to consider what you think about the most throughout your day. Today God is calling for your heart! He has treasures for you that you can't even imagine! He has plans for your life that you can't even begin to see or understand—plans that are good and plans that bring joy and happiness, love and excitement to your life. God loves you so much that he paid a very high price in order that he could be the treasure of your heart today and for all the days to come! Surrender your heart and life to him today and start living the abundant life that is full of the treasure of his love and faithfulness.

ARE YOU READY?

Be dressed ready for service and keep your lamps burning, like men watching for their master to return from a wedding banquet, so that when he comes and knocks they can immediately open the door for him. It will be good for those servants whose master finds them watching when he comes. I tell you the truth, he will dress himself to serve, will have them recline at the table and will come and wait on them. It will be good for those servants whose master finds them ready, even if he comes in the second or third watch of the night. But understand this: If the owner of the house had known at what hour the thief was coming, he would not have let the house be broken into. You also must be ready, because the Son of Man will come at an hour when you do not expect him.

Luke 12:35–40

Are you ready? Is your lamp burning? Or has the light been snuffed out by the worries, troubles, or temptations of this world? Maybe your light has never been lit; maybe you have been waiting to give your life to Jesus Christ at some time in the future when you feel more ready to take that step. Jesus is speaking of his return to earth here in this chapter in the book of Luke. Jesus says it can happen at any time and it will happen when you least expect it! When Jesus does come back to take all of his people that have trusted in him with their lives back to heaven, will you be on his list? What condition will he find your heart and life in? Will he find you giving your all for his Kingdom or will you be ashamed to see him because you have been wasting your life on pleasures of this world and self-indulgences? Will he find you with a heart that is full of forgiveness and love or will he see a heart that is bound up with bitterness, anger, and shame? Will he know you, and will you know him? Have you spent time getting to know him while you have been waiting for his return? He is coming and when he gets here it will be too late to change the decisions that you have made regarding the gift that he had left for you while he was gone. Accept that gift today into your heart before it is too late.

A SMALL ACT OF KINDNESS

Then Jesus asked, "What is the Kingdom of God like? What shall I compare it to? It is like a mustard seed, which a man took and planted in his garden. It grew and became a tree, and the birds of the air perched in its branches." Again He asked, "What shall I compare the Kingdom of God to? It is like yeast that a woman took and mixed into a large amount of flour until it worked all through the dough."

Luke 13:18–21

It must not have taken much effort to plant a mustard seed, as small as it is. No, not much effort at all, but look at the result. And an ever so small amount of yeast mixed into flour can and will have a huge effect on the end product. These analogies are true for us today as we as Christians obey the Holy Spirit by doing small acts of kindness to those people around us. These acts will indeed have a huge impact, not only on our own lives and relationship to God, but also on the lives of others. God can do so much with just one heart that is fully committed to him and is willing to obey his promptings at the smallest and seemingly insignificant times throughout our day. How much energy does it take to smile at a stranger, to take time to listen to someone who we might not normally associate with, to hold the door for someone, to genuinely ask how someone is doing and wait and listen to their answer, to tell someone that you love them, to pick up a piece of trash, to say thank you to someone else that has done a small act of kindness that normally would have never been noticed. The greatness of God can be seen in a human heart that first has surrendered to him and then has obeyed and served in the smallest, insignificant acts throughout an ordinary day. It is in these hearts that God can move like an ever so small amount of yeast to make a huge impact for his Kingdom! Today, look to make a difference by being obedient to God in the smallest of things and see for yourself how his power can move in your heart and in the hearts of others.

GOD IS NEAR AND IN CONTROL

We give thanks to you, O God, we give thanks to you for your Name
is near;
    Men tell of your wonderful deeds. You say,
    I choose the appointed time;
    It is I who judge uprightly.
    When the earth and all its people quake,
    It is I who hold its pillars firm.

Psalm 75:1–3

In the midst of this crazy world and all of the pressures and demands that we are up against, in the midst of all of the problems and disappointments, hurts and pains that seem to overwhelm us at times, isn't it refreshing to know that our God and Savior is near and in control of all that is happening in our lives? God loves you more than you can imagine and he is right next to you today, ready to walk the narrow road right beside you and see to it that you make it through to the other side! All he asks is that you trust in him, that you take his hand and let him guide you through this life. If you do this, then he will show you a whole new world through his eyes—a world that is full of love and fulfillment, joy and peace. Take his hand today!

ENTERING THROUGH THE NARROW DOOR

Make every effort to enter through the narrow door, because many, I tell you will try to enter and will not be able to. Once the owner of the house gets up and closes the door, you will stand outside knocking and pleading, "Sir, open the door for us."

But he will answer, "I don't know you or where you come from."

Then you will say, "We ate and drank with you, and you taught in our streets."

But he will reply, "I don't know you or where you come from. Away from me, all you evildoers!"

Luke 13:24–27

Isn't it sad that when Jesus was here on the earth that there were large crowds that were in his presence and many people that may have even eaten with him and listened to his teaching but only a few who truly responded to his teaching by surrendering their heart and life in obedience to him? The same is true of Christianity today in that there are many people who go to church and listen to God's teaching and many people who have felt the tug of the Holy Spirit on their heart who have been convicted to surrender their will and life to our loving Savior who do not respond inwardly and therefore—although they have experienced spiritual things—they have never entered into the narrow door to get to know Jesus Christ in a personal way. Unfortunately, these people will be in for a rude awakening when they go before the Lord at the end of this world and are given the response that we see in Luke 13:24–27. It is one thing to watch what the Lord is doing as an outsider looking in, but it is an altogether different thing to be a part of what he is doing by laying your life down at his feet, surrendering your will and your desires to him in order that he may begin to work in and through your life with his Spirit. Your goal should be that on that day there will be no question as to where you will spend eternity since he will have indeed known you as a result of being at the center of your life!

Have you responded to the promptings of his Spirit? Have you surrendered your will and your desires to him? Do you know him? Is his Spirit working within your life to reach a lost world for the Kingdom of God? Enter through the narrow door today.

SELF-INDULGENCE

Then Jesus said to his host, "When you give a luncheon or dinner, do not invite your friends, brothers or relatives, or your rich neighbors; if you do, they may invite you back and so you will be repaid. But when you give a banquet, invite the poor, the crippled, the lame, the blind, and you will be blessed. Although they cannot repay you, you will be repaid at the resurrection of the righteous."

Luke 14:12–14

Maybe it's because of my Italian heritage that I love to have people over for dinner and entertain guests in our home. After reading this passage in Luke I have to wonder if I may be missing the point of what this life is really about. Is this life really about selfishly spending time with friends and loved ones, eating and relaxing and soaking up all of the fun that this world has to give, or would I be better served by reaching out to the poor and the needy that are all around me and spending my time, energy, and resources preparing meals and entertaining people of this world that truly have a need to be fed and who truly have a need to see and experience the love of Christ in their lives? I will think twice in the future about how I spend my time. Many of us as Christians are just scratching the surface of the abundant life that Jesus promises us if we surrender our hearts and our lives to him. The reason for this is that we are trained by our culture and by society to be self-indulgent, but real blessing and fulfillment comes not in seeking pleasures for ourselves but in having a heart that gives and loves and is always looking out for the needs and interests of others. To give away all that God has given us is the secret to seeing and experiencing the power of God in our lives. So today, just for a little while, take your eyes off of yourself and all of your problems and personal goals and interests and look at the world around you with a different set of eyes. Look for how God would want you to share his love and give it away today.

SALT OF THE WORLD

Salt it good, but if it loses its saltiness, how can it be made salty again? It is fit neither for the soil nor for the manure pile; it is thrown out. He who has ears let him hear.

Luke 14:34–35

Just as salt is used in food to enhance the flavor and to preserve the food so that it lasts much longer, as Christians our very lives should enhance the lives of people around us and help to preserve their lives for eternity by pointing them to Jesus Christ! Our lives should be a reflection of God's love and humility, attractive and appealing to all who are watching us from afar. The only way to maintain our saltiness as Christians is to draw near to the one who provides the flavor, the one who is the only reason for anything good that comes out of the way that we live—our Lord and Savior Jesus Christ! So today, draw near to him and let his perfect love be reflected from your heart to others. Be the salt of the world today.

OUTREACH

Now the tax collectors and "sinners" were all gathering around to hear Him. But the Pharisees and the teachers of the law muttered, "This man welcomes sinners and eats with them."

Then Jesus told them this parable: "Suppose one of you has a hundred sheep and loses one of them. Does he not leave the ninety-nine in the open country and go after the lost sheep until he finds it? And when he finds it, he joyfully puts it on his shoulders and goes home. Then he calls his friends and neighbors together and says, Rejoice with me; I have found my lost sheep. I tell you that in the same way there will be more rejoicing in heaven over one sinner who repents than over ninety-nine righteous persons who do not need to repent."

Luke 15:1–7

As Christians, we do a very good job of getting together in various groups and encouraging each other, building each other up and developing strong Christ-centered relationships that are so very important in Christian life. But we could do a better job of reaching out to the lost people that are all around us; after all, that is why we are here isn't it? To go after the lost sheep of the world and point them to Christ by living our very lives for him, full of his Glory in the midst of everyone around us. How will they see and know that Jesus is real unless they see him in us, and how will they see him in us unless we are reaching out to them in love and spending our time interacting and loving them with the love of Christ? Jesus says here in this parable that all of heaven is full of rejoicing when just one soul comes to know our heavenly Father, repents of his or her sin, and surrenders his or her life to him! So today I encourage you to pray about how you spend your time. Ask God to show you how you can reach out in love to one of his sheep that are lost and point him or her toward Jesus so that he or she too may be saved!

KINGDOM OF GOD

Once, having been asked by the Pharisees when the Kingdom of God would come, Jesus replied, "The Kingdom of God does not come with your careful observation, nor will people say, 'Here it is,' or 'There it is,' because the Kingdom of God is within you."

Luke 17:20–21

Being a part of the Kingdom of God, the very essence of what it means to be a Christian, has nothing to do with external activities such as doing religious things or acting right and proper or going to church on Sunday or gaining a theological degree or even becoming a leader in the church. No, the Kingdom of God exists in the innermost parts of a person's heart and soul. It is inviting Jesus Christ to enter into your very own heart where his love for you becomes the reason and motivation for everything that you do in this life on earth! It is a personal relationship with him where you truly get to know our King and you let him lovingly change your way of thinking, you let him heal your hurts and pains that have scarred your heart, you enjoy his presence in your life minute by minute throughout the day, and you see the world with a different set of eyes that look beyond the external in order to see our great God at work to reach a lost world for him!

Being a part of the Kingdom of God is to be restored and renewed in order that you can live the life that your were originally meant to live and so you can enjoy this most precious relationship with your Creator and King once again, as he meant it to be from the start! Only you know for sure if you have entered in and have become of part of the Kingdom of God. Nothing that you do on the external side of life will ever even get you close to this amazing relationship with Jesus Christ. It takes a heart change; it happens on the inside. There is nothing that you can do to earn it and no one else can choose for you. You must make a decision to accept this free gift of salvation and abundant life that God has for you. He has paid the price already. The work is done. The Kingdom of God is alive, and it is in the heart of all who believe and who have put their trust in the one who gave his very life for their souls! Are you a part of the Kingdom of God? Do you know Jesus? Is he changing your heart and your mind to make you more like him? Only you know for sure. If you don't know Jesus, it is not too late; surrender your heart and life to him today and become a part of his Kingdom that will last for all eternity.

JESUS IS COMING

Just as it was in the days of Noah, so also will it be in the days of the Son of Man. People were eating, drinking, marrying and being given in marriage up to the day Noah entered the ark. Then the flood came and destroyed them all.

Luke 17:26–27

Very soon, Jesus is going to come back and wipe out this fallen world of sin and take all who have entrusted their lives to him up to an indescribably incredible place called heaven to live with him for eternity! Are you ready? It could happen today, it could happen tomorrow, or it may not happen in your lifetime, but one thing for sure is that he is coming back, and when he does it will be too late at that time to choose, him. If you haven't made that choice as of yet, then I encourage you to do so today! Not only will you receive eternal life, but even more, you will receive his Spirit to live with you during your time on this earth to guide and direct you into an incredible, abundant, and fulfilling life. Choose Christ today so that you will be ready when he does return to take his people home!

EMOTIONAL GOD OF LOVE

And God sent an angel to destroy Jerusalem. But as the angel was doing so, The Lord saw it and was grieved because of the calamity and said to the angel who was destroying the people, "Enough! Withdraw your hand."

1 Chronicles 22:15

Do you know that the way that you respond to God today by either obeying him and walking with him or turning from him and going your own way affects his emotions and makes him either very sad and grieved or so happy that he looks upon you with tears of joy in his eyes? We don't serve a God who is coldhearted and has no emotion. No, we serve a God who has characteristics and emotions of a person, just like us. The Bible says that God has created us in his image, so our God can feel joy and pain just like we can. So isn't it nice to know that whatever you are going through today that there is a God in heaven who in a very real way is sad when you are sad or celebrates with you with joyful tears when you are happy?

Just like God was grieved here in the text while watching Jerusalem being destroyed by an angel that he had sent, even more I think that God is grieved today as he watches millions of people that he so graciously gave his life for turn away from him and follow their own way instead of accepting his amazing gift of love in Jesus Christ, who reunites us with our Creator for the rest of eternity! All he wants and all that his heart aches for is to give you back the abundant life in his image that he originally meant for you to have. Make him happy today. Walk with him and let his love guide you, change you, and direct you into a life full of purpose that is lived for his glory all because of his great love.

PERSEVERANCE

Then Jesus told his disciples a parable to show them that they should always pray and not give up. He said: "In a certain town there was a judge who neither feared God nor cared about men. And there was a widow in that town who kept coming to him with the plea, 'Grant me justice against my adversary.'

For some time he refused. But finally he said to himself, 'Even though I don't fear God or care about men, yet because this widow keeps bothering me, I will see that she gets justice, so that she won't eventually wear me out with her coming!'

And the Lord said, 'Listen to what the unjust judge says. And will not God bring about justice for his chosen ones, who cry out to him day and night? Will He keep putting them off? I tell you, He will see that they get justice, and quickly. However, when the Son of Man comes, will He find faith on earth?'"

Luke 18:1–8

I recently spoke to a friend who has been struggling with sin in his life, just as we all do at times because of our old nature and the environment of this fallen world. My friend was frustrated and at the point of almost feeling like just giving up on trying to live a holy life because he had failed so many times in the past. But God is telling us here in Luke 18 not to ever give up but to keep persisting in prayer and obedience to him, as he will eventually answer our prayers and change our hearts and minds to make us more like him. It is not what we do or how effectively we obey that matters to God and makes a difference in our lives anyway; it is what God does in us as we draw near to him that changes us and makes a difference in the world around us! There is so much freedom in that, isn't there?

Our job on this earth as Christians is easy, we just keep persistently seeking the face of God every minute of every day, and he promises to always protect us from this world and to cover our sins and failures with his incredible grace and love up until the day that we meet him in heaven and are changed completely and perfectly back to his original glory! To stay faithful to him up until the day that he returns, even in the midst of failure is the goal and the mark for which we were called.

So today, if this world has beaten you down (as it so very easily can) then I challenge you to get up, dust yourself off, and persistently seek the face of God in your life. The Bible says in James 4:8, "Come near to God and He will come near to you." God wants to use you today to help reach this lost world for him!

CHILDLIKE FAITH

"But Jesus called the children to Him and said, "Let the little children come to me, and do not hinder them, for the Kingdom of God belongs to such as these. I tell you the truth; anyone who will not receive the Kingdom of God like a little child will never enter it."

Luke 18:16–17

Little children are totally dependant upon their parents for everything—food, protection, provisions, direction, you name it. Little children also have complete trust in their parents since they don't know any different and are very open and genuinely sincere. This is because little children have not been here long enough for their minds and their hearts to be tainted by this lost world!

The Bible says that if you have surrendered your heart and life to Jesus Christ that you are a new creation in him—a newborn baby, so to speak, with a new life in Christ! Just as little children, we are to receive this amazing gift of God and enter into this new life with childlike faith, trusting completely in him to meet all of our needs, depending upon his Spirit for direction as to how we should live our life, and being very genuine and completely sincere in the newfound faith that God has so graciously given to all of his children who have surrendered their hearts and lives into his precious care! Let go today of the worries and all of the other junk that this world throws at you and seek God and his spirit for comfort and peace, direction and safety. Put your life in his loving hands and enjoy the presence and care of your Father in heaven.

SACRIFICE FOR THE KINGDOM

Peter said to Him, "We have left all we have to follow you!"

" I tell you the truth," Jesus said to them, "no one who has left home or wife or brothers or parents or children for the sake of the Kingdom of God will fail to receive many times as much in this age and, in the age to come, eternal life."

Luke 18:28–30

Being a Christian is to take the path less traveled, to walk the narrow road, to act differently from the majority of the people that are all around you. Because of this, there will be sacrifices that you will make through leaving things of this world behind and following Jesus Christ! You may have a family member or a friend or a colleague that doesn't agree with your newfound faith. You may have to stop doing things that once brought you great pleasure or give up some of your free time in order to learn more about Jesus and to discover how to make him a part of your life and become more like him. You may have to set aside your own personal goals and agenda in order to discover and to live out the purpose that God has for your life. Look at the reward, though, that Jesus promises all who do sacrifice their very lives in order to follow him: he says that you will receive many times as much, both in this life as well as in the life to come. Personally, I can attest to the fact that to follow Jesus and to make him the number one priority in your life does indeed bring much more joy and fulfillment than anything this world has to offer! Whatever it is that is holding you back from experiencing this great joy and love in your life that comes from a personal relationship with Jesus, leave it behind today and start living the abundant life that only comes when you are willing to give up the things of this world and follow him.

ALL FOR YOU

Jesus took the twelve aside and told them, "We are going up to Jerusalem, and everything that is written by the prophets about the Son of Man will be fulfilled. He will be handed over to the Gentiles. They will mock Him, insult Him, spit on Him, flog Him, and kill Him. On the third day He will rise again."

Luke 18:31–33

Words cannot express the kind of love that God has for you when you read about this incredible sacrificial act of kindness that he eagerly suffered through all because of his desire to once again be united with his creation in spirit and in truth for the rest of eternity. He did it all for you because he loves you and he wants to give you an abundant life with him that will last forever. Even greater than that, though, is the fact that he loves you so much that he doesn't force himself on you because he wants the love that is shared to be genuine on your part, so he gives you the opportunity to either choose him and accept this extraordinary gift of love that will restore you once and for all back in relationship with him or to reject him and be separated from him for the rest of eternity. How could you say no to such an amazing God who humbled himself completely and gave his very life for you? Choose him today, walk with him, and let his love fill your heart and his Spirit control your mind and direct your actions. He has big plans for you today; don't miss out on the blessing that he has for you.

CRY OUT TO JESUS

As Jesus Approached Jericho, a blind man was sitting by the roadside begging. When he heard the crowd going by, he asked what was happening. They told him, "Jesus of Nazareth is passing by."

He called out, "Jesus, Son of David, have mercy on me!"

Those who led the way rebuked him and told him to be quiet, but he shouted all the more, "Son of David, have mercy on me!"

Jesus stopped and ordered the man to be brought to Him. When he came near, Jesus asked him, "What do you want me to do for you?"

"Lord, I want to see," he replied.

Jesus said to him, "Receive your sight; your faith has healed you." Immediately he received his sight and followed Jesus, praising God. When all the people saw it, they also praised God.

Luke 18:35–43

Just as this blind beggar faced resistance from other people of this world as he cried out to Jesus for the first time, so you too may face opposition from your friends and family and maybe even other church members as you cry out to Jesus for the first time. Don't let that discourage you. We live in a fallen world and there is an enemy that you can't see with your eyes that wants nothing more than for you to do nothing, to keep living with discouragement, pain, hurt, disappointment, and emptiness! Press on in the midst of the social norms and popular opinion of this age and seek this loving Savior with all of your heart! Yes, he knows what you need, but he wants to hear it come out of your mouth, just like he asked this blind man to vocalize his request even though he obviously knew what the man was longing for. God wants to hear from you. He wants to hear you tell him how much you love him, how great he is, how much you need him, what your hurts and pains are, what the deep desire of your heart is, and how he can make you whole and fulfill you in this life that we live! He wants a relationship with you where you cry out to him—in the midst of this unbelieving world—and for you to believe and have faith that he hears your prayer and will meet your needs. Look to him today—cry out to him and you will experience his peace, his grace, and his love like never before.

WHOLEHEARTED DEVOTION

And you, my son Solomon, acknowledge the God of your father, and serve Him with wholehearted devotion and with a willing mind, for the Lord searches every heart and understands every motive behind the thoughts. If you seek Him, He will be found in you; but if you forsake Him, He will reject you forever. Consider now, for the Lord has chosen you to build a temple as a sanctuary. Be strong then and do the work.

1 Chronicles 28:9–10

This is great advice from King David to his son Solomon as he prepares him to build a temple for the Lord. King David knew what it meant to serve the Lord with his whole heart; his mind was consumed with godly thoughts and his motives behind everything that he did and every thought he let enter into his mind had to do with his love for his God. Sure, he had his times of struggle throughout his life, but in this passage he has grown old and wise; he has an understanding that this life was meant to be all about God and not about us! And how much more important even today is such advice for your son or your daughter who is also building a temple for the Lord, as in the New Testament the Bible says that the temple of the Lord is your body: "Don't you know that you yourselves are God's temple and that God's Spirit lives in you?" (1 Corinthians 3:16). Be strong, then, and do the work as you, by your thoughts and your actions, are building a temple within your own body for the Spirit of the Lord to dwell! It says here that if you seek him, he will be found in you, but if you forsake him then he will reject your forever. To me, forever seems like a very long time. Serve the Lord then with wholehearted devotion today, let your mind and your heart be filled with his Word, his love, and his direction all because of the love that you have for the One who gave you life.

LIGHT IN THE TRENCHES

Jesus entered Jericho and was passing through. A man was there by the name of Zacchaeus; he was a chief tax collector and was wealthy. He wanted to see who Jesus was, but being a short man he could not, because of the crowd. So he ran ahead and climbed a sycamore-fig tree to see him, since Jesus was coming that way. When Jesus reached the spot, He looked up and said to him, "Zacchaeus, come down immediately. I must stay at your house today." So he came down at once and welcomed him gladly.

All the people saw this and began to mutter, "He has gone to be the guest of a sinner."

But Zacchaeus stood up and said to the Lord, "Look, Lord! Here and now I give half of my possessions to the poor, and if I have cheated anybody out of anything, I will pay back four times the amount."

Jesus said to him, "Today salvation has come to this house, because this man, too, is a son of Abraham. For the Son of Man came to seek and to save what was lost."

Luke 19:1–10

To seek and to save what was lost—that was Jesus' mission more than 2,000 years ago and that should be our mission today as his Spirit lives within each and every one of us that has accepted God's awesome gift of his Son into our lives! Hanging out in your comfort zone where you just spend time with other Christians and do "Christian things" can be fun, but real fun and abundant life comes in being a light in the trenches of this world where lost people are longing to just see a little glimpse of who God is, even if they have to run ahead and climb a sycamore tree to see him!

Do you want to grow as a Christian? Growth in Christ comes from giving away what God has already given to you by sharing his love with others all around you. You never know how God may use you today, whose heart he may touch through your life, whose life and eternal destiny may be changed because they see and experience the love of Christ though you today. So don't be afraid to hang out with people who are lost today; don't be judgmental, don't be critical of their actions, just love them and let them see God for who he really is by the way that you live your life today.

FUTURE HOPE

There is surely a future hope for you, and your hope will not be cut off.

Proverbs 23:18

I don't care where you are right now in your spiritual walk with the Lord, I don't care where you have been, what you have done, what other people say about you or even what you think about yourself, there is a future hope for you in Jesus Christ! God has a plan for your life. He knows exactly what is going on with you right now and he is waiting for you to give it all to him—your worries, your fears, your regrets, your dreams, everything—so that he can take all of the junk of your life and turn it into something beautiful that he can use for his Glory both now and for the rest of eternity! Seek him today with all of your heart and start living the abundant life that only comes when your hope is truly found in him.

STAY ALERT

Be careful, or your hearts will be weighed down with dissipation, drunkenness and the anxieties of life, and that day will close on you unexpectedly like a trap. For it will come upon all those who live on the face of the whole earth. Be always on the watch, and pray that you may be able to escape all that is about to happen, and that you may be able to stand before the Son of Man.

Luke 21:34–36

The dictionary defines dissipation as: "an amusement or diversion, useless or profitless activity, dissolute indulgence in sensual pleasure." I am convinced that up until the day that Christ returns the enemy will constantly try to divert our attention away from God and living your life for him and put it on all of these useless things that are mentioned above. Don't let him weigh your heart down with all of these things that do nothing but hinder your relationship with God and make you useless for his Kingdom. The only way to guard against this happening in your life is to stay close to Jesus and to stay alert, recognizing the enemy's schemes and turning away from them. Spend time each and every day in God's Word and in prayer, and you will see that Jesus himself will walk beside you and protect you as you relentlessly live your life for him and share his love with everyone that you meet! He will be back one day soon—it may be today, it may be tomorrow, it may be next week, or it may be twenty years from now. When he does come back, where will he find your heart? Draw near to him today.

SUN AND SHIELD

Better is one day in your courts than a thousand elsewhere;
I would rather be a doorkeeper in the house of my God than dwell in the tents of the wicked.
For the Lord God is a sun and shield;
the Lord bestows favor and honor;
no good thing does he withhold from those whose walk is blameless.
Oh Lord Almighty, blessed is the man who trusts in you.

Psalm 84:10–12

To have a "blameless walk" is to seek the Lord every day. It is to put him and his principles for living above yourself and your own desires. To trust in him is to turn from sin and to prayerfully commit your way to his guidance and direction for your life each and every day. If you do these two things, then you will experience this life like never before! There will be a light that gives you vision from the very source of light itself and you will be protected by the very shield of God from the peace- and joy-ending blows that this world uses to entices you! Look to him today. Trust in him. Start living the life of abundant blessing that is only found in walking side by side with our Lord and Savior, Jesus Christ!

ARE YOU SLEEPING?

Jesus went out as usual to the Mount of Olives, and his disciples followed Him. On reaching the place He said to them, "Pray that you will not fall into temptation."

He withdrew beyond them, knelt down and prayed, 'Father, if your are willing, take this cup from me; yet not my will, but yours be done." An angel from heaven appeared to Him and strengthened Him. And being in anguish, he prayed more earnestly, and His sweat was like drops of blood falling to the ground. When He rose from prayer and went back to the disciples, He found them asleep, exhausted from sorrow. "Why are you sleeping?" He asked them. "Get up and pray so that you will not fall into temptation."

Luke 22:39–46

I love the words "as usual" in this verse. Here is the Son of God and yet he consistently needed to go to the Mount of Olives to get alone with God and pray for strength, that he may not "fall into temptation." This time on the Mount of Olives, Jesus is struggling so much with what is about to happen to him that his sweat is intermixed with blood because of the extreme anguish of what he is about to do in order that you and I may be reunited with God for the rest of eternity! If the disciples back then had only understood the magnitude of what was happening then I doubt that they would have been sleeping during this time of prayer.

I don't know about you, but sometimes I race through this life so fast that I let the whole day go by, just going through the motions of life, without taking time to acknowledge the work of God that is happening all around me and without connecting with God in silent prayer throughout the day asking him for strength to persevere in my pursuit of holiness. It is like I am spiritually sleeping at times, and it is then that the enemy can break through and cause me to make decisions that will separate me from the work of God in my life, thus stealing away my joy and peace that is only found in God. Don't get caught sleeping today! Take time to ask God for help, acknowledge his presence in your life, and always be looking for how he may use you to make a difference in the world around you! There are angels waiting to strengthen you today. All you need to do is ask.

BETRAYED BY A FRIEND

While He was still speaking a crowd came up, and the man who was called Judas, one of the Twelve, was leading them. He approached Jesus to kiss Him, but Jesus asked him, "Judas, are you betraying the Son of Man with a kiss?"

Luke 22:47–48

Jesus spoke to thousands of people during his time on earth, he touched the lives of many but there were twelve, called disciples, who were his closest friends and allies. To be betrayed by one of these twelve must have really hurt, even though he knew it was going to happen. This is a good lesson for us in that our faith, hope, security, joy, and fulfillment in this life can only be found in only one man, and that man is Jesus Christ. People are going to let you down in this life. Close friends, Christian friends, role models, spouses, children, and even Christian leaders are going to disappoint you at times throughout your life. Do not look to other people for strength in this life, but look to God himself! God never changes. His love is never ending. His grace is always sufficient. Surrender your heart and life to him today.

HUMBLED BY OUR LOVING SAVIOR

That day Herod and Pilate became friends—before this they had been enemies.

Luke 23:12

I love this verse in the book of Luke! Both Herod and Pilate had just spent time with the Son of God and it appears as if their lives had dramatically changed as a result of being in the presence of God Almighty! Do you have an enemy? Is there hatred, bitterness, and anger in your heart of hearts that is keeping you from experiencing the peace of God in your life? Spend some time with Jesus and all of that junk that seems so heavy and such a burden today will become very insignificant in light of the magnitude of God's love and forgiveness.

There is something that is very humbling about being in the presence of God. He will heal your wounds and the mountains of your life that seem to be such an obstacle today will disappear and seem so silly when you truly experience God for who he really is and you grasp an understanding of his unconditional love and forgiveness that he has for you. Jesus is there today right next to you with love and tears in his eyes, longing for your attention and servitude. Seek him today with all of your heart and experience peace in this life like never before.

CARRYING HIS CROSS

As they led Him away, they seized Simon from Cyrene, who was on his way in from the country, and put the cross on him and made him carry it behind Jesus.

Luke 23:26

Jesus, the Son of God, beaten and flogged so badly that he couldn't carry a thirty- or forty-pound plank of wood as they dragged him to the place where they would finish the task of crucifying him on a cross of wood for all to see. Just imagine if that were you being forced, as Simon was, to carry the cross behind Jesus, with Jesus' blood and tears spattering in your face as he struggled with every last bit of strength to get to the place where he would give his life. If that were you carrying the cross, I have to believe that your vision and purpose on this earth would be crystal clear! After experiencing firsthand the amazing love and sacrifice of God that was done for you, the disruptions and distractions of this life that keep you from truly experiencing the abundant life that Jesus has for you would somehow seem very trivial and insignificant when compared to the ultimate sacrifice that was made in order that you wouldn't have to be a slave to the junk of this world any longer! Jesus says in Matthew 16:24: "If anyone would come after me, he must deny himself and take up his cross and follow me." How could you not deny yourself today after remembering all the suffering that Jesus went through in order that you could live free of the bondage of sin that this world places on our hearts. Seek him today with all of your heart, thank him for the sacrifice that he made, and walk with him as he guides and directs you both now and forevermore!

DIRECT ACCESS

It was now about the sixth hour, and darkness came over the whole land until the ninth hour, for the sun stopped shining. And the curtain of the temple was torn in two. Jesus called out with a loud voice, "Father, into your hands I commit my Spirit." When He had said this, he breathed His last.

Luke 23:44–46

From noon to three in the afternoon, by the Jewish method of keeping time, the sky was completely black, for they had indeed sacrificed the Son of God. The coolest thing, though, is the curtain that had been torn in two at the Temple! For this was the boundary between the most holy place and the rest of the Temple. It was only behind this curtain that a High Priest could encounter God and represent all of the people in order to make restitution for sin. That curtain had been supernaturally torn because now, because of Jesus' sacrifice, anyone can have direct access to God through Christ himself since the ultimate sacrifice for your sins has been paid by Jesus Christ. He was the lamb that was slaughtered for you and for me in order that we could once again be pure in the eyes of God and have a relationship with him that is much better than that of the most holy place in the temple since God becomes a part of our very hearts and souls! Three days later Jesus rose from the dead and today he is alive and wants to save you from this world of sin and from yourselves. He wants to reunite you with your Creator! Today, you can be forgiven, you can have eternal life, and you can start living the abundant life that Jesus promised all of us that surrender our lives to him. All you have to do is ask! Draw near to him today.

SELF-CONTROL

For the grace of God that brings salvation has appeared to all men. It teaches us to say "No" to ungodliness and worldly passions, and to live self-controlled, upright and godly lives in this present age, while we wait for the blessed hope—the glorious appearing of our great God and Savior, Jesus Christ, who gave Himself for us to redeem us from all wickedness and to purify for Himself a people that are His very own, eager to do what is good.

Titus 2:11–14

If you have surrendered your heart and life to Jesus Christ in order that you may live eternally in him, then you indeed belong to him, but you must understand that you still have your free will to either obey Christ who now lives in you or to obey your old nature, who will still be a part of your fleshly body until the time that you are fully redeemed and brought up to heaven to enjoy your God for the rest of eternity! So then, in order to experience the abundant life that Christ offers, even now, as you live for him on this earth, you must be self-controlled and not agree to give in to worldly passions that the enemy will try to entice you with. These things will only separate you from God and will lead to much disappointment and despair in this life. Instead, look for fulfillment in him! Be eager to do what is good, seek God with all of your heart every day, and you will indeed find a peace and joy in this life that no one can ever take away from you. You have been bought with a price. You are a man or woman of God; now, remain pure in him so that his purpose may be fulfilled in and through your life and in order that other people may see and believe.

CONTENTMENT

But godliness with contentment is great gain.

1 Timothy 6:6

There was a time in my life when I believed and lived the lie that we all hear and see in America, which says that success and happiness come with having more. Having more responsibility in your job, having more money, having a bigger house, bigger boat, more expensive car, nicer clothes, bigger diamonds—you name it, we can see that attitude being lived out on a daily basis all around us. Just recently Paula and I have been blessed beyond belief by being able to pay off a huge financial debt that we had built over the first ten years of our marriage as a result of buying into this idea that fulfillment comes with more stuff. Thanks be to God that he has shown us in the past years that the only thing that can bring true happiness and fulfillment in this life is a daily or even minute-by-minute relationship with Jesus Christ where he becomes the motivation in your life. Contentment, joy, and happiness come with the pursuit of godliness and the living out of God's purpose for you life! I gain much more joy and fulfillment from writing these daily devotionals and seeing God use them to encourage and challenge his people than anything else that I have ever acquired or strived for in my thirty-five years of living. Although I am not perfect by any means, and although God still has much more work to do on me in order to make me more like him, I am content with all that he has blessed me with, and I owe everything that I am and all that I ever hope to be to him! How great is the God that we serve! Find true fulfillment and contentment today. Surrender your heart, your life, your ambitions, and your desires to the living God who gave his very life for you.

FIGHT

But you man of God, flee from all this, and pursue righteousness, Godliness, faith, love, endurance and gentleness. Fight the good fight of faith. Take hold of the eternal life to which you were called when you made your good confession in the presence of many witnesses. In the sight of God, who gives life to everything, and of Christ Jesus, who while testifying before Pontius Pilate made the good confession, I charge you to keep this command without spot or blame until the appearing of your Lord Jesus Christ, which God will bring about in His own time—God, the blessed and only Ruler, the King of Kings and Lord of Lords, who alone is immortal and who lives in unapproachable light, whom no one has seen or can see. To Him be honor and might forever. Amen.

1 Timothy 6:11–16

Wow! How encouraging is that? It's like a pep talk given by a head coach to a sports team stepping out to play in a championship game. What an awesome brother in Christ and mentor that Timothy had in Paul. As Christians, we should be encouraging each other with the same amount of passion and to the same magnitude that we see in Paul's example here. We are strangers here in a fallen world with a purpose in life that is completely foreign to most of the people that we encounter on a daily basis. At times the Christian life can be very lonely and even discouraging. That is why we need each other to give pep talks from time to time—to encourage us to keep fighting the good fight in our pursuit of holiness. We need a brother or sister in Christ to clarify our vision and keep us focused on the one true God whom we serve. The King of Kings gives us everything worth living for in our short time on this earth. So today I encourage you to fight! Be intentional concerning your faith! Live you life for God, flee from selfish thoughts and distractions that the enemy tries to fill your head with, and look at the world around you with the eyes of your heart. Watch for ways you can be a servant of our awesome Savior today and take the time to encourage another brother or sister in Christ; be a friend and lift him or her up in God's name.

TAKE HOLD OF LIFE

Command them to do good, to be rich in good deeds, and to be gen-
erous and willing to share. In this way they will lay up treasure for
themselves as a firm foundation for the coming age, so that they may
take hold of the life that is truly life.

1 Timothy 6:18–19

As a young man making my own way in life, I used to think that
the way to take hold of all that this life has to offer was to acquire
great wealth, achieve power and prestige in the business world, and
finally to gain superior social status (basically to have lots of friends
who are impressed with your lifestyle and who want to spend time
with you). As I get older and wiser at the young age of thirty-five,
I wholeheartedly agree with Paul's instruction to Timothy that true
life is indeed found in giving away all that God has blessed me with.
All really means all and encompasses financial blessings, God-given
talents, time, and most importantly, the great love and compassion
that he has shown me. True, abundant life that brings great joy and
happiness, fulfillment and love comes only with a giving heart that
is willing to share its life with others in need.

Take hold of this abundant life today! Share your life and the
things that God has blessed you with with someone else that needs
to see and experience the love of God today.

ON FIRE FOR GOD

I thank God, whom I serve, as my forefathers did, with a clear conscience, as night and day I constantly remember you in my prayers. Recalling your tears, I long to see you, so that I may be filled with joy. I have been reminded of your sincere faith, which first lived in your grandmother Louis and in your mother Eunice and, I am persuaded, now lives in you also. For this reason I remind you to fan into flame the gift of God, which is in you through the laying on of my hands. For God did not give us a spirit of timidity, but a spirit of power, of love and of self-discipline.

2 Timothy 1:3–7

Paul is encouraging young Timothy here to live his life on fire for the Lord. If you have surrendered your heart and life to Jesus Christ, then there is a Spirit that lives inside of you that has more power than you could ever begin to imagine. God's Spirit gives you the power to love others as he loves us, the power to obey and to resist the devil's lies and schemes that are meant to drag you back into your old way of life, and the power to testify to others about how this great God that we serve has changed your heart and life for the better! Tap into this power today by spending time alone with Jesus and focusing your thoughts and attention on him. God wants to take your life and ignite a fire in your heart that can be seen by everybody and that will light the way for others around you that are still in the dark. The power is there; surrender your heart and life to Jesus today!

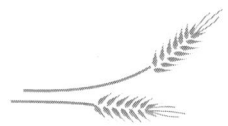

SOLDIER OF CHRIST

Endure hardship with us like a good soldier of Christ Jesus. No one serving as a soldier gets involved in civilian affairs—he wants to please his commanding officer.

2 Timothy 2:3–4

I can't imagine what it is like to be a soldier, representing the US over in Iraq. What I do know for sure is that these brave men are not concerned with some of the petty things that seem to consume our minds throughout the day. They are not concerned with what they are going to purchase any time soon, what clothes that they are going to wear, what house or neighborhood that they are going to live in, how successful they are or what their social status is, what their neighbors are saying about them, or what they are going to have for dinner that evening. No, their main concern is to accomplish their task for which they have been sent there. Likewise, if you have accepted Jesus Christ into your heart and life, then you are his soldier and your main concern on this earth should be living your life for him! The enemy will try to divert your attention to "civilian affairs"; don't let him distract you today from your primary purpose on earth as a new child of God! If you're a Christian, then you will suffer hardship here in this life! People will discount your beliefs, turn the other way, make fun of you, betray your friendship, and try their best to get you to stumble off of the new path that God has put you on. Don't be discouraged. First John 4:4 reminds us that "the one who is in you is greater than the one who is in the world." So today, do your best to please your commanding officer by loving the Lord your God with all of your heart and all of your mind and all of your strength. Make his purpose for your life the most important thing on your agenda today and you will be rewarded by him for your efforts.

DESERT ROSE

But mark this: There will be terrible times in the last days. People will be lovers of themselves, lovers of money, boastful, proud, abusive, disobedient to their parents, ungrateful, unholy, without love, unforgiving, slanderous, without self-control, brutal, not lovers of the good, treacherous, rash, conceited, lovers of pleasure rather than lovers of God—having a form of Godliness but denying it's power. Have nothing to do with them.

2 Timothy 3:1–5

It's no wonder that at times as a Christian you may feel unappreciated and incredibly lonely in the midst of the environment that we live here in the end times. You may even feel like giving up at times, wondering if you are making a difference in this world and if your light that you struggle so hard to keep shining in the midst of all this darkness can even be seen by the lost people that are all around you.

In the mid-eighties, White Heart wrote a song entitled "Desert Rose." The chorus line goes like this: "Desert Rose, don't you worry, don't be lonely, in a dry and weary land the flower grows." The flower grows because the God of this world is the gardener and he cares more for you than can ever imagine! He notices and so much appreciates your faithfulness to him! He promises never to leave you nor forsake you and says that there is nothing in this world that can ever separate you from his love! So be encouraged today because if you are living your life for Jesus Christ then you are making a difference, and despite what you may think or feel, people are watching you and noticing the work of God in your life, and God will continue to use you for his glory in this present life. So persevere, my brothers and sisters, and continue to live your life for him!

EQUIPPED FOR GODLINESS

All Scripture is God-breathed and is useful for teaching, rebuking, correcting, and training in righteousness, so that the man of God may be thoroughly equipped for every good work.

2 Timothy 3:16–17

I am convinced that spending just a few minutes with God in his Word and reflecting on what he has to teach you will make a huge difference in your walk with the Lord. The Bible says that if we love God then we must love his Word since the Word is God himself. God directs guides, teaches, rebukes, comforts, and loves us through this amazing book called the Bible that he gives as a gift for us to embrace and learn from each and every day. How blessed we are to be able to spend quality time with God, the Creator of everything, as he uses his Word to make us more like him. Thanks be to God.

FINISH THE RACE

For I am already being poured out like a drink offering, and the time has come for my departure. I have fought the good fight, I have finished the race, I have kept the faith ... At my first defense, no one came to my support, but everyone deserted me. May it not be held against them.

2 Timothy 4:6–7, 16

At the end of Paul's life, after an unbelievable journey where great things were accomplished for the Lord and thousands upon thousands of people were touched by the Apostle Paul's passion, love, and commitment for spreading the Gospel of Jesus Christ, there was a time that he was all alone and felt deserted by his friends and fellow believers. Even today, 2,000 years later, people are still being encouraged and inspired by this great man of God and yet, in the end, while he stood trial before the court, he felt all alone! Even still, he finishes the race with a faith and commitment that cannot be broken. You see, Paul's eyes were not focused on other people's commitment and faith. If that were the case then he would have indeed been discouraged and would have undoubtedly given up the pursuit of holiness. No, Paul's faith was rooted in something much deeper than another person or a pastor or a spouse or a close friend. Paul's faith was rooted in an unyielding love relationship with Jesus Christ. This relationship would never let him down, would always be there to comfort him, would bring joy in the darkest of circumstances, and would eventually see to it that he finished this incredible race that taught, touched, and encouraged so many people up to this present age. In this life, people are going to let you down. You are going to let yourself down. Don't focus on these things. Focus on Christ! Draw near to him today, look to him for strength, and finish the race, for the prize that awaits you in the end will be well worth your faith and commitment.

JOY

Be joyful always; pray continually; give thanks in all circumstances, for this is God's will for you in Christ Jesus.

1 Thessalonians 5:16–17

There is something that happens when you truly accept Jesus Christ as your personal Savior and you surrender your heart and life to him: he gives you a peace and a joy that is present in all circumstances; a peace and a joy that passes all understanding and cannot be explained but can only be experienced by those who have truly surrendered to him. I don't know what your circumstance is today or what difficult things that you may be facing in this life, but what I do know for sure is that if you take the focus off of yourself and you focus on what God is doing in your life and in the lives of those around you, then you will indeed have a joy just like Paul did here in his letter to the Thessalonians. His joy was present in the very worst circumstances of being locked up in prison and having his life threatened. The Bible says that there is nothing in this world that can separate you from God's love and the joy that results from a heart that is focused on him! So today, rise above your circumstances—look outside of yourself and focus your attention on God, draw near to him in prayer, and ask him to give you a peace and a joy that will last for all eternity!

HUMBLE PRAYER AND OBEDIENCE

If my people, who are called by my name, will humble themselves and pray and seek my face and turn from their wicked ways, then will I hear from heaven and will forgive their sin and will heal their land.

2 Chronicles 7:14

A pretty simple formula don't you think? But unfortunately, very few people, even ones that call themselves Christians and go to church, put this simplicity of humbly seeking the face of God into practice. You see, it's the sin that caused Satan to fall from heaven that keeps many people from truly surrendering their whole heart to the lordship of Jesus Christ—the sin of pride. Many people think that they have everything all figured out in this life. They want to be in control and they will never willingly surrender control of their life to anyone—not even God. The problem with that is that God is God; he created the world, he is in control, and he will eventually bring everyone to a place in his or her life where he or she understands that a relationship with him is what this life is really about and that nothing else can even come close to measuring up with the abundant life that he made possible for us by dying on the Cross. For some people it takes a major crisis in life to get to this point of realization of the need for God—a loss of a job, a death of a loved one, imprisonment, addiction to drugs or alcohol, a critical illness—for some people it takes drastic measures to get their attention off of themselves and on to the Creator of this world who just wants to love them!

Are you at that point in your life where you know, from the bottom of your heart, that he is the only one that can satisfy your hunger and thirst for fulfillment and joy in this life, so you humbly seek his face each and every day and you live your life in order to please him? If not, then what is it going to take to get you to this point? One thing that I know for sure is that one day he will get your attention and you will be humbled before him and know that it is only God that can truly bring you happiness in this life; I just hope that on that day it is not too late. Humble yourself before the Lord then today. Make a 180-degree turn from living your life for yourself to living your life for God and in truly surrendering to him you will receive power and blessing, joy and fulfillment like you could have never imagined! It will be the best decision that you have ever made and will change your life forever!

FRUITFUL GROWTH AND ENDURANCE

For this reason, since the day we heard about you, we have not stopped praying for you and asking God to fill you with the knowledge of His will through all spiritual wisdom and understanding. And we pray this in order that you may live a life worthy of the Lord and may please Him in every way: bearing fruit in every good work, growing in the knowledge of God, being strengthened with all power according to His glorious might so that you may have great endurance and patience, and joyfully giving thanks to the Father, who has qualified you to share in the inheritance of the saints in the Kingdom of Light. For He has rescued us from the dominion of darkness and brought us into the Kingdom of the Son He loves, in whom we have redemption, the forgiveness of sins.

Colossians 1:9–14

This Christian thing is much more than just praying a prayer and then sitting back and waiting for Christ to return. If you have indeed surrendered your heart to Christ and thus are called a Christian, then there should be evidence of Christ in the way that you live your life. You life should be bearing fruit for his glory. That means that other people should be able to see the attributes of God by looking at you! You should be growing in the knowledge of God through studying his Word, and your heart should be in the process of being transformed and strengthened by his power in order that you can endure and persevere in living your life for him and turning away from darkness, which is life without him and living your life for yourself.

Have you sincerely surrendered you heart to Jesus Christ? Do you see evidence of his Spirit working in you to make you more like him? Can other people see Jesus in you? If not, then it is not too late. All you have to do is ask. Pray now and ask Jesus into your heart. Ask him for forgiveness of your sins and tell him that you want to live your life for him. Start the process of obedience by being baptized, and then hang on for dear life, for God will consume you with his love and will begin to change your life forever!

If you prayed this prayer, then let someone know so that he or she can celebrate with you!

COMPLETENESS IN CHRIST

He is the image of the invisible God, the firstborn over all creation. For by Him all things were created: things in heaven and on earth, visible and invisible, whether thrones of powers or rulers or authorities; all things were created by Him and for Him. He is before all things, and in Him all things shall hold together. And He is the head of the body, the church; he is the beginning and the firstborn from among the dead, so that in everything He might have the supremacy. For God was pleased to have all His fullness dwell in Him, and through Him to reconcile to Himself all things, whether things on earth or things in heaven, by making peace through His blood shed on the cross. Once you were alienated from God and were enemies in your minds because of your evil behavior. But now He has reconciled you by Christ's physical body through death to present you Holy in His sight, without blemish and free from accusation—if you continue in your Faith, established and firm, not moved from the hope held out in the gospel. This is the Gospel that you heard and that has been proclaimed to every creature under heaven, and of which I, Paul, have become a servant.

Colossians 1:15–23

You were created by God. Your reason for living is to abide with him. The only thing in your life that will bring fulfillment and meaning—that will hold you together in this crazy world and will give you a reason to wake up in the morning is your relationship with him! A good life is found in him. Completeness, significance, joy, happiness, meaning, fulfillment, true love, and power is all there for you by the God who made you with his own hands and who shed his very own blood in order to bring you back together as one in him! So today, stop looking at external things in this life like your job or your spouse or your circumstances and blaming your unhappiness on them, for true happiness can only be found in looking internally at your heart and reconciling yourself to the Maker of your life by surrendering your very own life back to him. Seek him today with all your heart!

CONNECTED TO THE POWER SOURCE

To them God has chosen to make known among the Gentiles the glorious riches of this mystery, which is Christ in you, the hope of Glory. We proclaim Him, admonishing and teaching everyone with all wisdom, so that we may present everyone perfect in Christ. To this end I labor, struggling with all His energy, which so powerfully works in me.

Colossians 1:27–29

What an amazing concept to grasp and really understand. The God of this world is living inside of your very heart if you have accepted him and his sacrifice! He gives you power, just the like the power that the Apostle Paul speaks of here in Colossians, to live your life for him and to proclaim his glory to everyone around you by spreading his love and sharing this wonderful mystery to everyone who is in the dark. Through his Word and through prayer you can stay connected to the power source that will energize you to be a living sacrifice for the one that gave his life for you! I write this in hopes that you will spend just a few minutes of your day in his Word, in prayer, and reflecting on him in order that you can receive power from above to face this harsh and cold world. Ask him now to use you today. Pray that his Spirit would empower you to be an obedient saint, full of every good work and the joy that comes only from above.

RENEW YOUR MIND

Since then, you have been raised with Christ, set your hearts on things above, where Christ is seated at the right hand of God. Set your minds on things above, not on earthly things. For you died, and your life is now hidden with Christ in God. When Christ, who is your life, appears, then you also will appear with him in glory.

Colossians 3:1–4

One thing that you do have complete control of in this life is what you think about. The thoughts that you let dwell in your mind throughout the day are thoughts that you let stay there and hang out in your mind. Don't you know that the very first attack that the enemy will make on your newfound faith in God and Christian walk will be on your mind? He will tempt you with thoughts of self-ishness, lust, anger, resentment, greed, etc. to see if you will choose to entertain those thoughts and let them stay in your mind or if you will reject them through the power of Christ who now lives in you and set your mind instead on God and your relationship with him. A good barometer for the condition of your heart is to examine your thought life: what do you think about the most throughout your day? The Bible tells us in Philippians 4:8: "Finally, brothers, whatever is true, whatever is noble, whatever is right, whatever is pure, whatever is lovely, whatever is admirable—if anything is excellent or praiseworthy—think about such things." The battle for your heart begins in the mind! Guard your thought life today.

PEACE AND CONTENTMENT

Let the peace of Christ rule in your hearts, since as members of one body you were called to peace. And be thankful.

Colossians 3:15

I don't know about you, but for me, sometimes it is hard to just rest in God and enjoy the peace and contentment that a relationship with him brings. I think that this is because of the way that I was programmed as a child in our capitalistic society. We are trained at a very young age here to always be looking for the next thing. We think that we have got to go, got to go, got to get to work, got to get home, got to get to bed, got to go on vacation, got to get the next big sale, go to get the next big toy, got to do more for the church, got to have more control of life, got to eliminate debt, got to find the next big rush, got to do whatever it is that keeps us from truly living in the moment and enjoying the presence of God in our lives! So today, slow down, spend some time with your Creator, and instead of looking to the future and what you are going to do next, have a look at where you are right now, all that God has blessed you with, the people that he has placed in your life, the beauty of his creation, and the power and wonder of his love, and enjoy his presence! Soak in this peace of God that passes all understanding and be thankful for everything that God has done and the relationship that you now can have with him.

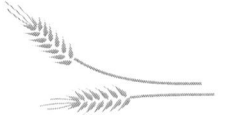

SEASONED WITH SALT

Be wise in the way you act toward outsiders; make the most of every opportunity. Let your conversation be always full of grace, seasoned with salt, so that you may know how to answer everyone.

Colossians 4:4–6

Salt is a tasty preservative and is used as an analogy here to describe conversations that we as Christians have with other people. Our conversations as Christians should be wholesome, always building up, encouraging, and appealing. "Full of grace" means that we should not go about condemning the world but we should offer the same grace that God offers us! One thing that I know for sure is that none of this ideal conversation that Paul describes here in the book of Colossians can be done on our own. No, in order to achieve such a high level of godliness in our speech, we must draw near to God and let him give us the words to say and let him control our attitudes and actions. Have you connected with the power source today? Are you ready to make a difference in the world around you by speaking unselfishly and full of grace to others in order that they too may come to know and have a relationship with the loving Savior, Jesus Christ, who you first saw in the life, actions, and speech of another believer? Draw near to him today and then draw near to others and love them with his unfailing love!

CONNECTED TO THE PEOPLE OF GOD

Tychicus will tell you all the news about me. He is a dear brother, a faithful minister and fellow servant in the Lord. I am sending him to you for the express purpose that you may know about our circumstances and that he may encourage your hearts. He is coming with Onesimus, our faithful and dear brother, who is one of you. They will tell you everything that is happening here. My fellow prisoner Aristarchus sends you his greetings as does Mark, the cousin of Barnabas. (You have received instructions about him; if he comes to you, welcome him.) Jesus, who is called Justus, also sends greetings. These are the only Jews among my fellow workers for the Kingdom of God, and they have proved a comfort to me. Epaphras, who is one of you and a servant of Christ Jesus, sends greetings. He is always wrestling in prayer for you, that you may stand firm in all the will of God, mature and fully assured. I vouch for him that he is working hard for you and for those at Laodicea and Hierapolis. Our dear friend Luke, the doctor, and Demas send greetings.

Colossians 4:7–14

Tychicus, Onesimus, Aristarchus, Mark, Justus, Epaphras, Luke, and Demas—these are all people who were connected to Paul and were connected to the church in Colossians. They were connected because of their common faith in Jesus Christ, and they spent hours upon hours praying for each other, learning from each other, and encouraging each other in the Lord. Paul, in chains in prison and in jeopardy of losing his life, spent his time writing letters of encouragement to fellow believers, praying for them, and gaining encouragement from them to press on and live a life of godliness. As good a man as Paul was, that fact remains that he couldn't do it alone. He needed the counsel and encouragement of other Christians. We need each other! We are the Church, and without real relationships that hold each other accountable and encourage, we will not experience God's best for our lives. Are you connected today? Do you have a friend that you can share even the most personal struggles and victories in regards to your faith in Jesus Christ with? Because of pride, it is easy in this world to try to live a godly life on your own, not really connecting with anyone to hold you accountable or to encourage you in your faith—I would not recommend this! Get connected today and you will make friendships that will last for the rest of eternity!

HUNGER AND THIRST FOR GOD

I spread out my hands to you; my soul thirsts for you like a parched land.

Psalm 143:6

Sometimes, as we continue on in this journey toward an abundant life with Christ, somewhere along the path you may find yourself distracted by things of the world that are not of God, and as a result, you may stray off the path a bit into the thorns and bushes that are along the edge. This happens because of sin in your life, and when it happens it does not take long before you may find yourself in the same state of mind that David was in here in the book of Psalms, where the peace and joy of his salvation that he once experienced in his life were gone and nothing was left but a hunger and thirst to once again be united to his Savior and made complete and whole again in him. At some point this will indeed happen in your journey since you are not perfected as of yet in your relationship with Jesus and will not be made completely holy until the day that he returns and brings us all who have trusted in him back to a perfect oneness with God. When this separation occurs, do not despair, for God promises to always restore your relationship with him, no matter how far you have strayed, as you seek his forgiveness and turn your heart back to the only one who will give you real, abundant joy in this life. His love never fails and his grace never runs out!

Seek him today with all of your heart; turn back to him and thirst no more!

MORE THAN YOU CAN THINK OR IMAGINE

I pray that out of His glorious riches He may strengthen you with power through His Spirit in your inner being, so that Christ may dwell in your hearts through faith. And I pray that you, being rooted and established in love, may have power, together with all the Saints, to grasp how wide and long and high and deep is the love of Christ, and to know this love that surpasses knowledge—that you may be filled to the measure of all the fullness of God. Now to Him who is able to do immeasurably more than all we ask or imagine, according to His power that is at work within us, to Him be the glory in the church and in Christ Jesus throughout all generations, for ever and ever! Amen.

Ephesians 3:16–21

Great love that surpasses knowledge! How could anyone live a normal life that has been rooted and established in this love and in the power of God himself living inside and changing you in ways that you could never begin to even know or understand. There is a war that is waging inside of your heart that is trying to keep you from believing that God can and will do the unimaginable in your life if you would just stop trying to understand it all and just surrender and let him fill you with this amazing, phenomenal, indescribable love and power that goes far beyond what your brain could ever begin to understand.

For a Christian, normality is a road block that will stifle the power of God in your life and cause you to miss out on the greatness of his power and love that he wants to express through your very life. So today, don't be discouraged if a friend or a loved one says that you are not normal because of your faith in Jesus Christ, for living a life of servitude in obedience to Christ and letting his unfathomable love and power change your heart and mind to be more like his is anything but normal! A heart that is being transformed by this amazing love cannot help but stand out in this world of sin. Don't try to fit in today; don't try to be "normal"; don't worry about what other people think; just let this love that surpasses knowledge spill out of your heart and make a difference to the world around you. Live you life for him today.

BEARING WITH ONE ANOTHER IN LOVE

As a prisoner for the Lord, then, I urge you to live a life worthy of the calling you have received. Be completely humble and gentle; be patient, bearing with one another in love.

Ephesians 4:1–2

The dictionary defines "bearing" as: "to hold up, to support, to carry from one place to another, to have a tolerance for, to be account-able for, and to carry in the mind." As Christians, when we become self-consumed with our own problems, failures, successes, etc. is when we run into trouble. Christian life was never meant to be lived alone. You are a very small part of a huge body of believers that need your gifts, your talents, your encouragement and participation in order to thrive as a church. Power and victory in the Christian walk comes only when we take our focus off of ourselves and redirect it on to others as we bear each other's burdens in love! When was the last time that you thought about someone else's faith rather than your own and how you could encourage that person in his or her walk with the Lord?

Humbly serve the Lord today by giving your life away to other believers who desperately need your love and encouragement!

FAITH THAT IS SEEN, NOT HEARD

And so you became a model to all the believers in Macedonia and Achaia. The Lord's message rang out from you not only in Macedonia and Achaia—your faith in God has become known everywhere.

1 Thessalonians 1:7–8

Does your faith ring out to the people around you? Do they know that you are a Christian, not because of words that come out of your mouth but because they see you living your life so radically different from everyone else by humbly loving and giving, being a servant to others that you come into contact with, showing a concern and love for the lost and hurting people that God has placed in your life so that they could see him in you and know that he is real? Being a Christian means that you no longer live for yourself but you now live for God. To be a Christian is to let God come into your heart, but it doesn't stop there. The reason his Spirit becomes a part of your life is so that he can work in you to make you more like him and at the same time work through you to touch the lives of people around you—to be his hands and feet! You shouldn't have to tell people about your faith in Christ, they should already know by the way that you live your life—they should be able to see Jesus in you! One of the most meaningful things that my wife Paula has ever said to me was said on Christmas Eve in San Antonio back in 2000. With tears in her eyes, she told me that she sees God in me, and that is something that I will never forget, for today that is the goal of my life—to live my life in a way that others will see and know that Jesus is real, and as a result they will believe and trust in him. I am not there yet and I will never be a perfect reflection of God in this life, but I must say that there is great joy in the journey of becoming more like him! Are you a Christian? Can other people see Jesus in you? Surrender you heart and life to him today!

UNITY

Make every effort to keep the unity of the Spirit through the bond of peace. There is one body and one Spirit—just as you were called to hope when you were called—one Lord, on faith, one baptism; one God and Father of all, who is over all and through all and in all.

Ephesians 4:3–6

In the world there are many different denominations of the Christian faith that vary in small details concerning communion and worship and many other things that are important but are not the most important aspect of our faith. The most important commonality that all Christian denominations have is Jesus Christ! There is no debating that he is the Son of God, has been crucified, has risen, and is living in the hearts of all of his people that have put their faith in him. Jesus Christ should be our focus as we bond together as one church and live out our lives as broken vessels for God to use to reach the world around us. Do not let the enemy distract your attention away from the Giver of life to the minor details that your particular denomination may differ on in interpretation, but instead, focus all of your attention on him, live your life for him, and he will take care of the details.

PLAYER OF SPECTATOR

It was he who gave some to be apostles, some to be prophets, some to be evangelists, and some to be pastors and teachers, to prepare God's people for works of service, so that the body of Christ may be built up until we all reach unity in faith and in the knowledge of the Son of God and become mature, attaining the whole measure of the fullness of Christ.

Ephesians 4:11–13

"To prepare God's people for works of service." I love this verse in Ephesians as it describes what the Christian life is all about. Too many people go to church and approach Christianity as a spectator instead of getting in the game! I have a customer that has just opened a location in a new city, and his store's famous quote is, "We are not here for batting practice, we are here to play." God's plan for you when he captured your heart and brought you into a relationship with him through his Son Jesus was for you to get into the game and play, not just to be a spectator on the sidelines. He has given you gifts to use so that you can play out your part in his body of believers called the church. It is only when you jump into the game and start using these gifts that he has given you to contribute to the cause of Christ that you will understand and fully comprehend the incredible joy and fulfillment that come when you live your life for him! Get into the game today!

SECURE AND MATURE IN CHRIST

Then we will no longer be infants, tossed back and forth by the waves, and blown here and there by every wind of teaching and by the cunning and craftiness of men in their deceitful scheming. Instead, speaking the truth in love, we will in all things grow up into Him who is the Head, that is, Christ. From Him the whole body, joined and held together by every supporting ligament, grows and builds itself up in love, as each part does its work.

Ephesians 4:14–16

Because of the weakness of my flesh, I feel like such an infant at times in my walk with Christ. Oh, to be mature and secure in him, not lacking anything, not worrying about the temptation of sin and failure, but simply enjoying his presence and soaking up his love and joy is what I truly strive for in this life! The truth is that I am just one small part of a much bigger body of believers called the Church. The direction, focus, and mission of the Church is to seek the face of Christ, to become more like him. As a Church we connect on an intimate level; we share our deepest needs, desires, longing, hurts, pains, failures, and successes in very real relationships where we hold each other accountable and seek his face together. As we struggle through this life in hopes that our lives will be a true reflection of Jesus Christ, we pray collectively for each other and for nonbelievers to come to know him. When we see his power at work in us and each one of us plays his or her part to the very best of his or her abilities, it is then and only then that we will be mature as a Church and we will see God move in a dramatic way within all of our hearts! Without the Church I am nothing, and the small part that I play outside of a committed body of believers to encourage me and supplement my gifts with gifts of their own would eventually be snuffed out by this fallen world of unbelief. We need each other in order to be mature and secure in our walk with the Lord. Get connected to the body of believers today!

PUT ON YOUR NEW SELF

So I tell you this, and insist on it in the Lord, that you must no longer live as the Gentiles do, in the futility of their thinking. They are darkened in their understanding and separated from the life of God because of the ignorance that it is in them due to the hardening of their hearts. Having lost all sensitivity, they have given themselves over to sensuality so as to indulge in every kind of impurity, with a continual lust for more. You, however, did not come to know Christ that way. Surely you heard of Him and were taught in Him in accordance with the Truth that is in Jesus. You were taught, with regard to your former way of life, to put off your old self, which is being corrupted by its deceitful desires, to be made new in the attitude of your minds; and put on the new self, created to be like God in true righteousness and Holiness.

Ephesians 4:17–24

Even though you are a new creation in Christ, if indeed you have accepted his sacrifice that he made for you on the Cross and surrendered your heart and life to his control, there is still your old self, your sinful nature that is called your flesh that will never go away until you are fully redeemed in Christ at his return. So then, each day, or really, every minute of every day, you have a choice as to which nature will rule in your heart: either your new nature that finds its purpose in a relationship with Jesus Christ or your old nature that has no purpose really, except to separate you from God. Of course, the only way to really experience the abundant life that Jesus describes is to walk with him in your new self, letting him control your mind, your thoughts, and your actions as you trust in his power and love to always see you through whatever it is that this world dishes out at you on any given day.

It will not be easy to always make the right choices, as there is indeed an enemy that is a liar and that will try to deceive you into thinking that what will really bring you happiness is to go your own way and do your own thing apart from God, but I promise that this path only leads to disappointment, despair, heartache, loneliness, and futility. Maybe this is where you are at right now in your life; maybe you have chosen to follow your fleshly desires and have discovered that your way is not the best way for your life. God will always forgive you if you come back to him! His grace and love cover a multitude of sins and will always be there for you when you lose your way to bring you back into the peaceful and joyful lifestyle that is full of purpose and meaning and is only found in giving your life away to the lordship of Jesus Christ! So come back to him today! Put on your new self in Christ and discover all of the great things that he has for you as you live your life for Him!

SPEAK WORDS OF ENCOURAGEMENT

Do not let any unwholesome talk come out of your mouths, but only what is helpful for building others up according to their needs, that it may benefit those who listen. And do not grieve the Holy Spirit of God, with whom you were sealed for the day of redemption. Get rid of all bitterness, rage and anger, brawling and slander, along with every kind of malice. Be kind and compassionate to one another, forgiving each other, just as Christ God forgave you.

Ephesians 4:29–32

There are people in this life that will do things to you that will be very difficult to forgive. One thing to keep in mind as you struggle through the feelings of anger and bitterness is that if you do not show them the same grace that God has shown you and forgive them completely, you will grieve the Holy Spirit's work in your life and will only hurt yourself and your own growth in Christ. The Holy Spirit cannot work in a heart that is disobedient or a heart that is full of anger, bitterness, rage, or malice. God has so much more of his love and fulfillment, purpose and meaning that he wants to play out in your life. He has a whole new world for you to experience and enjoy as he uses you to make a difference and to reach other people for him—you will never experience this world in this life, however, if you hang on to bitterness in your heart. So today, instead of being angry, instead of being bitter and resentful, speak words of encouragement and forgive that person that has stomped on your heart so many times, love them just as Christ has loved you and has forgiven you, and experience once again the peace and joy of God's Spirit working to make you more like him!

LOVE AND SACRIFICE

Be imitators of God, therefore, as dearly loved children and live a life of love, just as Christ loved us and gave Himself up for us as a fragrant offering and sacrifice to God.

Ephesians 5:1–2

To be an imitator of God and to live a life of love and sacrifice is such a high calling but it is expected of anyone who calls themselves a Christ follower. It is a life that yields great rewards, overwhelming peace and love, indescribable joy, crystal clear purpose and meaning, and it is something that we will never completely attain until Christ's return. The pursuit of such a life, however, is what drives us, every minute of every day. It is the reason that we are here and the sweet prize that awaits us at the end of the race! Oh to taste just a small morsel of the awesome unconditional love of Christ and be able to share that love with someone in need is what we long for and what makes us whole and complete in him! Be an imitator of God today; share his love with everyone you meet.

FAITHFUL—EVEN IN THE GOOD TIMES

After Rehoboam's position as king was established and he had become strong, he and all Israel with him abandoned the law of the Lord.

2 Chronicles 12:1

When things are going good—when tragedy and disappointments of this life have passed and God somehow has pulled you through the worst of circumstances and experiences in this life—it is then that it becomes very easy to forget about God and to go your own way in life. That is what happened here with King Rehoboam. After the first years of his kingdom were in turmoil and the Israelites rejected him as king, God had restored his position as king and made him strong, and then as thanks to God for his faithfulness, he turned his back on him once again. Who knows why this happens so easily and how we can so quickly forget all that God has done for us during the tough times in this life when all is well. Maybe it is because of our pride or our selfishness or our need to be in control that we believe the lie that we can make it on our own. The truth is that you cannot make it on your own, and if you choose to go your own way, then emptiness, disappointment, failure, and despair are not far behind! So today I encourage you to be faithful even in the good times! Draw near to God with a thankful heart for all he has done, remember his goodness, how he gave his life for you and all that he has done in your life, and surrender once again to him—give him your heart and your life and you will experience much more abundance and joy in this life as you daily seek his face.

CHILDREN OF THE LIGHT

For you were once darkness, but now you are light in the Lord. Live as children of light.

Ephesians 5:8

Some of my favorite paintings are those of the artist Thomas Kinkade who's well-known for being the "Painter of Light." Mr. Kinkade uses the imagery of light in his paintings to emphasize simple pleasures and inspiration messages as he successfully communicates and spreads inherent life-affirming values through his work. I believe that it is the light in the paintings that makes them unique and that captures and softens the hearts of the millions of people who enjoy his creations each and every day. These paintings are a good parallel as to how your life as a Christian should capture and soften the hearts of people with whom you come into contact as they see the light of Christ through the way you live your life. To live as children of the light means that your life will be much different from the world around you, as people will see and know that God is real because they see him living in you! Let your light shine today.

ONENESS IN MARRIAGE

For this reason a man will leave his father and mother and be united to his wife, and the two will become one flesh.

Ephesians 5:31

There have been probably thousands of books written on this subject, so a few paragraphs in a daily devotion can hardly do it justice; however, I would like to comment on just a few things that God has taught me so far on being one with my wife, Paula. Words cannot describe the joy that I experience each day as a result of this most precious gift that God has given me to share the most intimate of life experiences with both now and for the rest of eternity! I am humbled by the fact that I do not even come close to deserving her love and commitment that she provides on a daily basis. I try to love her with God's love, and although there are times of failure for both of us, his grace always prevails since we have a bond that holds us together that will never be broken as long as we stay committed to God and committed to each other. Paula is my best friend; she knows me better than anyone else and, surprisingly enough, even better than I know myself at times. Life experiences would mean nothing without having her to share them with. My prayer is that we grow in the years to come to know each other even more deeply so that we can love and encourage each other as we together become more like him! I pray that you are either working toward or will one day be growing together with a godly spouse in order to achieve this blessed gift from above of oneness in marriage.

I love you, Paula! Thank you for being my wife to share and enjoy this life with both now and forevermore!

ARMOR OF GOD

Finally, be strong in the Lord and in His mighty power. Put on the full armor of God so that you can take your stand against the devil's schemes. For our struggle is not against flesh and blood, but against the rulers, against the authorities, against the powers of this dark world and against the spiritual forces of evil in the heavenly realms. Therefore put on the full armor of God, so that when the day of evil comes, you may be able to stand your ground, and after you have done everything, to stand. Stand firm then, with the belt of Truth buckled around your waist, with the breastplate of righteousness in place, and with your feet fitted with the readiness that comes from the gospel of peace. In addition to all of this, take up the shield of faith, with which you can extinguish all the flaming arrows of the evil one. Take the helmet of salvation and the sword of the Spirit, which is the Word of God. And pray in the Spirit on all occasions with all kinds of prayers and requests. With this in mind, be alert and always keep on praying for all the Saints.

Ephesians 6:10–18

Whether you like it or not or whether you choose to acknowledge it or not, that doesn't change the fact that there is a spiritual battle taking place in a third realm all around you! There are angels and demons that are fighting for control of your mind and heart; they are fighting to try to stop the power of God from working in your life to make you more like him and from loving others with his love. The thing about our enemy is that he knows when to attack us, where we are vulnerable, and just what it will take to lead us astray. The very scary thing is that it all starts in the mind with a thought and escalates from there until we are rendered useless for the work of God in our lives.

You see, when you became a Christian, you received the power of God and his Spirit, but he also left you with the power to choose, and this is the very thing that the enemy tries to entice us with in order that we will not be effective for the cause of Christ in this lifetime. As Paul talks about in Ephesians here, it is blatantly apparent that the only way to be victorious in this Spiritual battle is to leave the fighting to God and his Spirit by staying as close to him as you can all of the time! This doesn't just happen; it takes a conscious effort to remain in his Word each day, to remain in communication with him throughout the day in prayer and to look for ways to give your life away for him as you go through your normal mundane tasks of the day. If you stay close to God, then it will be easy to make the right choice when the time of temptation comes and a thought is thrown your way from the enemy at the most vulnerable area of your life. One thing that I know for sure is that if you are making a difference for God and he is working in your heart to change you and to make you more like him, then you will be attacked and it is wise to prepare ahead of time for that moment and the response that you will give. You know where you are most vulnerable, you know where the enemy will try to invade your heart and mind, so plan now how you will respond and stay close to God. After all, the abundant life is found in staying close to him.

CRUCIFIED WITH CHRIST

I have been crucified with Christ and I no longer live, but Christ lives in me. The life I live in the body, I live by faith in the Son of God, who loved me and gave Himself for me.

Galatians 2:20

If you have surrendered your heart and life to Jesus Christ, then your old self should be dying a slow death as Jesus Christ changes you from within and begins to live through you by making you more like him! Your priorities, motivation, desires, ambitions, habits, goals, and even some friends may change as a result of your newfound faith in Jesus. What he has to offer you goes exceedingly above and beyond anything that you have given up as a result of him! The secret to living an abundant life is found only in surrendering the life that you know and are comfortable with and trusting in God to replace that life with a new life that is rooted in Christ. The peace, joy, fulfillment, and love that he offers go far beyond what any words can describe. The only way to know this life is to die to your old self and experience this abundant life for yourself. This process of dying to your old self will continue as you live your life here in this world, because you will not be made perfectly complete in him until he returns to take you to heaven with him to live forever. It is a daily, hourly, even minute-by-minute decision to choose him and to live for him and not for yourself. So choose him today. Put to death your old self and find new life in our awesome Lord and Savior Jesus Christ!

ALL ENCOMPASSING GRACE OF GOD

I do not set aside the grace of God, for if righteousness could be gained through the law, Christ died for nothing!

Galatians 2:21

So maybe today you feel like failure; maybe you feel like you can't quite measure up to the godly standards that we talk so much about; maybe you are struggling with some sort of sin or addiction in your life that you just can't seem to shake; maybe you even feel like giving up on the pursuit of holiness because you are not good enough. If this is you today then I have great news for you! Through repentance, because of what Jesus did for you on the Cross, the all-encompassing grace of God covers whatever sin or failures you might be struggling with today! Righteousness cannot ever be gained by doing everything perfect or living a godly life or following all of the rules impeccably. If this were possible, then we would not need Jesus, and as the verse in Galatians says, he would have died for nothing! All that God asks of you today is that you repent of your sins and seek him with all of your heart. If you do these two things, then he will do the rest. He will cover your failures as you ask his forgiveness and then he will begin to change you on the inside so that you will slowly become more and more like him and like the person that he originally created you to be! God loves you today more than you can imagine. Put your trust in him!

HUMAN EFFORT VS. FAITH AND BELIEF

You foolish Galatians! Who has bewitched you? Before your very eyes Jesus Christ was clearly portrayed as crucified. I would like to learn just one thing from you: Did you receive the Spirit by observing the law, or by believing what you heard? Are you so foolish? After beginning with the Spirit, are you now trying to attain your goal by human effort? Have you suffered so much for nothing—if it really was for nothing? Does God give you His Spirit and work miracles among you because you observe the law, or because you believe what you heard?

Galatians 3:1–5

I can relate to what Paul is speaking to the church in Galatia about in this passage, as I too at times try to attain righteousness through human effort rather than just believing and trusting in God to do the work in my life and staying close to him! Foolishness is correct in that our best efforts as humans do not even compare to the greatness, creativity, or the awesome power of God in our lives! I wonder what we could do as a Church if we would stop trying to humanize our efforts of evangelism, stop trying to market God, and just believe in a miracle through prayer, surrender, and just staying as close to him as we can! It would behoove us as Christians to stop our shallow discussions of the process of Christianity and to really open up our hearts to each other, to let our guards down, and to discuss what is really going on inside with our relationship to God. It is in those types of discussions where miracles happen and where the power of God is present and active in order to change hearts and lives. God wants to act out a miracle in the lives of people that are not afraid to be transparent about their faith, be willing to share their weaknesses and failures, and just believe God to be their strength to make them more like him! God wants to use you in ways that you have never even dreamed about or imagined. Draw near to him today and believe.

RIGHT WHERE YOU ARE:
A TESTIMONY FOR GOD

When I came to you, brothers, I did not come with eloquence or supe-rior wisdom as I proclaimed to you the testimony about God. For I resolved to know nothing while I was with you except Jesus Christ and Him crucified. I came to you in weakness and fear, and with much trembling. My message and my preaching were not with wise and persuasive words, but with a demonstration of the Spirit's power, so that your Faith might not rest on men's wisdom, but on God's power.

1 Corinthians 2:1–5

The Apostle Paul, probably the greatest preacher of all time, did not start his ministry after several years of Bible College, training on public speaking, leadership training, or any of the like. No, he started to be a witness for Jesus Christ shortly after his conver-sion, knowing very little about Christianity, feeling very inadequate and underqualified. It says in this verse that he came with fear and trembling, feeling weak and powerless within himself. What he did have was the power of the Holy Spirit living inside of him to give him the words to say and the courage to say them!

This example that God made of Paul's life was made to show you that you don't need to be a Bible expert or have everything all figured out in order for God to use you to impact the world for him. He can and wants to use you right where you are today. The key is to live by the Spirit and to stay close to Jesus, and if you do that then he will give you the words to say and will use you to impact the world around you for him! I can tell you that there is nothing more exciting than to be used by God in order to make a difference in another person's life! Ask God to use you today, right where you are, and then hang on for dear life because he will and you will be blown away with joy and fulfillment!

GOD'S TEMPLE

Don't you know that you yourselves are God's temple and that God's
Spirit lives in you?

1 Corinthians 3:16

How much more should you care, protect, and guard your fleshly
body knowing that God's Spirit lives inside of you and that your
body is in reality his temple if you have indeed surrendered your
heart and life to Jesus Christ? See, a church is not a building, but
a group of people that have accepted God's awesome gift of His
Spirit into their lives. I don't know about you, but I have not treated
my body as I should, knowing that the God of this world lives
inside of me! It would do us all well to keep this in mind today and
to pay a little more attention as to what we subject ourselves to and
thus subject Christ to also. Make every effort to treat your body as
the sacred temple that it is both today and in the days to come.

ALL THINGS REVEALED

Therefore judge nothing before the appointed time; wait till the Lord comes. He will bring to light what is hidden in darkness and will expose the motives of men's hearts. At the time each will receive his praise from God.

1 Corinthians 4:5

It is so easy to judge people that we interact with on a daily basis by looking at their external lives. Our flesh at times would take great delight in judging other people for how they treat their kids or their spouse or for committing blatant sins against their body or for their job performance or lack of performance or just how they live their life in general. The interesting thing to remember is that although external behavior that we can see with our eyes does indeed matter since the Bible says in James 2:26 that "so faith without deeds is dead," it is only God that can see the heart and only he who can know for sure the motives and faith of another person. That is why God tells us as Christians not to judge others. We are all imperfect because of our flesh and we all commit sins that we need to repent of as we continue on this journey to become more like Christ. One day God will reveal everyone's hidden thoughts and motives, but for now it is only God who can judge since only he can see the heart! I wonder what would happen if we as Christians would spend a little less time focusing on other people's behavior and a little more time focusing on our own relationship with God so that we could truly love those who are lost with the unconditional love of Christ that meets people right where they are—right where they desperately need to experience Jesus for who he really is!

Stay close to Jesus today and don't judge the lost people that are all around you; instead, love them with God's love so that they will see and know that God is real and believe.

NOT ALWAYS EASY

To this very hour we go hungry and thirsty, we are in rags, we are bru-tally treated, we are homeless. We work hard with our hands. When we are cursed, we bless; when we are persecuted, we endure it; when we are slandered, we answer kindly. Up to this moment we have become the scum of the earth, the refuse of the world.

1 Corinthians 4:11–13

As the Apostle Paul describes here to the church in Corinth, the Christian life is not always easy. Look at the early apostles and how they were beaten and persecuted for their faith. Consider how they eventually gave their livesfor the cause of Christ. We live in a world at war! Jesus has won the war; however, the enemy is still fighting for control of your mind and heart. The battle today may be less visual and dramatic as far as the physical realm goes; however, I believe that it is much more intense spiritually than in the early days of the Church. The Bible speaks about how many people will fall away spiritually in the end times, and I believe that we are in the end times. I experience this battle every day as I travel for work. I have had to become very proactive and transparent in order to survive this spiritual battle for my mind and heart while away from home. The key to living a successful Christian life and maintaining this great joy and peace that Jesus gives to those who accept him is to stay close to him in your mind and in your heart at all times. It is only Christ who can give you the power to remain in him in the midst of this fallen world that is crumbling all around us. So cling to him with everything that you have! Jesus is your shelter from the storm, your safe harbor. He is the Protector of your faith. Seek God with all of your heart and start living the life of victory that is only found in him.

SEXUAL IMMORALITY

Flee from sexual immorality. All other sins a man commits are outside his body, but he who sins sexually sins against his own body. Do you not know that you body is a temple of the Holy Spirit, who is in you, whom you have received from God? You are not your own; you have been bought at a price. Therefore honor God with your body.

1 Corinthians 6:18–20

We live in a society where sexual imagery is used to sell, to entice, to entertain—it is all around us and will only continue to get worse as this fallen world deteriorates here in the end times. On the Internet people can explore just about anything that you can imagine in private, the most popular television shows exploit and even promote homosexuality, and the trendy clothing of the day for young women is basically nightwear. As a Christian, the only way to escape all of these sexual images and keep a pure mind and heart is to draw near to Christ and to be proactive concerning your thought life and your actions.

One thing that I know for sure is that at the beginning of each day, that I will be tempted in this area of impure thoughts at sometime throughout the day because, let's face it, it is all around us in society. So, as a believer in Christ, who has been bought and paid for by the very blood of Jesus, I decide ahead of time how I will respond to that temptation and I put into practice an accountability system that will help me make the right decisions when that time of temptation comes. You must be proactive in order to win this war that is happening all around you for the control of your heart and mind! The best defense is to stay close to Jesus, in your mind and in your heart, at all times throughout the day! The Bible says in Proverbs 4:23, "Above all else, guard your heart, for it is the wellspring of life." If you want to serve the Lord with your whole heart and you want to realize the amazing joy and love and purpose that he has for you, then you must remain pure, both in thoughts and in actions, in this area of sexual immorality. Don't buy into the lie that what the world has to offer you will be more fulfilling than the plan that God has for your life. God loves you more than you can imagine and the only reason that he asks you to stay pure in this area is because he knows that his plan is the absolute best plan for your life and that a life that is fully surrendered to him will bring you so much more than you could have ever even dreamed about! So, guard your heart today—plan ahead of time how you will respond to temptation, and start living the abundant life that your soul has been longing for all along.

KNOWN BY GOD

Now about food sacrificed to idols: We know that we all possess knowledge. Knowledge puffs up, but love builds up. The man who thinks he knows something does not yet know as he ought to know. But the man who loves God is known by God.

1 Corinthians 8:1–3

The church in Corinth was arguing over trivial matters such as whether or not to eat meat that was sacrificed to idols. The Apostle Paul is telling them here in this Scripture that knowledge is good for knowing what to do and what not to do as it relates to their faith in Christ; however, knowing God and having a relationship with him is what they should be focusing on. Even today, many people get so wrapped up in the acts of Christianity that they miss the real joy and secret of what Christianity is all about, which is, of course, knowing God and having an intimate relationship with him!

God could care less whether or not the people ate this meat that was sacrificed to idols; all He wanted was for them to pay attention to him, to know him and love him, and then live their lives in a way that reflected his love to other people. And so the same is true today for us as Christians—God really doesn't care so much about the religious acts that separate us as a Church into the various denominations. What he does care about is knowing you in a personal way where his Spirit is free to live inside of you and transform your mind and lifestyle to be more like his! So, what's important is not where you go to church, not how you have failed him in the past or how much you know about Christianity, but what matters most to God is whether or not you are connecting with him in a personal way where he is becoming greater and you are becoming less. Seek him today with all of your heart, get to know the Creator of this universe, and watch your life be transformed into a new life that is a true reflection of God's love and power.

STRATEGIC APPROACH TO EVANGELISM

Though I am free and belong to no man, I make myself a slave to everyone, to win as many as possible. To the Jews I became like a Jew, to win the Jews. To those under the law I became like one under the law (though I myself am not under the law), so as to win those under the law. To those not having the law I became like one not having the law (though I am not free from God's law but am under Christ's law), so as to win those not having the law. To the weak I became weak, to win the weak. I have become all things to all men so that by all possible means I might save some. I do all this for the sake of the gospel that I may share in its blessings. Do you not know that in a race all the runners run, but only one gets the prize? Run in such a way as to get the prize. Everyone who competes in the games goes into strict training. They do it to get a crown that will not last; but we do it to get a crown that will last forever. Therefore I do not run like a man running aimlessly; I do not fight like a man beating the air. No, I beat my body and make it my slave so that after I have preached to others, I myself will not be disqualified for the prize.

1 Corinthians 9:19–27

Comfort and self-indulgence seem to be taking over modern-day America, even in the Christian social circles. Why do you think that we have so many denominations in the Christian faith? We have so many because people want to be comfortable where they go to church. They want to only worship to music that they are familiar with and like, they want to hear a message that is comforting or challenging or non-confrontational, or maybe they don't want to hear a message at all; maybe they just want to sing and dance and speak in tongues and hear prophecy. Today, it is much too easy to just hang out with people with whom you are comfortable and in a church where you are comfortable and thus become ineffective to reach this lost world for Christ.

Paul gives us an example here of his life and ministry and how he was anything but comfortable; in fact, he tells us how he intentionally hung out with all types of people: Jews, Gentiles, strong, weak, legalistic people, pagans, etc. Paul was willing to step out of his personal comfort zone in order to be a living example of someone who has fully committed his life to Jesus Christ to anyone who was willing to watch and listen.

Paula and I have a lot of friends who live a lifestyle that is much different than the lifestyle that we are striving for in our journey to become more like Christ. For me personally it would be much easier and more enjoyable to hang out with people who believe the same things that I believe and who are striving to be more like Jesus, just as I am. What good would that do, though, to live a life of comfort and self-indulgence that does nothing to win lost people to the Lord? I am now convinced that God calls each of us who professes to know and have a relationship with him to step out of our comfort zone and be willing to feel a little out of place in order that other people may see him living through us and believe.

TEMPTATION

No temptation has seized you except what is common to man. And God is faithful; He will not let you be temped beyond what you can bear. But when you are tempted, He will also provide a way out so that you can stand up under it.

1 Corinthians 10:13

I love this verse; I always have loved it ever since I was a young man in junior high school when I committed it to memory. There is so much hope in this verse as it has always encouraged me, letting me know that temptation itself is not wrong; in fact, everyone will be tempted to sin in this life. It is our response to temptation that can either cause us to sin and thus separate us from the joy that we have in Christ or bring us closer and more like Christ as we choose to be obedient to him. But there is more to it than that; it also tells us in this verse that there is always a way of escape when we are tempted—a refuge, a hiding place, a safe place where God will protect us and we won't have to yield to the desires of our flesh and the desires of this world that the enemy tries to entice us with on a daily basis. This is the part that has taken me years to figure out, as I could never seem to find this way of escape as a young Christian. The temptations seemed to be so overwhelming at times that in there was hardly a way of escape anywhere in sight. It has only been in my latter years as a Christian that I have understood and can see with a clear vision this way of escape that Paul is speaking of here to the church in Corinth.

The way of escape is Christ and his power and abiding in him! If you are not connected to the power source, then there is no way of escape; it is only in Christ that you can and will be victorious over sin in your life! It is only in being intentional about your relationship with Jesus by staying so close to him in your heart and in your mind that the way of escape will be clear to you and that you will have the power to be able to resist and be obedient! It is not easy and it will take all the strength that you have. You will have to be diligent in studying God's Word and in prayer; you will have to be transparent about your relationship to God with other Christians who can hold you accountable in your journey. As you step out of your comfort zone and open up to others in a very real and honest way, it is then that the power of God comes bolting into your life and real transformation begins to happen as your heart finally becomes solely committed to God. Your vision will be clear enough to see the way of escape, and you will be on your way to developing the mind of Christ. So, be intentional about your faith. Confess your struggles to other Christians so that they can help you stay accountable in the battle. Be diligent in reading God's Word and in listening for his voice in prayer; stay connected to the power source and experience a whole new life of victory in him!

ALL FOR THE GLORY OF GOD

So whether you eat or drink or whatever you do, do it all for the glory of God.

1 Corinthians 10:31

What a great verse this is to use as a barometer to measure everything that you think about or do throughout your day! If something doesn't bring glory to God, then as a Christian you shouldn't do it. For that matter you shouldn't let the thought of such things dwell in your mind. God teaches us that all sin starts by harboring a thought in your mind for too long. When such thoughts arise that do not glorify God, then you should do what Paul describes in 2 Corinthians 10:5 when he says, "And we take captive every thought to make it obedient to Christ." Never forget that it is a battle of the mind that we are fighting and that all thoughts lead to actions, whether good or bad. So today, glorify God in all that you think about and all that you do, and thus let his Spirit work in and through your life in order to make a difference in the world for him.

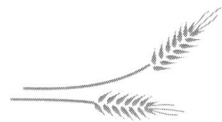

ABOUNDING IN LOVE

Praise the Lord, O my soul;
all my inmost being, praise His Holy name.
Praise the Lord, O my soul,
and forget not all His benefits—
who forgives all your sins
and heals all your diseases,
who redeems your life from the pit
and crowns you with love and compassion,
who satisfies your desires with good things
so that your youth is renewed like the eagle's.
The Lord works righteousness
and justice for all the oppressed.
He made know His ways to Moses,
His deeds to the people of Israel:
The Lord is compassionate and gracious,
slow to anger, abounding in love.
He will not always accuse,
nor will He harbor His anger forever;
He does not treat us as our sins deserve
or repay us according to our iniquities.
For as high as the heavens are above the earth,
so great is His love for those who fear Him;
as far as he east is from the west,
so far has he removed our transgressions from us.
As a father has compassion on his children,
so the Lord has compassion on those who fear Him.

Psalm 103:1–13

I feel so undeserved of this great love and compassion that David writes about here in the book of Psalms. That's the cool thing about God though: his love cannot be earned and his compassion has no boundaries! He gives limitless love and compassion away freely, doesn't keep any record of wrongs, and promises to carry us in his arms until the day that we are forever united again with him in Glory. All that he asks is that we continue to look to him for our strength; that we continue to love and worship him back with everything that we are—even in the midst of our failures—that we love him with our life!

Thank you, God, for your amazing love and compassion. Thank you for who you are and who we are in you. Today, we give back to you all that we have to give, we give to you our lives to use for your glory, so that your love may abound even more! Amen

OUT-OF-THE-BOX CHRISTIANITY

There are different kinds of gifts, but the same Spirit. There are different kinds of service, but the same Lord. There are different kinds of working, but the same God works all of them in all men.

1 Corinthians 12:4–6

As a Christian, I think that it is very easy at times to try to put God in a box. You see, all of us have had different life experiences and God has given us different kinds of gifts and has equipped us for different kinds of service. All of these things come together to form a filter through which we see God and see other people in the world. It is very easy, then—and just human nature—to want everyone to fit into our personal perspective of who God is, how his people should act, and what a Christian is supposed to look like.

Yesterday, we met a very talented and unique man of God with the gifts of art and evangelism. This young man had the story of Christ displayed with tattoos that covered almost his entire right arm. As I heard him describe the pictures and the meaning behind them, it was obvious to me that this young man was being used by God in a very unique and extraordinary way to tell the story of Christ and to reach people that probably would never be reached or hear about our loving Savior if it was not for him having this amazing story of love displayed in such vivid color and dramatic artistry on his arm. God is much bigger than our perspective and our personal world views. Many traditional, legalistic Christians would not consider a tattoo as a way to spread the Gospel and reach the lost. Today, set your own perspective aside and look at the world with a different set of eyes that are filtered through God's Spirit, and experience the great diversity of God, who displays a love so great that it has no boundaries! Get out of the box—step out of your comfort zone and let the God of this world use you in ways that you could have never imagined to make a difference in the world for him.

A GREAT DAY AWAITS ALL CHRISTIANS

But where there are prophecies, they will cease; where there are tongues, they will be stilled; where there is knowledge, is will pass away. For we know in part and we prophesy in part, but when perfection comes, the imperfection disappears. When I was a child, I talked like a child; I thought like a child, I reasoned like a child. When I became a man, I put childish ways behind me. Now we see but a poor reflection as in a mirror; then we shall see face to face. Now I know in part; then I shall know fully, even as I am fully known. And now these three remain: faith, hope and love. But the greatest of these is love.

1 Corinthians 13:8–13

One day when Jesus Christ returns to redeem his people and destroy whatever is left of this fallen world, our hope and faith in God will be made complete in that we will know him fully as we see him face to face and he reveals to us all the secret things of God that we could never have understood or comprehended without being restored back to our original glory in Christ where we are united to him and his Spirit in perfect unity. On this day, there will be no fleshly sin to separate us from his love! What a day that will be! Think of the most joy and love that you have ever felt on this earth and then multiply that times a thousand and you will have a good picture of what heaven will be like! Every day captured and dwelling in the perfect love of our Creator, enjoying his presence and the presence of all his people that have gone before us, being reunited with old friends and family members who have passed, having all of the junk of this world that separates us and keeps us from being fully united with God's people taken away so that there will be no barriers to our relationships with each other or our relationship with God, each one of us, enjoying each other and enjoying God.

Every minute of every day we'll spend safe in his loving arms and eternally secure forever!

Will you be there on that day? Do you acknowledge the sacrifice that he made with his life in order that you could indeed be reunited with him, partially now and completely when he returns? Have you surrendered your heart? The Bible says that you will know for sure if you have, that there will be no question as to your salvation.

Therefore, my brothers, be all the more eager to make your calling and election sure. For if you do these things, you will never fall, and you will receive a rich welcome into the eternal kingdom of our Lord and Savior Jesus Christ. 2 Peter 1:10–11

Surrender your heart and life today and reserve your spot for this party that will last for the rest of eternity!

STAND FIRM

Therefore, my dear brothers, stand firm. Let nothing move you. Always give yourselves fully to the work of the Lord, because you know that your labor in the Lord is not in vain.

1 Corinthians 15:58

There are many things that will happen to you in this life as a Christian that will make you feel like giving up on living your life for Christ. Some of these things might include failure from the weakness of your flesh, being distracted by the sins of other believers, discouragement from unanswered prayer, fear of failure, ridicule by friends and family, or distraction by the things that this world will try to entice you with so that your focus is diverted away from your relationship with God. Life is hard, the world is cruel, and your personal walk with God will not always be easy. But let me encourage you today to stand firm in your walk with the Lord, because one day very soon this world will pass away and all of the things in this world that people looked to to bring them life and happiness will be destroyed, and the only thing that will remain will be your faith in Christ and what you did during your life to enrich and strengthen that relationship, which is the only thing that will last forever! The work that you do for the Kingdom will be rewarded in the end, if not before, and God will always be with you during your journey here on this earth in order to comfort you and hold you in his loving arms as you fight the good fight for his glory. Be strong in the Lord today.

NO ONE LIKE YOU

Then Asa called to the Lord his God and said, "Lord, there is no one like you to help the powerless against the mighty. Help us, O Lord our God, for we rely on you, and in your name we have come against this vast army. O Lord, you are God; do not let man prevail against you.

2 Chronicles 14:11

Sometimes in this life we come up against obstacles and problems that are so gigantic in that they make us seem powerless to overcome them on our own. People react in many different ways when the huge problems of life arise. Some people become very bitter at God and try to face the issues on their own, only to end up in a downward spiral of disappointment, anger, and bitterness. When this life throws a problem or circumstance at you that is so overwhelming that you don't see any way of escape or any light at the end of the tunnel, the right thing to do is to trust your Creator, who promises the very best for you, to do his work within your circumstance. There is no one like God! He has a much bigger perspective on the world and what happens in the world since, after all, it was God who created the world!

There is no one else that can change a heart; there is no one else that can bring great joy, peace, and hope, even in the midst of great tragedy in this life. You see, that problem or circumstance that you have come up against in your life is there for a reason. That reason is so that you will learn to trust in God to perform a miracle in your life. That reason is so that you will surrender your will and all of your goals, dreams, and desires to him so that he can then give you what you have been really longing for in this life. He wants you to become the reflection of him that he originally created you to be. He wants to bring you back to your original glory that is rooted in his love! When you have tasted just a small morsel of this faith that we are speaking of, it is then that you will know and understand what it means to really trust in our Savior to carry you through the storms of this life. King Asa set a great example for all of us when he was up against an army so great that it made him seem powerless to win any battle against them, and in the midst of this huge obstacle, he trusted God! Today, give that huge problem of yours that is consuming your life over to God and just watch what happens! It could be that God is just waiting to see if you will indeed trust in him.

OUR RESPONSE

Then He opened their minds so they could understand the scriptures. He told them, "This is what is written: The Christ will suffer and rise from the dead on the third day, and repentance and forgiveness of sins will be preached in His name to all the nations, beginning at Jerusalem."

Luke 24:45–47

It is done! Christ has risen from the dead, and now it is time for you and me to respond! How should we respond to this, you ask? Well, our response is so simple, yet we see so little of it today in this fallen world! The first response is to turn from your sins, to repent, to ask for forgiveness, and then not to consciously do things any more that separate you from God. You know what those things are. God says that the law is written on our hearts, so we all know deep inside what separates us from God. His Spirit convicts us of these things. So today, stop making excuses, stop denying the truth, repent of your sins. Turn from them and turn to God so that you can with a pure heart accept this most awesome gift of forgiveness that he has made possible because of his death on the Cross! Lastly, our final response should be to tell others of the new life that you have found in him. How would you have known of these great treasures if someone had not told you? In the same way then, share your experiences of living your life in Christ with other people so that they too can repent, be forgiven, and have the abundant, eternal life that you and I have so undeservedly been given by our awesome Lord and Savior. You can pray a prayer right now wherever you are and start the process of Christ coming into your life and giving you the peace and joy that you hear so many people talk about but have never experienced for yourself.

Ask God right now to forgive you of your sins. Tell him that you accept his free gift of forgiveness and salvation and that right now, today, you repent of your sins and will make a 180-degree turn to start living your life for him and not for yourself. Thank him for the price that he paid on the Cross so that you could have a relationship with God Almighty that will last for the rest of eternity.

If you prayed this prayer above, then welcome to the family of Christ! Thank you for stepping out in faith and responding to the miracle of Easter!

COMFORT FROM ABOVE

Praise be to the God and Father of our Lord Jesus Christ, the Father of compassion and the God of all comfort, who comforts us in all our troubles, so that we can comfort those in any trouble with the comfort we ourselves have received from God.

2 Corinthians 1:3–4

I recently had one of those days where at the end of the day I felt anything but comfort. I was betrayed by a good friend who has betrayed me in the same way in the past several times. I also received some disturbing news about some other friends of ours that are having trouble with their marriage. It's like in a moment, everything came crashing down and feelings of anger, bitterness, and hurt set in. This morning I realized that I was looking for comfort in other people and the sad reality of life is that other people can and will at some time let you down, no matter who they are or what your relationship is with them. True comfort that is certain, eternal, and that you can always count on only comes from our heavenly Father! It is only in a relationship with him that you will experience real comfort and peace that you can then share with others who are hurting and who need to experience the all-encompassing love of God that heals and comforts, fulfills, and brings peace and joy into your life like you could have never imagined. Seek him today with all of your heart! Let his comfort enter your heart and experience peace that passes all understanding in the midst of whatever circumstance you find yourself in today.

MARKED WITH A SEAL

Now it is God who makes both us and you stand firm in Christ. He anointed us, set His seal of ownership on us, and put His Spirit in our hearts as a deposit, guaranteeing what is to come.

2 Corinthians 1:21–22

Be encouraged today, for if you have surrendered your heart and life to Jesus Christ then you are marked with his seal of redemption and forgiveness, the seal of belonging to him for the rest of eternity! It is God that enables you to stand firm in your faith! It is his Spirit that gives you the strength to face a new day and all of the challenges that are ahead of you; it is his Spirit that will work in and through your life to use you in a miraculous way to make a difference in the lives and hearts of all of the people you encounter today! In and of yourself you can do nothing, so knowing that, spend some time with your Father in heaven today. Seek him with all of your heart and set your mind on heavenly things—look at the world with the eyes of your heart and don't let the enemy distract you with things that won't matter 100 years from now. The good news today is that your Spirit is going to live exponentially longer than 100 years, and the decisions that you make today with how you spend your time will enrich not only your life here on earth but will prepare you for what is ahead in the life to come when your time on this earth is through. You have been blessed beyond belief with the gift of God's Spirit living inside of you. Now it is up to you to tap into this great mystery by letting his Spirit control your thoughts and actions as you give your life away to him!

THE AROMA OF CHRIST

But thanks be to God, who always leads us in triumphal procession in Christ and through us spreads everywhere the fragrance of the knowledge of Him. For we are the aroma of Christ among those who are being saved and those who are perishing.

2 Corinthians 2:14–15

Back in the Roman times, a "triumphal procession" was a festival procession where the victorious general would lead his soldiers and the captives they had taken down the street while the people watched and applauded and the air was filled with a sweet smell released by burning spices as they marched. This was a march of victory, and I am sure that everyone was filled with joy, as their loved ones had made it home safely and their freedom was secured through the efforts of their fighting soldiers! So Paul is using this analogy here in writing to the church in Corinth, reminding them that their church and the lives of each and every one of them who had surrendered his heart and life to Jesus Christ was spreading the knowledge of God! God was spreading through them the sweet smell of having defeated Satan and the opportunity to engage in this newfound freedom in Christ and receive abundant life for the rest of eternity. Nothing has changed for you and I today—no, if you have accepted Jesus into your heart, then God is using your very life today, just as he did with the early Church, to spread the wonderful aroma of him to the people around you that are lost and desperately need Christ in their lives! So today, no matter what situation you find yourself in, do not be discouraged, for God has already won the war and he is in control of everything that is happening in your life! If you have accepted him, then you are marching in his triumphal procession, and the saints that have gone before us as well as his people that are still alive today are cheering you on as your life spreads the sweet aroma of our Lord and Savior Jesus Christ to the world around you. March on, my brothers and sisters, in Christ, and live your life for him.

COMPETENCE IN CHRIST

Such confidence as this is ours through Christ before God. Not that we are competent in ourselves to claim anything for ourselves, but our competence comes from God. He has made us competent as ministers of a new covenant—not of the letter but of the Spirit; for the letter kills, but the Spirit gives life.

2 Corinthians 3:4–6

I was talking to a friend the other day who goes to a church that has been without a pastor that they could call their own for more than five years. It was very sad to listen to his story of how disappointed he had become as a result of the congregation voting down a very dynamic pastor all because of a very conservative and legalistic environment that exists within his church. He described the church as spiritually dead. Christianity is not a set of rules, and if that is how you see it then you are missing the whole essence of why Jesus Christ died on the Cross! Christ died so that you and I could have a relationship with God forever and so that we are not bound by our own obedience to the law, for if this was the case then none of us would ever measure up to the standards of God. Through his death there is grace for our failures but more importantly, he gives us his Spirit to live inside of us to transform our hearts and minds to be more like him! See, a relationship with Jesus Christ is all about change! As the very core of who we are is changed to become more like our Creator so, as a result of this change, what we did and how we acted five, ten, or twenty years ago should be totally different than what we do and how we act today. So our competence then comes from Christ and our relationship with him and not from ourselves and how obedient we are to a law that we could never uphold on our own. The Christian life is all about falling in love with the Creator of the world and because of that love, being submissive to his will for your life and letting his Spirit first come into your heart and then change your heart and your mind to be more like him so that he can use you to point the rest of the lost people in this world to a similar relationship with God Almighty. As the verse here says, God's Spirit gives life—abundant life that is the life that you have been searching for all along. Accept him today and start living a life like you could never have imagined.

SPIRITUAL PERSPECTIVE

Therefore we do not lose heart. Though outwardly we are wasting away, yet inwardly we are being renewed day by day. For our light and momentary troubles are achieving for us an eternal glory that far outweighs them all. So we fix our eyes not on what is seen, but on what is unseen. For what is seen is temporary, but what is unseen is eternal.

2 Corinthians 4:16–18

I love the words of author John Eldridge in Wild at Heart (2001, Thomas Nelson) when he tells us to "look at the world with the eyes of your heart." To look at the world with the eyes of your heart is to focus your attention on what is unseen as opposed to just focusing on the externals. There are circumstances and issues that are present in all of our lives, many of which are discouraging, painful, and even life-threatening at times. What Paul is explaining to the church in Corinth here is that all of those external things that happen to you while on this earth are temporary and will eventually pass away; however, your Spiritual condition or the unseen part of your every-day life will last forever. Because of this, you should focus on the condition of your heart and your relationship with God because this is the only part of your life that will last for the rest of eternity! The enemy uses the obvious things of this world to distract us from the not-so-obvious, unseen Spiritual realm that is the only thing that will bring you eternal life and true happiness and fulfillment, both in this life and in the life to come! There is another quote by Eldridge that comes to mind: "Things are not what they seem." There is something much bigger going on all around you that you can't see with your eyes, but that you can fully see and participate in with your heart. So today, look at the world with the eyes of your heart, focus your attention on your relationship with God and how you can know him more and be used by him more; watch for him in the people that you meet, and look for his work in your life and the lives of those around you. When you learn to embrace this perspective on life, it is then that you will find life; it is then that you will find joy and peace, fulfillment, and purpose.

LIVE FOR HIM

For Christ's love compels us, because we are convinced that one died for all, and therefore all died. And He died for all, that those who live should no longer live for themselves but for Him who died for them and was raised again.

2 Corinthians 5:14–15

Out of love for the one who gave his life and suffered much pain and agony so that you and I could live with him forever, we live our lives to glorify him! Life in Christ is everything that I am and everything that I ever hope to be! It is the secret to unspeakable joy and fulfillment in this life. It is the reason that I get up in the morning and the driving force behind everything that I do. His love is the rock that keeps me secure when the storms of life come; he is my comforter and my strength, the one that I can always count on to meet my needs, keep me safe, and hold me in his arms when the battles of this life are more than I can handle. The hope that I have in him of being transformed back to the way that he originally created me to be in order that I can live out the purpose that he created me for is the target that I am shooting for with my life. I live my life for him because of his awesome love for me and because true abundant life is only found in a relationship with him! Have you found it? If not, then all you have to do is ask. Seek Christ today with all of your heart, surrender your heart and life to him, and search for love no more.

AMBASSADORS OF CHRIST

We are therefore Christ's ambassadors, as though God were making His appeal through us. We implore you on Christ's behalf: Be reconciled to God. God made Him who had no sin for us, so that in Him we might become the righteousness of God.

2 Corinthians 5:20–21

What a call this is for all of us who claim to know and have a relationship with Jesus Christ! To be his ambassador here on this earth is to be obedient to his will by letting his Spirit live in and through our lives in order that we may point other people to Christ! It is an awesome privilege that we have and one that should not be taken lightly. How are you doing? Are you representing your King to the best of your ability? Are you spending time with him in his Word and in prayer in order that your life will truly reflect his love? Are you being obedient to his principles and thus standing on firm ground so that you cannot be shaken by the enemy, or have the pleasures and enticements of this world bound you up so that the only things that you are representing here in this world are your own selfish desires and weak flesh that can do nothing to advance the cause of Christ? It is not too late to start living the life of the ambassador of Christ that God has called you to live! All it takes is an act of surrender—the surrender of your will to his and the dying of your old self in order that his love and power that you have received can shine through you so that others may see him. He is there; he is just waiting for you to let him reign over the throne of your life. Surrender to him today.

ENDURANCE IN CHRIST

We put no stumbling block in anyone's path, so that our ministry will not be discredited. Rather, as servants of God we commend ourselves in every way: in great endurance; in troubles, hardships and distresses; in beatings, imprisonments and riots; in hard work, sleepless nights and hunger; in purity, understanding, patience and kindness; in the Holy Spirit and in sincere love; in truthful speech and in the power of God; with weapons of righteousness in the right hand and in the left; through glory and dishonor, bad report and good report; genuine yet regarded as imposters; known, yet regarded as unknown; dying, and yet we live on; beaten, and not yet killed; sorrowful, yet always rejoicing; poor, yet making many rich; having nothing, and yet possessing everything.

2 Corinthians 6:3–10

This life can be very hard; especially if you are trying to live your life for Christ and are walking down the narrow path where his Spirit is in control of everything that you do and you are making a difference in the world for him. The reason that there are so many difficulties in this life is because of the fact that we live in a fallen world and if your are genuinely trying to make a difference then you will be opposed by an enemy who is very real and who hates to see any more people come into a life-saving relationship with Jesus Christ. You will feel very alone at times; you will feel like you are the only one who is trying to live a righteous life and will feel like an outcast from the crowd; you will be laughed at and called a hypocrite, and everything that you do will be under a microscope for the world to see. Don't give up! Keep seeking the Lord no matter what other people say or do or how you feel, as there is something much bigger going on all around you that you can't see with your eyes! The enemy will try to distract you and make you feel like you are not doing the right thing by obeying Christ, but do not believe his lies! God is right there beside you with his army of angels to fight battles for you so that he can continue his work in and through your very life, so that other people may see him and believe! Take heed here of Paul's example and all of the pain and hardship that he endured and yet look at how many lives have been impacted by the life that he lived! I don't think that Paul could have ever known at the time how many millions of brothers and sisters in Christ would be encouraged and inspired all because of his faithfulness and endurance in the midst of much pain, suffering, and disappointment! God promises in Philippians 1:6 to complete the work that he started in you, and he came to give you and abundant life even in the midst of hardships! So, hang in there as the bell is about to ring and God is using your faithfulness to reach more people than you could have ever imagined. Draw near to him today, even in the midst of this fallen world, and let his love carry you, comfort you, protect you, and guide you into an abundant life that is full of his love and a true reflection of him.

FULLY COMMITTED TO CHRIST

For the eyes of the Lord range throughout the earth to strengthen those whose hearts are fully committed to him.

2 Chronicles 16:9

This is one of my all-time favorite verses in the Bible! If only I could act out the part about being "fully committed"! Life doesn't have to be as hard as we make it. No, if you surrender everything to Christ—and by everything I mean you job, your spouse, your children, your money, your secret sins, your pride, your entertainment, absolutely everything—bringing it all under the authority of Jesus Christ, then he promises to move in a major way, in and through your very life, giving you all the strength and power that you will ever need to live an abundant life in him! See, I think that the problem with Christianity today is that it just becomes another thing that we do, just one part of our life that we keep separate from everything else. This kind of Christianity will never bring real joy, purpose, or fulfillment in our lives. No, Jesus didn't die just to be one of many aspects or our life; no, he came to be our life—to consume and transform our hearts and minds back to their original glory in him. It is only when you are willing to die to yourself and surrender everything that you are that life will get easier and more fulfilling since God will be there to strengthen you and move in a radical way in order that your life will be an example for all of the world to see! God loves you today and is waiting for you to completely surrender to him. He has a life waiting for you that you could never have even dreamed, so don't wait any longer: fully commit your heart and life to him today!

A PURE HEART

Since we have these promises, dear friends, let us purify ourselves from everything that contaminates body and spirit, perfecting holiness out of reverence for God.

2 Corinthians 7:1

Jesus died on the Cross, and if you believe in him and the sacrifice that he made and have accepted him into your heart; then you are a new creation in him and he has given you a new heart that is pure and holy in the eyes of God! Your part now is to protect this new heart from being bound up once again from the things of this world that are not of God! The way that you do this is to seek him every day in prayer and in the study of his Word. As you grow and become more like him it will be much easier for your heart and your mind to remain pure and free from the contaminates of this world! You will fail at this attempt to remain pure, that is a given as a result of your old self or what the Bible calls your "flesh," but do not despair when this happens, for God's unconditional love, grace, and forgiveness never changes and will always be there for you as you seek his forgiveness. The key is to learn from your mistakes and to always be striving to know him more and to become more like him.

The real joy in the Christian life is found not in being perfect, but in the pursuit of holiness. As you humble yourself before God, knowing that you can't do anything on your own, you will see and experience the work of his Spirit in and through your life! So the key to remaining pure is to continually surrender your fleshly will to his will for your life as you remain in him throughout your day. Jesus wants more than anything to know you in a personal way, to have the kind of relationship with you where he guides and directs you into the abundant life that you hear so many people talk about. The cool thing is that he leaves more room for failure than you will ever need and he promises to do the work in your life if you would only let him. Seek Christ today with all of your heart, surrender everything that you are and everything that you hope to be to him, let his Spirit guide and direct your actions as you live your life for him out of a pure and perfect heart from God.

SOWING GENEROUSLY

Remember this: Whoever sows sparingly will also reap sparingly, and whoever sows generously will also reap generously. Each man should give what he has decided in his heart to give, not reluctantly or under compulsion, for God loves a cheerful giver. And God is able to make all grace abound to you, so that in all things at all times, having all that you need, you will abound in every good work.

2 Corinthians 9:6–8

My wife, Paula, and I can personally attest to the fact that God is faithful to keep this promise of making grace abound to you when it comes to giving! There was a time in our marriage when we were in so much debt that we could barely make our monthly payments and we lived day to day, burdened by our own sin of overspending, wondering how we were ever going to pay off everything that we owed. To give 10% of our income at that time would have been unrealistic in that we wouldn't have been able to pay our bills, so we gave what God had placed on our hearts to give, which was a lesser amount. I began to listen to a program on the radio called Money Matters, which is a Christian-based program that gives financial advice to listeners. Through time, God enabled us to give 10% and still make our monthly payments, and so that is what we did. I was convinced through listening to this radio program that the only way to financial freedom was to be faithful in this area of giving back to God what is his first and then to live on a budget and to stop overspending. Long story short, we have been faithful to give back to God at least 10% of our income for the past several years and for the first time in our marriage we have a positive net worth and God has definitely been faithful in blessing our obedience to him! I don't tell you this story to brag, for we are still learning how to avoid overspending and how to live within a budget, but I tell you this story to encourage you to sow generously what God has blessed you with, not only your money, but your time and God-given talents as well! One thing that I know for sure is that you cannot out-give God. For he has already given you everything that you could have ever hoped or imagined in the gift of life that can be lived in him! Now it is time to give back to him, for it is only in giving that you will reap the rewards of an abundant life.

GROWING OR FALLING AWAY

We ought always to thank God for you, brothers, and rightly so, because your faith is growing more and more, and the love every one of you has for each other is increasing. Therefore, among God's churches we boast about your perseverance and faith in all the persecutions and trials you are enduring.

2 Thessalonians 1:3–4

In a relationship with Jesus Christ, where he is transforming your heart and mind to be more like his and where you are getting to know him more and falling in love with your Creator, there is no such thing as being stagnant. You are either growing in your faith or falling away. Be careful, then, how you live, for if you are not obeying God and his Spirit, if you are making even the smallest choices of disobedience and not seeking his forgiveness and direction on a daily basis, then you will begin to move farther and farther away from his will for your life and before you know it, you will be at a very low place in your life as a result of the choices that you have made to live your life within yourself and apart from God. I have been there, even as a Christian, and it is not fun! The habits and lifestyle that you develop apart from God will be hard to break and will cause you much hurt and pain. The other option is to always be growing more and more to be like Christ, learning from your mistakes and seeking his face on a daily basis through prayer and spending time in his Word, asking his forgiveness for times of failure, and just letting him be in control of everything that you do every day! This is what was happening in the church of the Thessalonians and that is why the Apostle Paul was boasting about them in his travels. Would he be boasting about you? Are you growing in your faith or are you letting the enemy gain a foothold as you make small compromises to live your life apart from God? Life apart from Christ brings nothing but disappointment, emptiness, shame, and despair. If this is you, then God wants to pick you up today and start you on the journey again to an abundant life in him! His grace and love is big enough to cover and forgive anything that you could have possibly done to disobey him! Rest in God's unconditional grace and love today and get back to living life in him.

LORD JESUS REVEALED

All this evidence that God's judgment is right, and as a result you will be counted worthy of the Kingdom of God, for which you are suffering. God is just: He will pay back trouble to those who trouble you and give relief to you who are troubled, and to us as well. This will happen when the Lord Jesus is revealed from Heaven in blazing fire with His powerful angels. He will punish those who do not know God and do not obey the gospel of our Lord Jesus. They will be punished with everlasting destruction and shut out from the presence of the Lord and from the majesty of His power on the day He comes to be glorified in His Holy people and to be marveled at among all those who have believed. This includes you, because you believed our testimony to you.

2 Thessalonians 1:5–10

Today, you may feel a bit discouraged or weak or like an outsider from the fast-paced world that is spinning all around you. Be encouraged! For one day, our Lord Jesus will be back and this time he won't be the humble servant like he was during his first visit on earth. No, this time he will be seen by the whole world in all his glory. He will be here to destroy all of those who did not put their trust in him and to rescue his people from this world of sin! What a day that will be, and it could happen very soon. Are you ready to meet your creator? Which side will you be on? Will Jesus be here to be glorified in you and to perfect your relationship with him for the rest of eternity, or will he be here to destroy you because you have decided to live your life apart from him? If the first is true then be encouraged today and keep running the race toward him, for one day you will receive your prize in full! If the latter is true then it is not too late to put your trust in him! Ask him today to forgive you of your sins; tell him that you want to surrender your heart and life to him and join the rest of God's people who will live an abundant life in Christ for the rest of eternity!

LOVE AND PERSEVERANCE

May the Lord direct your hearts into God's love and Christ's perseverance.

2 Thessalonians 3:5

We live in a world that is in the midst of a spiritual war, and as a Christian, love and perseverance are the only two things that will sustain you and fulfill you in the midst of this great battle. God's love is the reason that we do everything that we do—it is the trophy that awaits us at the end of the race as well as the rush of the pursuit that brings us joy in the midst of the battle. The way that we persevere in this life is to remain in Christ—to have Jesus Christ be the Lord and Master of everything that we do, every minute of every day! To remain in him by renewing our mind and choosing godly thoughts is the key to success in this great battle for control of our hearts. So today, take the gift of God's love and let it shine through you to others as you remain in Christ, and persevere in order that those around you may see and believe!

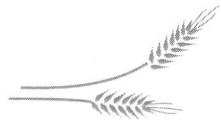

IT'S NOT ABOUT US, IT'S ALL ABOUT HIM

To Him who loves us and has freed us from our sins by His blood, and has made us to be a Kingdom and priests to serve His God and Father—to Him be the glory and power for ever and ever! Amen.

Revelation 1:5–6

As a child, years ago, I still remember the goose bumps that I would get at the end of each service on Sunday morning when the choir would sing the last part of this verse as a doxology to send us on our way to face another week. Whatever situation or circumstance that you may find yourself in today, please remember that everything that happens to you now as a Christian has nothing to do with you and is all about serving the King of kings and Lord of lords who has by his blood given you the power to live an abundant life in him! It is because of him and the sacrifice that he made on the Cross that you are free to live for the rest of eternity, reunited in a loving relationship with your Creator. It is because of him that you are able to face another day in this fallen world in which we live. It is because of him that your needs are provided for and because of him that you are connected to other believers with a love bond that is so amazingly awesome and brings us all together as one church to reflect his image to the world! It is because of him that you are gifted to serve and because of him that you can and will be successful here in this life! It is because of him that you will breathe your next breath, see the next sunset, and be able to rest in the knowledge that he is in control of your life and only wants the best for you. Every good thing comes from him and everything that happens to you is needed to mold and shape you back to the original masterpiece that he has planned for your life! Today and every day, it is not about us, it is all about him!

FIRST LOVE

I know your deeds, your hard work and your perseverance. I know that you cannot tolerate wicked men, that you have tested those who claim to be apostles but are not, and have found them false. You have persevered and have endured hardships for my name, and have not grown weary. Yet I hold this against you: You have forsaken your first love. Remember the height from which you have fallen! Repent and do the things you did at first. If you do not repent, I will come and remove your lampstand from its place.

Revelation 2:2–5

Sometimes we as Christians can get so wrapped up in church and in serving and in living the Christian life that we forget why we are even doing it in the first place. The life that we live comes out of a genuine, unexplainable, deep, and passionate love that we have for Jesus Christ, all because of the love and sacrifice that he made for us. Also, love for our Creator is at the very core of who we are and why we were even created in the first place—to love and worship the one true God, the Alpha and Omega! The Christian life is really much more simple than we make it out to be and can be summed up like this: the Christian life is learning to fall in love with Jesus Christ so that one can be restored once again to the perfect fellowship that existed before sin entered the world! The writer of Corinthians says it this way: "And now these three remain: faith, hope, and love. But the greatest of these is love" (1 Corinthians 13:13). So the challenge that Jesus is giving the church of Ephesus here is the same challenge that faces you and me today: to live our lives, every minute of every day, consumed by the awesome love of Christ, not letting anything that exists in this world distract our attention away from this most extraordinary love relationship that we as Christians are so privileged to have with our Father in heaven! Fall in love with him today!

PARADISE

He who has an ear, let him hear what the Spirit says to the churches.
To him who overcomes, I will give the right to eat from the tree of life,
which is in the paradise of God.

Revelation 2:7

The paradise of God—what a huge incentive that should encourage us as Christians not to give in to all of the junk that this world throws at us to try and separate us from the abundant life that you and I can find in Jesus Christ! To overcome these things means to obey God, to submit to his authority by remaining pure, and to stay in his will for your life. The "tree of life" is a metaphor describing a perfect fellowship with your Creator that is not tainted by sin that separates but is whole and complete and brings total fulfillment, perfect love, unspeakable joy, and a peace that passes all understanding. This paradise, this abundant life, is out there waiting for you and is available for you to live in every minute of every day from now through the rest of eternity. The price has been paid for you to enter through Jesus' blood on the Cross; the choice is up to you. You have the choice every day whether to live in paradise by walking with Jesus as the Lord of everything that you say and do or to give in to Satan's enticements and instead of overcoming them to be overcome by them and thus separated from God's best for your life. So to overcome is to remain in him by living your life the way that he would want you live. There is an old saying that says that the grass is always greener on the other side. In this case I can attest to the fact that the grass is definitely greener for the Christian who daily chooses to obey Christ over the world and as a result eats from the tree of life that our loving Father so graciously wants to give to all of his children that he created to have this love relationship with forever! Enter paradise today my friend! Seek God with all of your heart and live your life for him.

HIDDEN MANNA FROM HEAVEN

He who has an ear, let him hear what the Spirit says to the churches. To him who overcomes, I will give some of the hidden manna. I will also give him a white stone with a new name written on it, known only to him who receives it.

Revelation 2:17

Are you hungry today? God has for you some "hidden manna" from heaven that he so desperately wants you to receive. This is heavenly food that will quench your thirst and satisfy your soul, filling you completely so that your search for significance and purpose will be complete! And not only that, he also wants to give you a new name that is written on a white stone that will be your entrance pass into paradise! You see, in him you will have a new life with a new name and will be completely satisfied, totally fulfilled, and eternally safe from sin and death forever! To overcome is to remain in him in order that you can experience all of these great things that God has planned for your life. Today, surrender your life and overcome the temptation to live for yourself. If you do this then you will receive an abundant life like no other, as well as an eternal life with your heavenly Father that no one can ever take away. Seek him today with all of your heart.

ALIVE IN CHRIST

To the angel of the church in Sardis write: These are the words of Him who holds the seven spirits of God and the seven stars. I know your deeds; you have a reputation of being alive, but you are dead. Wake up! Strengthen what remains and is about to die, for I have not found your deeds complete in the sight of my God. Remember therefore, what you have received and heard; obey it and repent.

Revelation 3:1–2

The church in Sardis was the capital of the ancient kingdom of Lydia; it was a city full of great wealth and fame. I am sure that like a few famous cities in America today, these people of Sardis had the reputation of being very alive because of all their worldly treasures and busyness and popularity. Isn't it interesting that despite all of their material possessions and activity that they were considered spiritually dead by Jesus and were on the verge of disaster? Even more interesting than that is the fact that they had heard and received the Gospel of Jesus but had not obeyed it. To be alive in Christ takes much more effort than just hearing and receiving the Word of God! To be alive in Christ is more than just going to church on Sunday morning to fulfill your religious duty for the week. Spirituality and the Christian life cannot be compartmentalized into just one area of your life; it was designed to consume your whole life so that Jesus could be a part of everything that you do and so that you can become more like him in the process! To be alive in Christ is to obey what you learn on Sunday throughout the week; it is to commit every minute of every day to him and to surrender your will for your life to God's will and to live as he would want you to live. To be alive in Christ is to put into action the words that you read and the sermons that you hear. What is God telling you to do as a first step of obedience today? Is it to be baptized; is it to turn from a blatant sin or habit; is it to forgive that person that has so wrongly offended you; is it to start spending time with him in his Word? Or maybe it is to start at the very beginning and ask him into your heart, committing your life and everything that you do to him. Whatever it is, I would challenge you to jump in today with both feet! Wake up! Start living the abundant life that is alive in Christ, full of joy, and eternally secure.

LUKEWARM

These are the words of the Amen, the faithful and true witness, the ruler of God's creation. I know your deeds, that you are neither cold nor hot. I with you were either one or the other! So, because you are luke-warm—neither hot nor cold—I am about to spit you out of my mouth. You say 'I am rich; I have acquired wealth and do not need a thing.' But you do not realize that you are wretched, pitiful, poor, blind and naked.

Revelation 3:14–17

This passage makes it very clear that our God in heaven does not like mediocrity! He does not like casual Christianity! He wants you and me to be sold out for him. He wants us to be on fire for his cause, earnestly seeking his will for our lives and wanting desperately, every day, to be more like him. He wants us to choose to either live our lives in obedience to him, laying down our own wills and seeking his face every day, or to do the opposite and just be consumed by worldly things. We have all met people who go to church on Sunday but who live totally different lives during the week. What kind of picture does that paint to the lost people of the world who are desperately seeking purpose and fulfillment in this life? What does that say to them about our faith and our God when they see such hypocrisy? Are they convinced that God is real? Are they convinced that this Christianity thing is real and can change even their lives if they were to surrender? Hardly so. Maybe that is why God takes such a strong stand against being a lukewarm Christian since such mediocrity would turn anyone away from wanting to know Jesus for who he really is! Now, don't get me wrong and think that you have to be perfect to be a Christian; we all fail at times and this process of becoming more like Christ is just that—a process. But the point here is to make a choice each and every day, despite our failures, to live our lives for Jesus and to let him transform our hearts and minds to be more like him. To make a choice to surrender and not to give in to the world, no matter what obstacles we are up against and how high that next barrier is that is right in front of you. To make a choice to trust God that he will sustain you and believe his promise that he will finish the work that he started in your life. To make a choice to be so much on fire for him that people around you will see and know that God is real because of the work that he is doing in and through your very life. Today it is time to choose. Choose Jesus! Start living your life on fire for him and then hang on for dear life, for you will see and experience the power of God like never before!

OPEN THE DOOR

Here I am! I stand at the door and knock. If anyone hears my voice and opens the door, I will come in and eat with him, and he with me.

Revelation 3:20

There are many people in this world who believe that since God is God he can do anything and they don't really need to act in order for him to be a part of their lives. Sadly enough, unless they open the door by asking him to be a part of their lives, these people will never have a relationship with him. You see, our God is such a relational God that when he created us, he gave us the ability to choose whether or not we would want anything to do with him. He did this so that our devotion to him would be real. As a result, many people have made the wrong choice and sin has entered the world and the amazing thing to me is that God knew ahead of time that all of this was going to happen. Guess what, he created us anyway! He created us because his love for you and me is so great that he knew what was going to have to be done in order to restore mankind's relationship with him; he knew that Jesus was going to have to die on the Cross to make amends for our wrong choices. He knew all of this and yet his compassion and love was so incredibly real that he carried on with his plan in order that he could have sons and daughters that love and worship him for the rest of eternity! Isn't that awesome? But don't miss the point of the verse here—you must act in order to start this process of a relationship with God. It is one thing to believe in God; it is another thing to "open the door" by putting your trust and faith in him! Let me illustrate the point this way: I can tell you that if I am standing in front of you with my back facing you and fall backward that I believe that you would catch me and not let me fall. To tell you that I believe this is one thing; to actually fall backward and expect you to catch me is something totally different. Fall backward into the loving hands of God today! Open the door of your heart and commit everything that you are to him. Ask him to be a part of your life and start the process of this most amazing relationship with Jesus Christ.

GOD IS WORTHY

You are worthy, our Lord and God, to receive glory and honor and power, for you created all things, and by your will they were created and have their being.

Revelation 4:11

All things were created by our Lord and God in heaven! God created you to be unique from every other person or thing that was a part of his creation. The Bible says that he has numbered the hairs on your head and that he has a most awesome plan for your life. He created you so that he could live in relationship with you. He loves you and wants to give you so much more than you could ever dream or imagine. He created you with the ability to choose—the ability to choose to surrender your life to him and thus be rewarded with an abundant life that has purpose and meaning, fulfillment and agape love, or to choose to live a life that in the end only leads to loneliness and despair. God created you with a longing deep inside that can only be filled by him. Today, why don't you taste and see that he is good! Ask him to fill that void in your life that only the Creator of your life can fill. He is worthy! He is God! In him there is power, in him there is love, in Him there is joy—surrender your heart and life to him today.

LION OF THE TRIBE OF JUDAH

Then one of the elders said to me, "Do not weep! See, the Lion of the tribe of Judah, the Root of David, has triumphed. He is able to open the scroll and its seven seals."

Revelation 5:5

Just as God had prophesied about early on in biblical times, more than 2,000 years before his arrival, a descendent of David—Jesus Christ—came. He came and lived among us in the flesh, lived a perfect life, and then paid the ultimate price to atone for our sins so that you and I could be restored in relationship to the God of this world and could live forever with him! He has won! The battle for eternal life is over and you can enter in to this victorious life in Christ today. All you have to do is ask. Even in the midst of this fallen, sinful world, you can have joy and fulfillment. You can have a peace that passes all understanding and a clear vision of your purpose here on earth as God himself will enter your heart if you let him and will transform your life to be more like him, preparing you to do the work and be the person that he had planned for you to be all along. If you are already on this journey, then you know that this process can be painful as you die to your old self in order for Christ to be revealed more in and through your life, but don't despair, as the reward that awaits you in the end will be more than satisfying, more than anything that you could have hoped or imagined. You will be made perfect and complete, not lacking anything, in perfect union with your Creator who loves you more than you could ever know. The alternative is separation and regret forever from God himself and from anything that is good. Don't let this happen to you! Seek him today with all of your heart and surrender your life to him!

PURCHASED ALL MEN FOR GOD

And they sang a new song: 'You are worthy to take the scroll and to open its seals, because you were slain, and with your blood you purchases men for God from every tribe and language and people and nation. You have made them to be a Kingdom and priests to serve our God, and they will reign on earth.

Revelation 5:9–10

Whatever your nationality, whatever your gender, whatever your skin color, whatever you have done in your past, and whatever you will do in your future does not matter when it comes to the saving grace of God! No matter who you are or where you are or what you have done, Jesus, through his blood on the Cross, has made it possible for you to be a part of God's Kingdom forever! For me to grasp this idea of grace and forgiveness has been a lifelong process. There are times when I fail and times when I feel like such a stranger to the holiness of our Creator, and somehow it is in these times that God shows me how desperately I need him and how great his love and forgiveness are! If you have accepted Jesus into your heart and life, then there is nothing that you have done or can do that will separate you from his love. As you seek his forgiveness and his direction in your life, he will always be there to wrap his arms around you and tell you that it is okay, that he has purchased you for God, that he has paid the price for your sin, and that his strength will be made perfect in your weakness so that all will see and know that he is God.

HEAVENLY WORSHIP

Then I looked and heard the voice of many angels, numbering thousands upon thousands, and ten thousand times ten thousand. They encircled the throne and the living creatures and the elders. In a loud voice they sang:"Worthy is the Lamb, who was slain, to receive power and wealth and wisdom and strength and honor and glory and praise!"

Revelation 5:11–12

Now that's what I call worship! More than 100 million angels in song, praising the King of kings and Lord of lords. The Apostle John was blessed to have just a glimpse of the throne in heaven and the awesome glory of God and his Son Jesus surrounded by more than 100 million angels. The cool thing is that this same power can be lived out in you and me today. This same worship can be lived out in our lives because Jesus himself lives in our hearts and is transforming each and every one of us that has accepted him to live out a lifestyle of worship for all of the world to see. Worship is indeed a lifestyle. It is the way that you, as a Christian, live your life as a servant, dying to your own selfish desires and looking out for the needs of others.

I was talking with one of the senior managers at our company this week and he was explaining to me his need to have more "Christianity" in his life than just the weekly Sunday service that his family attends. So, he has been reading through the Bible each day, and that is a phenomenal start to the Christian life! It is only the beginning, though, of what God wants to do and will do in his life. See, understanding your need for God is just the beginning of living the Christian life; eventually, as the Spirit of God moves in your life, you will come to the understanding that what you really need is to give your life away to others for the cause of Christ. What will ultimately fill the void in your life and give you purpose and meaning is to live a lifestyle of worship by looking out for the needs of others with humility and loving them unconditionally with God's love that he has so undeservedly given to you! Jesus was explaining to the religious people of the day what the greatest commandment was in Matthew 22:37 when he said: "Love the Lord your God with all your heart and with all your soul and with all your mind. This is the first and greatest commandment. And the second is like it: Love your neighbor as yourself."

You want to worship God? Do you want to have purpose and meaning in your life? Do you want that emptiness inside to be filled with something that will last for the rest of eternity? Then start giving your life away today to the people around you—start living a life of worship that will have an impact on this fallen world!

PATIENT ENDURANCE

This calls for patient endurance on the part of the saints who obey God's commandments and remain faithful to Jesus.

Revelation 14:12

This phrase is seen several times in the book of Revelation. The reason that it is repeated is because we are called to endure and to obey even in the worst of circumstances such as in the end times when all Christians will be tormented and martyred because of their faith in Jesus Christ. Now, I am not going to predict when the end of the world is going to come, as God himself tells us that not one of us will know the hour and that the "day of the Lord will come like a thief in the night" (1 Thessalonians 5:2). What I do know is that the times that we live in, even today, make it extremely difficult to be a believer and that it is only going to get even worse in the coming years. As a Christian, you will have times of failure, will be ridiculed for your faith in Christ, will be strongly opposed by the enemy, and will even feel like giving up at times. Don't be discouraged! Jesus has won the war! He loves you even in the midst of your failures and just wants you to keep seeking his face each and every day, no matter what happens in the world around you. His grace and love and forgiveness and strength are much more powerful than anything that the world can throw at you to distract your attention away from him. Rest in his grace and love today! Have patience as he molds and shapes you to be more like him. Seek him today with all of your heart and live your life for him.

GOD'S BATTLE

He said: "Listen, King Jehoshaphat and all who live in Judah and Jerusalem! This is what the Lord says to you: 'Do not be afraid or discouraged because of this vast army. For the battle is not yours, but God's."

2 Chronicles 20:15

When King Jehoshaphat was faced with an army that was headed his way that greatly outnumbered his people and defeat was almost inevitable, he did what many of us need to do today when we are up against insurmountable odds in life: he fasted and prayed and sought the Lord's help! You see, sometimes God will test us to see if our faith in him is real. Sometimes he does this by allowing us to face mountains and obstacles in this life that are way out of our reach. He does this to see if we will just give up or if we really have faith that he is in control of everything. You see, many of the obstacles that we face every day, we could never overcome on our own; they are God's battle and the only way that we will ever see and experience victory is to surrender and trust completely in him! When will we learn that we are nothing without him? When will we learn that his ways are way outside of our scope and vision and that it is not about us but all about him? Don't try to fight God's battles on your own—let him do the fighting as you seek him with all of your heart and draw near to him in the midst of the great disappointments and struggles that we have in this life. Heed Jehoshaphat's example today and stop trying to control your own destiny; instead, seek the Lord and stay close to him and watch what he will do in your life.

THE BOOK OF LIFE

Then I saw a great white thrown and him who was seated on it. Earth and sky fled from His presence, and there was no place for them. And I saw the dead, great and small, standing before the throne, and books were opened. Another book was opened, which was the book of life. The dead were judged according to what they had done as recorded in the books. The sea gave up the dead that were in it, and death and Hades gave up the dead that were in them, and each person was judged according to what he had done. Then death and Hades were thrown into the lake of fire. The lake of fire is the second death. If anyone's name was not found written in the book of life, he was thrown into the lake of fire.

Revelation 20:11–15

There are several books here in this story. One set of books has a record of everything that you and I have done in our lifetimes here on earth. The other book (the only one that really matters) is called the Book of Life. The only way to get your name printed in the Book of Life is to have known the one who paid the ultimate price for your sins in order that you could live forever with God, free and clear of the penalty for sin in your life. To know and have a relationship with Jesus Christ is the only way to avoid the lake of fire and complete separation from God forever. This is why our mission as Christians on this earth is so vitally important. We must let Jesus live through us in order that the lost people that are all around us would see him living through our lives and believe, in order that they won't perish at this great Day of Judgment. You are the hands and feet of God Almighty. You are the Church in which he wants to use to reach the lost people of the world. You may be the only hope for someone that you know to see that Jesus is real and want to have a personal relationship with him in order that they too may live forever with him in glory. The days are short, the hour is coming, and your mission is a very tall order and of utmost importance! Live your life for him today in order that other people will see him living through your life and believe.

LIGHT IN HEAVEN

I did not see a temple in the city, because the Lord God Almighty and the Lamb are its Temple. The city does not need sun or the moon to shine on it, for the glory of God gives it light, and the Lamb is its lamp.

Revelation 21:22–23

We read here a description of a place that you will see in person one day if you have accepted Jesus Christ and thus have eternal life and will have the opportunity to live forever with him in glory. I think that it is interesting to read about the glory of God and the light he gives off. Do you know that if you are a Christian then this same glory of God lives inside of you and that this same light that will light up heaven one day is present in your life? Do you know that even today, here on this earth, your life has a radiance to it because of Christ living in you and that God's glory can be seen in you? Your life lights up the world around you, exposing the darkness and letting all the world have a sneak preview of God's love and his radiant light that will one day never be covered by this dark world but will shine ever so brightly forever. In Matthew 5:16 Jesus says, "In the same way, let your light shine before men, that they may see your good deeds and praise your Father in heaven." You see, it is impossible to blend in with this world and not sick out if you are a Christian. It is impossible for God's Glory not to be seen in your life if you have truly accepted him and are living your life surrendered to his Spirit. So, keep this in mind today as you live your life. Know that people are watching you, for you can't help but stand out from the crowd. Be sure that you represent Jesus well in everything that you say and do. Let your light shine so that others will see and believe.

OBEDIENCE BRINGS FREEDOM

For a man's ways are in full view of the Lord,
and He examines all of his paths.
The evil deeds of a wicked man ensnare him;
the cords of sin hold him fast.
He will die for lack of discipline,
led astray by his own great folly.

Proverbs 5:21–23

God has rules and principles for us to live by not to ruin our fun here on earth but to increase our joy by protecting us from ourselves. I know what it is like to be held captive to habitual sin, and let me assure you that it is no fun! I have seen many people's lives destroyed by them choosing to chase after their own fleshly appetites, ignoring God's direction, thinking that they are making choices that will fulfill them and make them happy when, on the contrary, they are making choices that keep them bound up by their own selfishness, sin, and shame. After a recent telephone conversation with a close friend, I was heartbroken to hear how this person is being led astray by her own folly. She is running from her family, running from this country even, in search of freedom, but what she is actually doing is creating a web of sin and selfishness that is destroying people's lives all around her, including her own. You see, true freedom is only found in surrendering your heart and life to Jesus Christ and then living for him, obeying his principles and direction for your life. Who knows better what will make you happy than the one who created you in the first place? The one who created you with that burning desire for purpose and meaning, that burning desire for joy and fulfillment, that burning desire that can only be found in the person of Jesus Christ! Start giving your life away today to other people for him; start seeking his direction for your life and you will see and know what freedom in Christ is all about.

THE ROOT

I, Jesus, have sent my angel to give you this testimony for the churches. I am the Root and the Offspring of David, and the bright Morning Star.

Revelation 22:16

The dictionary defines "root" as: "a part of the body of a plant that develops, typically, from the radicle and grows downward into the soil, anchoring the plant and absorbing nutriment and moisture; the fundamental or essential part." Jesus is our root that had been testified about many years before his birth. To Christians, Jesus is your anchor; he offers everything that brings life to your soul. Jesus is the essential part of understanding and realizing what it means to be alive, what it means to have purpose and meaning, and what it means to finally be complete, not lacking anything. Jesus should be the fundamental and essential part of everything that you do and say. This concept sounds simple and yet many Christians leave him out of their life during the week, they only acknowledge him on Sunday in church, and the rest of the week they go at it on their own, making their own decisions apart from him. This reminds me of a plant in our home that we forget to water at times throughout the week. The plant almost always appears as if it is on its last leg, droopy and dying, until it gets so bad that we remember to water it and it comes to life for a few days until the cycle of droopiness starts again. If we were to water that plant every day, then it would always appear vibrant and would be growing and healthy. This is not so different than your life as a Christian. If you feed the spiritual part of your life every day through living a life of servanthood and obedience and through studying his Word and communicating with him in prayer and by loving God and loving people with everything that you are, then your life will be vibrant and full of purpose and meaning, for others will be able to see God overflowing from the way that you live your life. Jesus is the source of life, the fundamental part of what you are all about. Don't leave him out of your life today; let him be a part of everything you think about, everything that you say and do. If you do this then your heart will be overflowing with love for the entire world to see and believe.

COME

The Spirit and the bride say "Come!" And let him who hears say, "Come!" Whoever is thirsty, let him come; and whoever wishes, let him take the free gift of the water of life.

Revelation 22:17

God is not going to force your hand when it comes to accepting him into your heart and accepting this free gift of salvation that he has offered to all of his children. No, it is up to you to come to him. It is up to you to make the first move by choosing to surrender your heart and life to his control because of his great love for you, because of all that he has to offer you both now and in the life to come, and because of the incredible sacrifice that he made for you on the Cross in order to make all of this possible. You must make the first move by asking his forgiveness for your sins and by asking him to come into your life to change it to be more like him. In Matthew 7:7 Jesus tells us in this way: "Ask and it will be given to you; seek and you will find; knock and the door will be opened to you." Even as a Christian, every day you have a choice to either move toward God, invite him to be a part of your day, or go it alone and leave him out. God tells us all today to "come!" He tells us all to invite him into our world—he has so much to offer, so much that our small minds cannot even comprehend it all. So "come" to him today; start you day in prayer, asking him to be a part of everything that you say, everything that you do, everything that you think about, and everything that you stand for or dream to be. Jesus is telling you to "come!" Make a move toward him today.

ALTARS AND IDOLS

Jehoiada then made a covenant that he and the people and the king would be the Lord's people. All the people went to the temple of Baal and tore it down. They smashed the altars and idols and killed Mattan the priest of Baal in from of the altars.

2 Chronicles 23:16–17

Once again we see here in the Old Testament a newly named royal family that had a desire to obey the Lord and to rule the people under God's direction. The first thing that almost always happened when a godly king was appointed after a time of turning from the Lord was to tear down and destroy the altars and idols that the people had been worshipping rather than worshipping God Almighty. Many, many times in the Old Testament we see God's people turn from him in order to worship lifeless statues, gold and silver pieces of material that may have been nice to look at but that could not protect them and bring them the hope of salvation that they had been seeking. This act of disobedience is not unlike many of us today. Many of us turn from God and spend more time thinking about and chasing idols of this world rather than spending our time becoming more like Christ. Many of us chase the almighty dollar, the job that will finally qualify us as being a success in the world's eyes, the house or boat or car that we think will bring us joy and fill the void that we feel in our heart of hearts. The truth of the matter is that none of these things can fill that void in your heart. Yes, they may fill it for a short period of time, but soon after acquiring whatever it is that you are chasing after in this life, soon after you will be hungry for more as the only thing that can satisfy your hunger and fulfill you completely and forever is a relationship with Jesus Christ! Many of us need to smash the altars and idols in our lives that are separating us from a deeper relationship with God Almighty. You know that that thing is in this world that is keeping you from total surrender to God—that thing that you feel like you cannot live without and are trying to keep hidden in secret as you are trying to somehow keep a foot in both worlds and serve two gods. Jesus tells us in Matthew 6:24, "No one can serve two masters. Either he will hate the one and love the other, or he will be devoted to the one and despise the other. You cannot serve both God and money." Heed Jehoiada's example today and destroy whatever it is in your life that is distracting your attention away from your loving Savior who wants only to give you the best of everything in this life! Turn that idol over to God—lift your hands to heaven this morning and surrender everything to him. It is only in true surrender that God can move in your heart where he will give you everything that you could have ever dreamed or imagined. Surrender you heart and life to him today.

CONVICTION OF THE SPIRIT

Although the Lord sent prophets to the people to bring them back to
Him, and though they testified against them, they would not listen.

2 Chronicles 24:19

In the Old Testament, prior to the resurrection of Jesus and the
dwelling of the Spirit of God in his children's heart, the Father had
to send prophets to warn his people when they were doing wrong
and not following his commands. In today's time, we have an amazing gift of the Spirit that lives inside each and every person that has
surrendered his heart and life to Jesus Christ. It is the Spirit's job to
guide and direct us as we journey on in this life toward becoming
more like Christ. It is the Spirit's job to convict us of sin in our life
and encourage us in our walk with the Lord. Many of you who are
reading these daily devotions can feel the prompting of the Spirit
as he is pushing you and encouraging you to make changes in your
life in order that you can live out the life that God has planned for
you all along. The Spirit is prompting many of you to accept Jesus
in your heart for the first time in order that you can become a part
of the family of God and live forever with him. And in others the
Spirit is prompting to fully surrender everything that you are and
everything that you have to the lordship of Jesus Christ in order that
God can do great things in and through your life! Don't ignore these
promptings on your heart. God Almighty is calling you into a life
with him that is full of unimaginable joy and fulfillment, peace and
love that will last for the rest of eternity. It is up to you to respond;
he can't choose for you. All he can do is make his presence known
by his Spirit as he is pleading with you today to accept his gift of
love that he gave his very life for in order that you could finally be
reunited with the for whom your heart has been longing all along.
Choose him today, pray, and ask him into your heart—surrender all
that you are to Jesus.

PLAN

Do not those who plot evil go astray? But those who plan what is good find love and faithfulness.

Proverbs 14:22

To win the war against evil and live a successful Christian life takes planning! As a Christian, if you do not plan for times of weakness and plan for Spiritual growth in your life, then you will never come to a deeper relationship with Jesus Christ. Several times in Scripture God tells us to "come," to "open the door," to "enter in"; he wants us to be proactive and intentional concerning our faith in God. If you just live your life and leave things to happen by chance then you unfortunately will become a victim of this fallen world. God tells us to choose him each and every day, to choose to live our lives under his direction and control. To do this successfully takes a solid plan. You should plan how you are going to respond the next time that you are tempted to live your life apart from God and his principles. You should plan time to spend in God's Word and in prayer, where you really get to know him in a personal way. You should plan how you are going to keep your mind on good things as Philippians 4:8 discusses. You should plan for the worst, hope for the best, and always be moving forward in this incredible journey toward becoming more like Christ! It is you who develops the plan for Spiritual growth in your life; it is God that gives you the strength, commitment, grace, and compassion to carry it out.

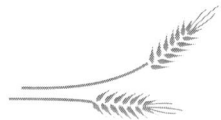

SECRET OF SUCCESS

He sought God during the days of Zechariah, who instructed him in the fear of God. As long as he sought the Lord, God gave him success.

2 Chronicles 26:5

As King Uzziah learned from Zechariah, there is only one way to truly be successful in this life, and that is to seek God's direction and plan for your life as you grow to become more like him! As God works in and through your life to do great things for his Kingdom, you need to be careful not to let your pride get the best of you. That is what happened to King Uzziah—at first he sought the Lord, who made him very successful as a king, but later on in life his pride got the best of him and he rebelled against God, who immediately humbled him to die a leopard's death. Now, don't get me wrong, God does not love us any more or any less as a result of our obedience to him. The point is that he has the perfect plan for our lives and to live in submission and obedience to him is to live out the life that he originally created us to live. At times, when people become more successful, as a result of their pride they think that they don't need to obey God and his principles for life any longer and slowly start to move out of God's will, making decisions about their actions apart from him. God has the very best plan for you! He is the secret of success in this life! Seek him today with all of your heart and live your life for him.

STEADFAST FAITH

Jotham grew powerful because he walked steadfastly before the Lord his God.

2 Chronicles 27:6

The dictionary defines "steadfast" as: "fixed or unchanging, firmly loyal or constant." King Jotham was king of Judah for sixteen years and in that sixteen years he consistently obeyed God and stood firm before him. He was rewarded by God for his steadfast obedience and servitude. God calls all of us to have a "steadfast" faith in him! Our world here is consistently changing and there are many distractions and disappointments and successes and failures and tragedies and all sorts of things that try to distract our attention and direction in our Journey toward becoming more like Christ. The encouraging thing is that God never changes and even in the midst of all of this chaos that is happening all around us, because of the one who lives inside of us, we have the power to hold firm to our faith and to consistently let him change our hearts and lives as he comforts us with his amazing love!

Don't you know that during King Jotham's reign that the same enemy that is present today and trying his best to make you swerve off of the narrow road was present back then? And I am sure they are very upset at King Jotham's steadfast faith. This godly king did not let that distract him, though; he kept his eyes focused on the only one who could pull him through and make him a success. This is a good lesson for all of us today who are trying to walk this narrow road and who are being pulled in all directions and tempted in seemingly every was possible. I would encourage you today to keep your focus on Jesus. Stay firmly loyal to him, and your reward will be great, both in this life and even more in the life to come!

PRAYER

But I call to God, and the Lord saves me. Evening, morning and noon
I cry out in distress, and he hears my voice ...
Cast your cares on the Lord and He will sustain you;
He will never let the righteous fall.

Psalm 55:16–17, 22

Today we live in a world of such self-sufficiency that I think at times, even as Christians, we try to tackle problems and issues on our own and sometimes forget to lift them up to the Lord in prayer. You see, the world today is so full of self-help strategies and ideas and proven business models for success that at times we feel like if we just follow the proven system for success that we read about or see acted out in other people's lives and other churches, then we will be successful and don't necessarily need to bother God with the details. What we forget is that God's plan for each one of us is different. God's plan for each church is different; he has many different churches with different types of worship and different ways of reaching people for him. It is in prayer, as we seek his direction in our lives and in our church, that we change. It is in prayer that our hearts and lives are transformed to be more like him as we enter in to this most amazing relationship with God Almighty. God loves you more than you could ever imagine and he wants more than anything for the lines of communication between you and him to be flowing, day and night. He gave His life to make this possible. He has plans for you that you could never read about in a book about someone else's life. No, your purpose here on earth is unique to you. He has gifted you to do things that no one else can do. The only way to know what this purpose is and the only way to live out your life in sync with his precious will is to enter into a daily relationship and a daily dialogue with your heavenly Father. The Bible calls this daily dialogue "prayer." Start communicating with your Lord today and you will begin living the abundant life that he promises to all of those who seek him with all of their heart!

SIGHTS AND SOUNDS

Ears that hear and eyes that see—The Lord has made them both.

Proverbs 20:12

One of my favorite sights in life is about to happen as the fall season approaches and the leaves on the trees are about to change to beautiful, vivid colors that are refreshing to the soul to gaze upon. Another is that of a sunset on the lake that illuminates both the sky and the water with endless color and depth—the right sunset will transpose feelings of peace and quiet, calm and stillness as a busy day nears the end with such a grand finale. One of my favorite sounds is the sound of the water crashing on the rocks along the shore on a windy day and the sound of chirping birds as they awake at sunrise to enjoy a new day under God's care. What a blessing most of us have to be able to hear and to see such amazing sights and sounds utilizing our eyes and ears that God Almighty has blessed us with. Not only does he give us the instruments in order to process the stimuli, but he creates for us such amazing and beautiful acts in creation for us to enjoy! Slow down today and take time to enjoy this great drama called life that is playing out all around you! The Director is creating scenes that are just for you to enjoy and to bring you peace and comfort in this chaotic world. Don't miss what he has to show you today.

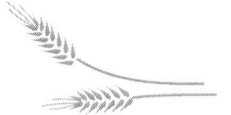

GIVE TO THE POOR

If a man shuts his ears to the cry of the poor,
he too will cry out and not be answered.

Proverbs 21:13

Some of our most memorable times as a couple are when we did something together to help other people and when we made a small sacrifice and gave to another person who was less fortunate. There is a feeling that reaches deep down into your soul that is indescribable and very fulfilling when you take time to give to the poor. Many tears of joy have been shed by us as a couple over the smallest acts of kindness to help others. Please remember that the act or amount of your gift is not important, but what is important is your heart and motive in being willing to help those who are in need. During Jesus' ministry he spoke many times about giving to the poor and needy. Successful icons such as Bono from U2 have made it their life's mission to help the poor people of the world. The Church should be the one who is leading this effort; the Church should be the first to try to meet the needs of all the less fortunate people in the world today. The cool thing is that many blessings come and an abundance of joy comes when you obey our heavenly Father and give of your time and resources to poor people with whom you come into contact. Don't miss out on these blessings today—take some time to help other people in need and you too will experience the joy that comes from loving others.

FISHERS OF MEN

As Jesus walked beside the Sea of Galilee, he saw Simon and his brother Andrew casting a net into the lake, for they were fishermen. "Come follow me," Jesus said, "and I will make you fishers of men." At once they left their nets and followed him.

Mark 1:16–18

There is more to Christianity than just going to church on Sunday and going through the motions of what it means to be a "good Christian." There is much more to it than just being good or making a stand for what you believe. It is more than giving financially or teaching Sunday school or serving in other capacities in the church. It is even more than just having your own personal relationship with God. To be a Christian means that you live your life in such a way, connected in relationship to Jesus Christ, so that other people can see him in and through your life and believe! To be a Christian means to be a "fisher of men" by letting Christ live in you so that more people will choose to accept the awesome gift of forgiveness, salvation, and abundant life that you have chosen to build your life around. God has chosen you to be the avenue in which other people will see him and believe. Live your life for him today.

SPIRIT WORLD

Just then a man in their synagogue who was possessed by an evil spirit cried out, "What do you want with us, Jesus of Nazareth? Have you come to destroy us? I know who you are—the Holy One of God!"

"Be quiet!" said Jesus sternly. "Come out of him!" The evil spirit shook the man violently and came out of him with a shriek.

Mark 1:23–25

At one of his first teachings at Capernaum, Jesus was confronted by an evil spirit from the third realm. This spirit knew what Jesus was about to do for you and me and what his ministry was all about. Needless to say, the evil spirit didn't like Jesus very much, because he knew that God was about to open the door for redemption of his people through the sacrifice of his Son, Jesus Christ. Today the evil spirits are still there and, although defeated in view of eternity, the battle still rages on. The battle today is for control of your heart. You see, God wants more than anything for you to surrender control of your heart and life to him in order that he can live through you and that you can live forever in relationship with him! Satan, on the other hand, wants more than anything for you to stubbornly refuse to accept the free gift of salvation that God has for you. Satan will try to deceive you into believing that to surrender control of your heart and life to God will be boring and unfulfilling and a total drag. Just the opposite of that lie is the Truth!

To surrender your life to the lordship of Jesus Christ is the most fulfilling and rewarding thing that you could ever do, it will bring you much joy, perfect peace, purpose, and meaning, both now and for the rest of eternity as you live your life in relationship once again to God Almighty who loves you more than you can ever know! So, remember today that things are not as they seem; that there is a spiritual realm all around you and that angels and demons are fighting for your attention. Be sure to make the right choice and to stay connected today to the one who loves you and wants the very best for your life.

LIVE FOR TODAY

Do not boast about tomorrow, for you do not know what a day may bring forth.

Proverbs 27:1

I used to have a colleague in business that would always boast about the great things that were going to happen and the future success that he was going to have in the months and years to come. This excitement and optimism was very appealing for a while; however, after many letdowns and disappointments because things did not quite work out the way that he had planned, it was then that he lost trust in some of the people that worked for him. This particular fellow was always talking about what was going to happen next instead of just enjoying his present success and achievement. This thought process is not uncommon in America, where for many people the present circumstances or material wealth or social status is never acceptable. It is greed and ambition that drive this capitalistic economy. For a Christian, this thought process should be different. God has many blessings for you today, right where you are in life and in your relationship to him. It is up to you to open your eyes and just enjoy his presence and what he is doing in your life today, right now! Enjoy and soak in the beauty of his creation and the people that will cross your path today that he has strategically placed in your life to bless your journey toward becoming more like Christ. Live for the moment and enjoy this day, for tomorrow it will be gone, never to return!

ACT OF COMPASSION

A man with leprosy came to Him and begged Him on his knees, "If you are willing, you can make me clean."

Filled with compassion, Jesus reached out His hand and touched the man. "I am willing," He said, "Be clean!" Immediately the leprosy left him and he was cured.

Mark 1:40–42

According to the Mosaic law, to touch a man with leprosy would bring defilement. It was not an accepted thing to do in the culture at the time. That's what I love about Jesus! He wasn't concerned about appropriateness or being politically correct; the only thing he was concerned about was to have great compassion and love for people and do whatever it took to express this love. He had so much love that he eventually gave his very life for all of us in order that we could live in relationship with him for eternity! Be on the lookout today for people who God may put in your path to love and have compassion for. Don't follow the skewed worldly view of political correctness. Step out in faith and walk as Jesus did. Show compassion and love to those that the world has left behind.

LONELY PLACES

Instead he went out and began to talk freely, spreading the news. As a result, Jesus could no longer enter a town openly but stayed outside in lonely places. Yet the people still came to Him from everywhere.

Mark 1:45

As a result of the man with leprosy spreading the news of his miracle of healing by Jesus, Jesus could no longer enter the city. The text here describes the places outside of the city as "lonely places." It is interesting, though, that God was still there in these lonely places and that God brought people to Jesus even out in the most remote of places to be touched and healed by him. As a traveling salesman, I can relate to the term "lonely places." At times on the road, away from my friends and family and church and comfort zone, at these times, life in general—especially trying to live a holy life—can be very lonely. The thing that God is teaching me here recently is that he is still there, no matter where I am or how far away from home I travel. What God is teaching me is that he still has a plan and purpose for me, even when I am away from home and feel very alone. What God is teaching me is that he wants to use me to reach people for him even when I am 500 or 1,000 miles away from home. What God is teaching me is that he will bring people to the lonely places to love with his love and to reflect his glory upon, even in the midst of loneliness! The same is true for you today. God has a plan and purpose for your life, no matter where you are or what circumstance you find yourself in today. He wants other people to see him in and through your life. This Christian life that we live is not about us! It is all about him! Let his love shine through your life today, no matter where you are, even if you are far from home, for God has put you there for a reason and you will be greatly blessed for your faithfulness in him.

HEALING FAITH

A few days later, when Jesus again entered Capernaum, the people heard that He had come home. So many gathered that there was no room left, not even outside the door, and He preached the Word to them. Some men came, bringing to Him a paralytic, carried by four of them. Since they could not get him to Jesus because of the crowd, they made an opening in the roof above Jesus and after digging through it, lowered the mat the paralyzed man was lying on. When Jesus saw their faith, He said to the paralytic, "Son, your sins are forgiven."

Mark 2:1–5

I had a youth pastor one time tell me a definition of faith that I never forgot. His name was Tom Benardo and his definition of faith was acting like it's so, when it's not so, because God said it would be so, and he'll make it so." You want God to heal your marriage? If you want this then you must first believe that he will and then you must take action as if he is going to! Do you want God to heal your sickness? you must first believe so much that you are willing to "act" upon your faith or belief. You want God to save your spouse or family member or friend or colleague? You must then have faith enough that he is going to, and then you must "act" on this faith by living your life in a way that God can touch and heal that person through you. These people went through some pretty extreme measures in order to heal their friend who was paralyzed. I mean, they dug a whole in the roof! The text says that God forgave them of their sins because of their faith in him and later on in the chapter he heals the paralytic of his disease. What extreme measure have you taken lately as a result of your faith in God? How have you acted on your faith, knowing and believing that God lives inside of you and that he has a plan for your life and wants to use you in a mighty way to reach other people for him? The paralytic had to get up off of the mat in front of all those people and try to walk. How is God asking you to step out of your comfort zone today in order that you may prove to him that your faith is real? Faith requires action; step out in faith today.

APOSTLES OF CHRIST

Jesus went up on a mountainside and called to Him those He wanted, and they came to Him. He appointed twelve—designating them apostles—that they might be with Him and that He might send them out to preach and to have authority to drive out demons.

Mark 3: 13–15

I love what the NIV study notes have to say about this verse: "The training of the Twelve included not only instruction and practice in various forms of ministry but also continuous association and intimate fellowship with Jesus Himself." To me, this is a great definition of what it means to be a Christ follower. The only difference for us today is that as Christians after Jesus' death and resurrection, Jesus actually lives inside of our hearts and minds. You want to be successful and victorious in your walk with the Lord? Then make sure that you have "continuous association and intimate fellowship with Jesus" every minute of every day. It is only when we take our eyes off of Jesus that the enemy gains a foothold in our lives; he will try to distract your attention and before you know it you will have veered off of the narrow road altogether. The only reason that Jesus died on the Cross was for this very thing—so that God could once again be a part of your life in a very real and intimate way where you communicate and relate to him continually as he works within you to make a difference in the world for him. And when your work on this earth is done, then you will be reunited in perfect unity with your Maker once again to live in this awesome love relationship for the rest of eternity! So there it is, the secret to living a victorious life in Christ is to stay connected and to keep your focus on him in prayer and in mind-set, every minute of every day as you live your life for him and do everything out of this great love that you have for the one who is living inside of you. Enjoy your time with Jesus today.

BEYOND YOUR SCOPE AND VISION

Then Jesus entered a house, and again a crowd gathered, so that He and His disciples were not even able to eat. When His family heard about this, they went to take charge of Him, for they said, "He is out of His mind."

Mark 3:20–21

Sometimes God's plan for your life may seem like foolishness to others, even those who are closest to you. God's perspective is eternal and much greater than our feeble minds could ever begin to comprehend. That is what faith is all about—believing and trusting God even when his promptings don't make sense to us or to others. As you live out the Christian life, you may encounter ridicule and resistance from loved ones who think that you have lost your mind, for they are the ones who know you the best and who have seen you at your worst prior to accepting Jesus Christ into your heart and life. As we see in the text here, even Jesus had this resistance from his family as he started his ministry on earth. When this happens, do not lose heart! God wants to do great things in and through your life; things that you now may not even be able to understand or see fully how they are going to play out in your life. He has a plan for you and that plan may currently be out of your scope and vision in this life, but don't let that stop you from pursuing him! Seek him no matter what other people may say, and you will encounter greatness as he changes you to become more like him.

FAMILY IN CHRIST

Then He looked at those seated in a circle around Him and said, "Here are my mother and my brothers! Whoever does God's will is my brother and sister and mother."

Mark 3:34–35

If you have accepted Jesus into your heart, then immediately you have been adopted into a new family of believers. This family is somewhat different than your physical, natural family of your youth. In this family everyone has the same goal, and that is to become more like Christ. In this family everyone is moving to the same place to live forever: heaven. In this family, there is one Father who is perfect and complete and who has compassion and grace and love like you have never experienced before. In this family there is a tie that binds us all together that goes deeper than blood and that makes us all one in him! In this family there is a peace and love for each other that is present yet indescribable. The mission of this family is to add more to its numbers so that all people could experience the greatness that comes from being a part of the body of Christ. Spend some time with your family members today—encourage them and let them encourage you as we all enjoy being a part of the family of God.

MYSTERIOUS POWER IN THE GOSPEL

He also said, "This is what the Kingdom of God is like. A man scatters seed on the ground. Night and day, whether he sleeps or gets up, the seed sprouts and grows, though he does not know how. All by itself the soil produces grain–first the stalk, then the head, then the full kernel in the head. As soon as the grain is ripe, he puts the sickle to it, because the harvest has come."

Mark 4:26–29

There is mysterious power in spreading the Gospel of Jesus Christ. Jesus describes here in the book of Mark using the parable and analogy of seed to represent the Word, and grain to represent people who hear the Gospel. Even if they don't consciously know it at the time, the Word of God changes people. It transforms hearts and minds and brings people to a place where they have no choice but to accept the amazing gift of love that it describes. Then they grow to become more like Christ so they too can start sharing this amazing message of abundant life and transformation to other people who don't yet know what it means to be a part of the Kingdom of God. The best way, by the way, to scatter seed or to spread the Gospel of Jesus Christ is to live it out through your own life on a daily basis by totally surrendering everything that you are to the lordship of Jesus Christ. This way people will be able to see the Gospel acted out by the way that you live your life; they will be able to see Jesus in you and then will know that he is real and will want to be a part of what they have seen through your obedience and submission to his will. There is power in the Gospel; there is power in surrender.

GREATNESS COMES IN SMALL PACKAGES

Again he said, "What shall we say the Kingdom of God is like, or what parable shall we use to describe it? It is like a mustard seed, which is the smallest seed you plant in the ground. Yet when planted, it grows and becomes the largest of all garden plants, with such big branches that the birds of the air can perch in its shade."

Mark 4:30–32

Do you want to become great in the Kingdom of God? Do you want to become more like Jesus and realize the abundance of blessing that he offers for anyone who will seek him with all of his/her heart? Do you want to be successful and have a peace that passes all understanding? Do you want to have vision and focus and purpose for you life here on earth? All of these things that can be described as "greatness" come by you making the smallest decisions and smallest acts of obedience because of your love for God! The Kingdom of God is described here in the text as the smallest seed possible that when planted becomes the largest of all garden plants. That, my friend, is exactly what it means to be a Christian.

To be a Christian is to make the smallest choices, choices that may seem insignificant to your friends and colleagues and other people in this world, but it is indeed in these seemingly insignificant choices that God's Spirit begins to move in your heart and make you more like him—choices to look away from an image that will cause you to think a thought that you don't want to think; choices to forgive someone when they inadvertently trample on your heart; choices to smile and have compassion on someone, maybe even a stranger who is obviously having a bad day; choices to continue on working diligently throughout the day, even when you don't feel like working; choices to look beyond the person to the need; choices to share even your deepest and most intimate feelings with a trusted friend; choices to give back, just a little, of what God has blessed you and your family with; choices to spend a few minutes communicating with God each day in his Word and in prayer; choices to say small prayers throughout the day as his Spirit would prompt you; choices to love those who don't love you; choices to never tell a lie, no matter how small. Choose to embrace change in your life today, if only in the smallest of things, and you will be on your way to greatness!

A CHEERFUL HEART

A cheerful heart is good medicine, but a crushed spirit dries up the bones.

Proverbs 17:22

I heard a saying last week that said, "A good way to cheer yourself up is to cheer someone else up." How true is that! I sometimes am accused of being too enthusiastic. It sometimes comes across to my colleagues and close friends as being immature or naïve. I couldn't disagree more with this assessment, for outside of my relationship with God, it is a positive attitude that I can attribute to any successes that I have had in my life. I heard another quote that said, "Life is 10% how you make it and 90% how you take it." How will you "take it" today? God is in control! Take whatever circumstances that you have been dealt today and live them out with joy, knowing that there is a master plan for you in this world and that abundant life is yours for the taking. Spread a little cheer to someone else today; give your life away for him.

EYES THAT SEE

Jesus left there and went to his hometown, accompanied by His disciples. When the Sabbath came, he began to teach in the synagogue, and many who heard him were amazed. "Where did this man get these things?" they asked. "What's this wisdom that has been given Him that He even does miracles! Isn't this the carpenter? Isn't this Mary's son and the brother of James, Joseph, Judas and Simon? Aren't His sisters here with us?" And they took offense at Him.

Jesus said to them, "Only in his hometown, among His relatives and in His own house is a prophet without honor." He could not do any miracles there, except lay His hands on a few sick people and heal them. And He was amazed at their lack of faith.

Mark 6:1–6

The enemy had blinded the eyes of those closest to Jesus during his childhood so that they could not see the larger story of what he was about to do for them and what he could do for them in the present if they would have only believed. The text says that because of their lack of faith, there were very few miracles performed among them. If only they would have had eyes to see the bigger picture of God's amazing love for them and the sacred romance of God's redemption that they were right in the middle of at the time!

The problem back then was the same problem that I see played out even today over and over again in our world. There are too many of us that are so wrapped up in our smaller stories, focused so much on ourselves that we are blinded to the larger story that is happening all around us! There are many of us, even Christians, who are victims of the enemy's ploys to distract our attention from the God of love that only wants an intimate, loving relationship with us. The enemy wishes to turn our attention to self-indulgences and busywork in an attempt to satisfy our hunger and desire for this intimate relationship with God with other things. Do you want to see a miracle happen in your life? Do you want to experience fulfillment and joy and adventure? Do you want your life to make sense and your purpose on earth to be fulfilled? Do you want to be victorious over the sin or addiction that has been keeping you in bondage and enslaving your heart so that it cannot be free to experience and become all that God has created it to be? If so, then stop hiding behind busywork or Christian service or self-indulgence, and ask God to give you a set of eyes that see! Engage your heart into this most amazing love relationship with God, trusting him for your future, trusting him for fulfillment, and loving him because of his amazing unconditional love for you! Get connected to him today.

REPENTANCE

They went out and preached that the people should repent.

Mark 6:12

Paula and I, along with others from Journey Church, recently had the opportunity to visit a mission in Charlotte, North Carolina. In this particular mission, unlike others that just feed the homeless and give them a place to stay, there is a ninety-day program that helps people who have been addicted to drugs or alcohol repent and come clean in their heart and in their minds as the wonderful volunteers and staff of the Charlotte Rescue Mission teach them what it means to repent. They teach them what is means to turn from their sins to righteousness and what it looks like to turn from the bondage and slavery that they had in their addiction to a loving God who always forgives when his people repent and seek him! The joy and freedom that I saw last night in the eyes of these brave men who at one time in their lives most likely had almost lost everything was simply a miracle! The stories that they told of how their lives had been changed for the better all because of the mission introducing them to the person of Jesus Christ would bring tears to your eyes.

One gentleman said something profound that provoked much thought. He said: "Many people suffer from addictions in their lives, it's just that most people hide it, keep it under the rug, and it never comes to the forefront until it is too late and they have lost everything." These men, many on their last string, had committed to the program. They had truly repented as they turned from their sin and had a plan on how they were going to be obedient in the future by participating in this wonderful recovery program that the Charlotte Rescue Mission provides.

God honors repentance! In this politically correct world we don't hear the Word spoken much in public. Even from many pulpits we hear feel-good messages that steer away from speaking of true repentance and turning from the sins that hold us in bondage from a righteous, loving, and forgiving God whose grace and unconditional love is big enough to cover any sin that you have committed. With repentance comes the freedom to truly know and have an intimate relationship with Jesus Christ. True repentance opens the door to a whole new world where your life has purpose and meaning and where God takes you on an adventure to make a difference in this world for him. The adventure is exciting and fulfilling and will last for eternity! Sin leads to death. Repentance leads to a free, abundant life in Christ. Repent today and seek God with your whole heart; he will make all difference in your life as you turn to him.

GOD OF LOVE

The Lord is gracious and compassionate; slow to anger and rich in love.

The Lord is good to all; He has compassion on all He has made.

All you have made will praise you O Lord; your Saints will extol you.

They will tell of the Glory of your Kingdom and speak of your might,

so that all men may know of your mighty acts and the glorious splendor of your Kingdom.

Your Kingdom is an everlasting Kingdom, and your dominion endures through all generations.

The Lord is Faithful to all His promises and loving toward all He has made.

The Lord upholds all those who fall and lifts up all who are bowed down. The eyes of all look to you, and you give them their food at the proper time.

You open your hand and satisfy the desires of every living thing. The Lord is righteous in all His ways and loving toward all He has made.

The Lord is near to all who call on Him, to all who call on Him in Truth.

He fulfills the desires of those who fear Him; He hears their cry and saves them.

The Lord watches over all who love Him, but all the wicked He will destroy.

My mouth will speak in praise of the Lord. Let every creature praise His Holy name, for ever and ever.

Psalm 145:8–21

My God of love fulfills all of my heart's desires as I look to him and call on him each day for strength and direction. He promises to be near me, to uphold me when I fall, and to lift me up when I am down. He hears my cry and loves me with a love that is unconditional and so great that it is indescribable by words and will never be taken away no matter what I do. I did not earn any of this great compassion and love, but he gives it freely to me because his desire is to dwell in the innermost places of my heart and to be one with me as he changes me to be the creation that he had originally planned who is one with him in purpose and meaning. This loving relationship is the ultimate relationship with the God of this universe who delivers abundant life that is full of peace and harmony, perfect in every way and so fulfilling beyond belief! So, today, I have the best present that I could have ever dreamed or imagined—an open door to this intimate relationship that each one of us longs for way down deep in our hearts. The door is open for you to today! Have you called on him? Do you know him in this way? Have you accepted his free gift of love? Does he dwell in your heart of hearts? Is he making you more like him and fulfilling your innermost desires? All you have to do is ask! He says in Matthew 7:7, "Ask and it will be given to you; seek and you will find; knock and the door will be opened for you." Don't wait any longer; jump in to this love relationship today!

POLITICS, POWER, AND WINNING

For Herod himself had given orders to have John arrested, and he had him bound and put in prison. He did this because of Herodias, his Brother Philip's wife, whom he had married. For John had been saying to Herod, "It is not lawful for you to have your brother's wife." So Herodias nursed a grudge against John and wanted to kill him. But she was not able to, because Herod feared John and protected him, knowing him to be a righteous and holy man. When Herod heard John, he was greatly puzzled; yet he liked to listen to him. Finally the opportune time came. On his birthday Herod gave a banquet for his high officials and military commanders and the leading men of Galilee. When the daughter of Herodias came in and danced, she pleased Herod and his dinner guests. The King said to the girl, "Ask me for anything you want, and I'll give it to you." And he promised her with an oath, "Whatever you ask I will give it to you, up to half my kingdom."

She went out and asked her mother, "What shall I ask for?"

"The head of John the Baptist," she answered.

At once the girl hurried in to the king with the request: "I want you to give me right now the head of John the Baptist on a platter." The king was greatly distressed, but because of his oaths and his dinner guests, he did not want to refuse her. So he immediately sent an executioner with orders to bring John's head. The man went, beheaded John in prison, and brought back his head on a platter. He presented it to the girl, and she gave it to her mother. On hearing of this, John's disciples came and took his body and laid it in a tomb.

Mark 6:17–29

John the Baptist was a threat to Herodias' lifestyle as the king's wife and all the fringe benefits that came with such a high position. She used a political situation to manipulate the king into doing something that he did not want to do. After all, all of his leaders and very important people that helped him to rule his kingdom where there at the party to hear the oath that he had made to Herodias' daughter. In the world's eyes, he had no choice but to comply with the request, for if he didn't then trust would have been gone with his leadership team and that would have been sure disaster for his kingdom—or so he probably thought at the time. What Herodias did not know at the time she was playing out this grudge on her self-declared enemy is that John the Baptist actually won in the end!

Listen, if you are a Christian trying to live a godly life in this fallen world, then do not be surprised to find that you do have enemies that will try to use politics and power to beat you down and discourage you in your journey to become more like Christ. Do not lose heart when this happens, as there is nothing that this world can do to you that will separate you from the love of God that is in Christ Jesus! John the Baptist is in the loving hands of our Father in heaven right now; he is experiencing a perfect union with the God that he gave his life for. Even in death there is victory since the death of a Christian means life everlasting with our heavenly Father. Stand strong today in Christ. Make an impact on this world for Jesus! Don't let the power and politics of this world discourage you in your pursuit of knowing God and being used by him. God has already won the war!

SURRENDERED HEART VERSUS
CEREMONIAL TRADITION

He replied, "Isaiah was right when he prophesied about you hypo-
crites; as it is written: 'These people honor me with lips, but their
hearts are far from me. They worship me in vain; their teachings are
but rules taught by men.' You have let go of the commands of God and
are holding on to traditions of men."

Mark 7:6–8

Jesus was upset with the Pharisees and teachers of the law because
they followed "religious" traditions but did not truly worship God
with their heart. God could care less whether you go to church
every Sunday, teach Sunday school, take communion, say grace
before a meal, or do any other religious tradition that you carry
out in your life. Now don't get me wrong, each and every one of
these things in itself is good and will help you in your journey to
become more like Christ; however, God is not looking for you to go
through the motions of Christianity; what God is looking for is for
you to have an intimate relationship with him where your heart is
totally surrendered and you are living your life in communion with
him because of his great love for you and no other reason. Get connected with him today and you will reap the rewards of an abundant
life versus a life full of tedious tradition.

NO NONSENSE

When they came back from the tomb, they told all these things to the eleven and to all of the others. It was Mary Magdalene, Joanna, Mary the mother of James, and the others with them who told this to the apostles. But they did not believe the women, because their words seemed to them like nonsense.

Luke 24:9–11

We live in a world where there is a third realm present that we cannot see. In this third realm are angels and demons that are fighting for your soul. It was in this realm that the ultimate battle for your forgiveness of sins and your eternal destiny was fought and won when Jesus was resurrected from the dead! Now today there is a battle that is raging in order to keep you distracted from understanding and accepting this free gift that Jesus has earned for you, as well as an effort to keep those who have accepted Christ distracted with worldly things so that their lives will be ineffective in reaching others for him. All of this may seem like nonsense to people whose eyes are still blinded from the truth. When you have experienced the power of God in your life and when you live your life trying to stay connected to Jesus Christ with a vision and purpose that goes much deeper than what anyone can see with their eyes today in the physical realm, it will seem like nonsense to people around you. Do not let that discourage you! At some point God will open their eyes and they will realize that your life has been changed for the better and that God is indeed a God of love and that Jesus has indeed been raised from the dead and is living in and through your very life! Today, continue to look at this world with they eyes of your heart. Focus on what is unseen; don't let the enemy distract you by what other people say or do. Live you life for him today!

DAMAGED HEART

Again, Jesus called the crowd to Him and said, "Listen to me, everyone, and understand this. Nothing outside a man can make him unclean by going into him. Rather, it is what comes out of a man that makes him unclean."

Mark 7:14–16

What comes out of a man? Your speech, your attitude, your actions, your obedience or disobedience, your thoughts, and your perspective on life, all of which have been molded and shaped and are filtered by your life experiences here on this earth. We have all been pierced at one time or another by the arrows that this fallen world throws at our hearts, both when we were very young and even when we are more mature and can see them coming. What Jesus is telling us here is that our failures in this life come not from external things but are a result of the condition of our heart. Outside of Christ, we all have damaged hearts that need to be healed, restored, and redeemed by the Master Healer who promises to make us new. You try to live a holy life and continue to miss the mark day after day. You change your circumstances in order to be victorious, but to no avail. You dive into more Christian service in order to try and drown out your broken heart with business and Christian duty, and even that just wears you down so much that you don't experience even a glimpse of this abundant life that Jesus speaks so much about. The problem lies in your heart and my heart. We all need the healing touch of Jesus and that healing and redemption only comes from abiding in him! It amazes me how at times I try to complicate the Christian life when the reality is that true healing and holiness and abundance come not from our actions or any external activity but from the condition of our heart that is only healed from its brokenness when we stay connected to the Savior and abide in him. He will heal your scars and make you new.

THREE DAYS WITHOUT FOOD

During those days another large crowd gathered. Since they had nothing to eat, Jesus called His disciples to Him and said, "I have compassion for these people; they have already been with me three days and have nothing to eat. If I send them home hungry, they will collapse on the way, because some of them have come a long distance."

Mark 8:1–3

A group of 4,000 people had been following Jesus around for three days straight without anything to eat. For three days, they were just trying to get close enough to be touched by Jesus or were just soaking in all of his teaching that gave them hope and made them feel loved and directed, like a lost sheep that has been found by the shepherd. Food was the last thing on their minds, even for three whole days, for they just wanted to be with Jesus as he was there in there presence. As I thought about this, I wondered if people would respond the same way today. I wondered if Jesus was here in the flesh, if people would follow him and not be concerned with their appetites for food or anything else. I wondered if people would take a break from their jobs or their hobbies or their families or friends or entertainment to just be touched by the Savior of the world. I wondered if I would throw everything aside to just be with him. And then I realized that the Truth of the Gospel is that Jesus is indeed here with us today, even in a much better and more personal way, as he resides in our hearts if we have accepted him in.

Jesus tells us in the Gospel of John 15 verse 4, "Remain in me, and I will remain in you. No branch can bear fruit by itself; it must remain in the vine. Neither can you bear fruit unless you remain in me." It is like Jesus is longing for us just to notice him—to put our own agendas and appetites aside and just spend time with him, as he is already here, right in our hearts, ready and willing to give us the desires of our hearts and abundance like we could have never imagined. And all we have to do is to acknowledge him in our lives and remember that he is here. I can imagine him saying to me way too often, " I gave my very life so that I can be here with you all the time, for the rest of eternity, and you at times forget that I am a part of you now and how much I love you and want to fill you and heal you. I will wait here inside your heart until you notice me enough to let me live through you and give you all that you really need and all that your lonely heart is longing for."

Father, forgive us for letting our appetites and our own agendas and desires distract our attention away from you. Thank you for all that you have done in order that we could be together forever. We love you!

DO YOU STILL NOT UNDERSTAND?

The disciples had forgotten to bring bread, except for one loaf they had with them in the boat. "Be careful," Jesus warned them. "Watch out for the yeast of the Pharisees and that of Herod."

They discussed this with one another and said, "It is because we have no bread."

Aware of their discussion, Jesus asked them: "Why are you talking about having no bread? Do you still not see or understand? Are you hearts hardened? Do you have eyes but fail to see, and ears but fail to hear? And don't you remember? When I broke the five loaves for the five thousand, how many basketfuls of pieces did you pick up?"

"Twelve," they replied. "And when I broke the seven loaves for the four thousand, how many basketfuls of pieces did you pick up?"

They answered "Seven."

He said to them, "Do you still not understand?"

Mark 8: 14–21

Jesus had just earlier in the day fed 4,000 people with seven loaves of bread, and yet just a few hours later, his disciples were so worried about not having any bread with them in the boat that they could not see the big picture of what was happening all around them. Jesus was trying to explain to them about the Pharisees and warn them about what was about to take place and yet all they could surmise from his words were that they did not have enough to eat on the boat.

Isn't this a perfect example of how we as Christians sometimes act today? God does miraculous things in our life, blesses us beyond belief, and yet just a short time later we bound ourselves up with worry about our circumstances when we know from experience that God has the power to meet our needs no matter what situation we find ourselves in. The problem is that when we worry about such pointless things, just like the early disciples, we miss the big picture of what God is doing all around us. We have "eyes that do not see" and "ears that do not hear" because our hearts are hardened as a result of our unfaithfulness to God. When we totally trust God with our lives by remembering what he has done in the past, we are free to see clearly the situation with the eyes of our heart. We can see God in the midst of many trials and tribulations if our vision is not clouded by worry and selfishness. So today, remember what God has done in the past. Don't forget the miracle that he has performed in your life. Trust him with your whole heart and watch closely what he is doing all around you, for you have a very important role to play in order that other people may also see and believe in him!

TAKE UP YOUR CROSS DAILY

Then He called the crowd to Him along with His disciples and said: "If anyone would come after me, he must deny himself and take up his cross and follow me. For whoever wants to save his life will lose it, but whoever loses his life for me and for the gospel will save it. What good is it for a man to gain the whole world, yet forfeit his soul? Or what can a man give in exchange for his soul? If anyone is ashamed of me and my words in this adulterous and sinful generation, the Son of Man will be ashamed of him when he comes in his Father's Glory with the holy angels."

Mark 8:34–38

What does it mean to "deny" yourself and to "take up your cross"? What is this business of "losing your life" for the sake of the Gospel? What does it mean to "gain the whole world"? For me it means that I keep the same character and integrity when I am on the road, far away from home where nobody is watching. For me it means that I make a habit of guarding my eyes from seeing things that would cause me to have an unclean thought. For me it means that I try to think more about my relationship with God throughout the day than being successful, or making more money or satisfying my own desires. For me it means that I try to be "others-minded" by looking out for the interests of others before myself. Now, I have by no means perfected any of this; however, what I would tell you is that there is much more joy and fulfillment in giving your life away by "taking up your cross" and following him than in anything that you may give up in the process! The reason is because as you are intentional about your faith and actually "act out your salvation by sacrificing your own fleshly desires, you will become more like Christ and begin to know him in a very personal way. This, my friend, is what your heart has been longing for; this is why your are here and the only thing that will bring you happiness that will last! Take up your cross today and follow him.

SPIRITUAL REALM

After six days Jesus took Peter, James and John with Him and led them up a high mountain, where they were all alone. There He was transfigured before them. His clothes became dazzling white, whiter than anyone in the world could bleach them. And there appeared before them Elijah and Moses, who were talking with Jesus.

Mark 9:2–4

Moses and Elijah had been gone from this world for some time, and here Jesus was talking with both of them face to face! A real-life ghost story! The truth is that this world is only temporary. Each one of us has a Spirit inside that will live on for the rest of eternity. What is determined during our time here on earth is where that Spirit will spend eternity when your time on this earth is through. If you have accepted Jesus Christ into your heart and made him the Lord of your life, then you will spend the rest of eternity with him in paradise. If not then you will spend the rest of eternity in separation from God, which the Bible calls hell.

There is a spiritual realm all around us; a third realm with angels and demons and those who have gone before us that are fighting for control of your mind and heart. Many things that happen to you on this earth are a result of this battle that is raging on in the spirit world. This Christianity thing is not a game, it is very real and the smallest decisions that you make today may have an eternal impact on other people and where they spend the rest of eternity. God has already won the war! The battle now is for your heart and for the choices that you make. Victory and abundant and eternal life is yours for the taking if you choose wisely and don't forget that other people are always affected by the decisions that you make. How will you choose today?

LISTEN

Then a cloud appeared and enveloped them, and a voice came from the cloud: "This is my Son, whom I love. Listen to Him!"

Mark 9:7

My wife often tells me that I need to do a better job of listening to her and to others. She sometimes tells me that I may hear what she is saying but that I obviously have not been listening. To listen to Jesus means to first hear what he is saying by reading his Word and spending time with him in prayer and then to obey what he is telling you. Are you listening to him today? Can you even hear what he is saying to you about how much he loves you and the abundant life that he wants to give you? Are you giving him an opportunity to speak to you through his Word and in the quietness of your mind? Or are his words being drowned out by the busyness of this world and the many distractions that the enemy throws up at us so that we do not hear? God has much to say to you and he has many blessings to give you today. All that he asks is that you first take time to hear his words and then to simply obey.

SALTED WITH FIRE

Everyone will be salted with fire. Salt is good, but if it loses its saltiness, how can you make it salty again? Have salt in yourselves, and be at peace with each other.

Mark 9:49–50

Think of your favorite Christian hero, your favorite Christian speaker or motivator—the person that has impacted you the most by hearing their story. The thing that all of these great motivators have in common is that they all have a story to tell. They all have overcome some type of adversity in their lives, they all have gone through the fires of life, and now their lives are used just as salt is used on food—to appeal to the appetites of people so that their lives may be preserved in knowing Jesus Christ as their personal Savior. God wants to use you and your experiences to help encourage others and to show others that his love is real. As I look back on my own life and relive some of the fires that Paula and I have been through in our marriage, I am encouraged as I see how God is using those very experiences to encourage some close friends that are presently going through some of the same struggles that God ultimately brought us through in our marriage years ago. I think about my childhood and the horrors that I faced growing up in a very dysfunctional family and then I see that dysfunctional families are the norm today, and I am encouraged by all the people that need to hear my story in order to get through a difficult time with their family. That very thing that you are embarrassed about, that very thing that you wish no one else in the world knew, that is the very thing that God wants to use as salt to the world in order that they would know that he is real and alive and can heal and transform any situation in order to use it for his Glory. Tell your story today. Share with others how God has healed and blessed your life. Be the salt of the world so that others may see and believe!

ONE FLESH

Jesus then left that place and went into the region of Judea and across the Jordan. Again crowds of people came to Him, and as was His custom, He taught them. Some Pharisees came and tested Him by asking, "Is it lawful for a man to divorce his wife?"

"What did Moses command you?" He replied.

They said, "Moses permitted a man to write a certificate of divorce and send her away."

"It was because your hearts were hard that Moses wrote you this law," Jesus replied. "But at the beginning of creation God made them male and female. For this reason a man will leave his father and mother and be united to his wife, and the two will become one flesh. So they are no longer two, but one. Therefore what God had joined together, let no man separate." When they were in the house again, the disciples asked Jesus about this. He answered, "Anyone who divorces his wife and marries another woman commits adultery against her. And if she divorces her husband and marries another man, she commits adultery."

Mark 10:1–12

Of this passage, the NIV Study Bible says this: "Divorce was an accommodation to human weakness and was used to bring order in a society that had disregarded God's will, but it was not the standard God had originally intended, as verses 6–9 clearly indicate. The purpose of Deuteronomy 24:1 was not to make divorce acceptable, but to reduce the hardship of its consequences." With the divorce rate in America being above 50%, I must say that this is one principle in Scripture that our society has misunderstood and abused in recent times. God tells us in other Scriptures in the New Testament that there are certainly situations where divorce is acceptable in God's eyes, for instance in a situation where there has been unfaithfulness in marriage; however, it appears as if our society has expanded this rule to include many other reasons in order that people could simply move on instead of working to become one in Christ. I have been married for twelve years and can say from experience that it is indeed a lot of work to be a godly husband and to make a marriage work. There have been many times in years past that Paula and I have felt like throwing in the towel and giving up when whatever situation that we were in at the time was all that we could see and there was no light at the end of the tunnel. After plowing through these times, mainly because of our faith in God and the commitment that we have made to each other for a lifetime, we have not only resolved some of these issues that seemed like insurmountable mountains at the time, but even more importantly we have fallen deeply in love and are continuing to become one and become more like Christ. I can't imagine being separated from my wife. My heart goes out to anyone who has gone through a divorce and whose hearts have been ripped apart from the spouse that God has chosen to unite him or her with. There is healing for those of you that have gone through this terrible tragedy in your life in the person of Jesus. His love is big enough to cover anything that has happened in the past.

For those of you that are contemplating such an act, please give it one more try, as it is not God's desire to see you go through so much pain. The pain that comes from plowing through a difficult circumstance does not even come close to the pain that will come when your heart is torn in two from the one that God has united you with. The joy that comes after sacrifices have been made and problems are solved in your marriage is a joy and a love that is one of the most awesome blessings that God will ever give you. Make a commitment today to stay married and to make it work no matter how hard it seems or how rocky it might get in your marriage. Once this is done, then I can attest to the fact that any problem can be overcome when you both have made this commitment to each other and even more importantly to our Father in heaven who has given you a treasure and friend for a lifetime, an awesome blessing in your husband or wife to enjoy for eternity.

OUR GOD REIGNS

The Lord reigns, He is robed in majesty; the Lord is robed in majesty
    and is armed with strength.
    The world is firmly established, in cannot be moved. Your throne
was established long
    ago; you are from all eternity.
    The seas have lifted up, O Lord; the seas have lifted up their
voice;
    the seas have lifted up their pounding waves.
    Mightier than the thunder of the great waters, mightier than the
breakers of the sea–
    the Lord on high is mighty.
    Your statutes stand firm;
    holiness adorns your house for endless days, O Lord.

Psalm 93:1–5

Isn't it nice to know as we start a new day that we serve and worship a great God that reigns and is in control of anything that the world throws our way today! I love to gaze out upon the ocean and watch as the waves come crashing into the shore. There is something magical and powerful about seeing nothing but this powerful body of water as far as one can look and to know that nothing can restrain its reach as the tide comes crashing in upon the sand. Our God is much more powerful than even the ocean tide; he is able and willing to move mountains for you today because of his great love and compassion. All that he asks is that you notice him and spend just a little time enjoying his presence in your life. He is waiting today to woo you into a love relationship that will last for all eternity. How could you say no so such a powerful, all-encompassing God of love? Seek him today with all of your heart and live your life for him.

ROOT OF ALL EVIL

As Jesus started on His way, a man ran up to Him and fell on his knees before Him. "Good Teacher," he asked, "what must I do to inherit eternal life?"

"Why do you call me good?' No one is good—except God alone. You know the commandments: Do no murder, no not commit adultery, do not steal, do not give false testimony, do not defraud, honor you father and mother."

"Teacher," he declared, "all these I have kept since I was a boy." Jesus looked at him and loved him.

"One thing you lack," he said. "Go, sell everything you have and give to the poor, and you will have treasure in heaven. Then come, follow me." At this the man's face fell. He went away sad, because he had great wealth. Jesus looked around and said to His disciples, "How hard it is for the rich to enter the Kingdom of God!"

Mark 10:17–23

Do not let the riches of this world come between you and your relationship to God! Money will distract your attention away from what really matters in the scope of eternity if you let it. You cannot buy your way into heaven; you cannot take any wages that you earn on this earth with you when you die. Money and things purchased with money will never fill the void that is in your heart and soul that is thirsting for a relationship with God Almighty! I can speak from experience when I say that it is easy to get distracted in this life by chasing the almighty dollar and miss the abundant life that comes from surrendering your heart to a relationship with God instead of selling it short by focusing it on worldly riches that are temporary and empty. Don't be distracted today by the false notion that financial gain will make you happy and bring you joy; seek the only one who can bring such joy to your life; surrender your heart and life to Jesus Christ today.

DAILY SURRENDER TO GOD'S DIVINE POWER

The disciples were amazed at His words. But Jesus said again, "Children, how hard it is to enter the Kingdom of God! It is easier for a camel to go through the eye of a needle than for a rich man to enter the Kingdom of God."

The disciples were even more amazed, and said to each other, "Who then can be saved?"

Jesus looked at them and said, "With man this is impossible, but not with God; all things are possible with God."

Mark 10:24–27

The life that you have chosen as a Christian, to live a holy life that is pleasing to God Almighty is about as reachable as stuffing a camel through the eye of a needle if you try to do it within your own power. To live a successful Christian life takes a daily surrender to God—a daily connection with him where he consumes your heart and soul with his Spirit and supernaturally guides and directs your thoughts and actions as you go throughout the day. If this thought of being spiritually and relationally connected to Jesus is foreign to you; if your thoughts of God are just on Sunday morning, then I would venture to say that you will not be victorious in your pursuit of joy and fulfillment in this life. You were created to be in relationship with him, not just on Sunday, not just at the beginning of the day during your quiet time, not just at prayer before meals, but at every minute of every day. You were created for a purpose, so that God could have a love relationship with you where he sustains you all throughout your day; a relationship where he molds and shapes you to be more like him; a relationship where he uses your gifts and talents to show the world that his love is real and that they too can know him in a personal way if they would only respond to his courting of their hearts. Ask him and he will show you today how to live your life connected to him, where Jesus is Lord, Savior, Lover, and Forever Friend who will hold you in his arms and never let you go. Take hold of this great love today.

PRIDE

Then James and John, the sons of Zebedee, came to Him. "Teacher," they said, "we want you to do for us whatever we ask."

"What do you want me to do for you?" He asked.

They replied, "Let one of us sit at your right and the other at your left in glory."

"You don't know what you are asking," Jesus said. "Can you drink the cup I drink or be baptized with the baptism I am baptized with?"

"We can," they answered.

Jesus said to them, "You will drink the cup I drink and be baptized with the baptism I am baptized with, but to sit at my right and left is not for me to grant. These places belong to those for whom they have been prepared."

When the ten heard about this, they became indignant with James and John. Jesus called them together and said, "You know that those who are regarded as rulers of the Gentiles lord it over them, and their officials exercise authority over them. Not so with you. Instead, whoever wants to become great among you must be your servant, and whoever wants to be first must be slave of all. For even the Son of Man did not come to be served, but to serve, and to give His life as a ransom for many."

Mark 10:35–45

James and John didn't quite get it, did they? Jesus had just finished explaining how he was going to be humiliated, flogged and killed all because of his great love for them and the response that they had was one of pride in wanting a place of prestige and power next to him in heaven. The life of a disciple is much different than the value system that we have here on earth. There is no place for pride in a disciple's life. If you have accepted Jesus Christ as your personal Savior then you are a disciple as well, and there is no place for pride in your life either. In fact, the secret to becoming great in the Kingdom of God is just the opposite. Humble and loving service are the two attributes that will set you apart from the rest of the world! Do you want to be great in God's Kingdom? Then serve someone today, love others with his unconditional love, and you will know and understand what it means to be a Christ follower.

FAITH AND BELIEF

Throwing his cloak aside, he jumped to his feet and came to Jesus.
"What do you want me to do for you?" Jesus asked him.
The blind man said, "Rabbi, I want to see."
"Go," said Jesus, "your faith has healed you." Immediately he received his sight and followed Jesus along the road.

Mark 10:50–52

We can learn much from this blind man's actions as Jesus passed along the roadside where the blind man was sitting and begging in Jericho. The first thing that is clear is that he wanted his sight back; he wanted to be healed. The second thing that is clear is that he came to Jesus to be healed; he stepped out of his comfort zone and first called out to Jesus from alongside the road and then got up and walked toward him. The third thing that is clear from the text is that he told Jesus exactly what it was that he wanted. The fourth thing that can be learned is that he believed that Jesus could and would give his sight back, and it is because of that belief, according to Jesus, that his sight we returned. And lastly, after Jesus had healed him, he didn't turn and walk the other way; instead, he followed him! What about you today? Do you want to be healed? Do you have a need or circumstance that is out of your control that only God can change? Is there something about your life that needs to change? Are you willing to let that change happen?

The first step to a better life is wanting your life to be better, wanting to see a change in your life. The next step is a little more difficult; it will require you to step out of your comfort zone, to be intentional about your faith by reaching out to Jesus for his help. You can do this in a number of ways—in the quietness of your own mind and heart, by asking a friend to pray with you and for you, by walking up to the altar at church for prayer, or by seeking direction in his Word, etc. However this step looks for you, one thing that I know for sure is that it will not be comfortable at first; God calls this stretching your faith. It is like when you work out at the gym and break down your muscles in order that they will grow back bigger and stronger. Next, and probably the most difficult step, is to believe what God says is true, to believe that he wants only the very best for you and that he will indeed heal your scars and change your life for the better as he makes you more like him. And lastly, after God has begun to make a difference in your life, don't ever turn your back on him; continue to press on in the journey of becoming more like him. Believe today that God can and will make a change for the better in your life; take a step toward him and your life will never be the same!

BELIEF AND FORGIVENESS

"Have faith in God," Jesus answered, "I tell you the truth, if anyone says to this mountain, Go, throw yourself into the sea, and does not doubt in his heart but believes that what he says will happen, it will be done for him. Therefore I tell you, whatever you ask for in prayer, believe that you have received it, and it will be yours. And when you stand praying, if you hold anything against anyone, forgive him, so that your Father in heaven may forgive your sins."

Mark 11:22–25

Two things need to happen for God to hear your prayers and for him to respond to the desires of your heart. The first thing is that you have to actually believe that he is going to answer your prayer; you have to believe in your heart of hearts without any doubt in his sovereignty and control over any situation or circumstance. This means you have to gain a different perspective than the one that you can see with your eyes; you have to have a perspective from your soul that knows that God is able to do more than you could ever think or imagine. The only way to have this belief is to know him in a personal way, such that he enters your heart and gives you a supernatural outlook and confidence that can only come from him. The author Anne Rice in a footnote to her most recent work entitled Christ the Lord (Ballantine Books, 2006) speaks of her experience like this:

> Well, what happened to me on that Sunday that I returned to faith was this: I received a glimpse into what I can only call the infinite Mercy of God. It worked something like this. I realized that none of my theological or social questions really made any difference. I didn't have to know the answers to these questions precisely because God did. He was the God who made the Universe in which I existed. That meant that He had made the

Big Bang, He had made DNA, He had made the black holes in space, and the wind and the rain and the individual snowflakes that fall from the sky. He had done all that. So surely He could do virtually anything and He could solve virtually everything. And how could I possibly know what He knew? And why should I remain apart from Him because I could not grasp all that He could grasp? What came over me then was an infinite trust, trust in His power and His love.

Things in this world do not have to make sense for us in order to believe; the only thing that needs to happen is for you to let Jesus grab a hold of your heart, just like he did to Anne Rice's heart, and you will have a peace and a belief like you never had before.

The second thing that has to happen is to forgive, just as you have been forgiven. This too can be hard and can be almost impossible without the power that comes from a relationship with Jesus Christ. Let him in today! Start communicating with him out of a new heart and a clear conscience and see for yourself what amazing things can happen in your life as a result of your faith, belief, and forgiveness.

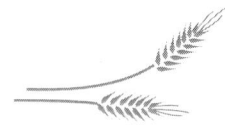

FAITHFUL FRIEND

Perfume and incense bring joy to the heart,
    and the pleasantness of one's friend springs from his earnest counsel.

Proverbs 27:9

There is something about being an honest friend who speaks the truth in love that is healing and pleasant and brings about joy and fulfillment. It is rare in this world to find another person that sincerely cares enough about you that he or she is willing to speak to you honestly and give you his or her opinion about your life and how you can be a better person; how you can be a better spouse; how you can be a better employee; how you can be a better friend, or most importantly, how you can be more like Christ. I have a few friends like this and I treasure them greatly. I only hope that I can be the same kind of friend to them and to others that they are to me. Don't take your friends for granted; tell them how much you love and appreciate them today and be sure to reinvest your life into someone else's by being a friend. By doing this you will build something that will last for all eternity.

STEADFAST SPIRIT

Have mercy on me, O God, have mercy on me,
for in you my soul takes refuge.
I will take refuge in the shadow of your wings
until the disaster has passed.
I cry out to God Most High,
to God who fulfills His purpose for me.
He sends from heaven and saves me,
rebuking those who hotly pursue me;
God sends His love and His faithfulness.
I am in the midst of lions; I lie among ravenous beasts—
men whose teeth are spears and arrows,
whose tongues are sharp swords.
Be exalted, O God, above the heavens;
let your glory be over all the earth.
They spread a net for my feet—I was bowed down in distress.
They dug a pit in my path—but they have fallen into it themselves.
My heart is steadfast, O God, my heart is steadfast;
I will sing and make music.
Awake, my soul! Awake, harp and lyre!
I will awaken the dawn.
I will praise you, O Lord, among the nations;
I will sing of you among the peoples.
For great is your love, reaching to the heavens;
your faithfulness reaches to the skies.
Be exalted, O God, above the heavens;
let your glory be over all the earth.

Psalm 57

I am the kind of guy that likes to control things. I like to control situations and circumstances and people and business and relationships—you name it. Sometimes, when life is a complete disaster and I want so much to clean it up and make it right, when I want so much to control the situation and try to fix it within my own means but I can't, despite countless efforts, it is then that God has me exactly where he wants me. You see, he wants you and me more than anything to just rest in his love and protection with a steadfast spirit, knowing that he is in control, and to let him and his providence do the work in our lives. That is all that our God longs for—for you and me to trust completely in him. He longs for us to let him love us with his unfailing love and faithfulness. To let him hold us like a little child in his arms, perfectly at peace, knowing that he would never do anything to harm us and that he will never let us go! Rest in him today!

NAKED AND ASHAMED

"Am I leading a rebellion," said Jesus, "that you have come out with swords and clubs to capture me? Every day I was with you, teaching in the temple courts, and you did not arrest me. But the Scriptures must be fulfilled." Then everyone deserted Him and fled. A young man, wearing nothing but a linen garment, was following Jesus. When they seized him, he fled naked, leaving his garment behind.

Mark 14:48–52

Just as Jesus had predicted, all of his disciples had deserted him in his greatest time of need; one of them even fled completely naked, leaving his clothes behind. This is not so different than when you and I run from Jesus in today's times. Of course, we don't run naked in the streets, but somehow, when we choose to leave the shelter and protection of Jesus' providence and direction in our lives, we eventually will feel just as naked and ashamed as this young man must have felt more than two thousand years ago. That is because we can do nothing apart from Christ! He is our strength; he gives us our drive and motivation for our jobs, he gives us enthusiasm and purpose for living; he covers us in our nakedness with his unfailing, unconditional love when we fail; his compassion and understanding and graciousness and direction in our lives is the only thing that could ever bring satisfaction and ultimate fulfillment!

There are times in your life when you may choose for one reason or another to be disobedient to God, thinking that you may be missing out on something that the world has to offer. When this happens, do not lose heart, for you will soon find that the only thing that happens at the end of the day when you choose to live your life outside of God's will is that you will find yourself naked and ashamed. The good news is that God's love is bigger than anything that you could ever do and it will always be there to welcome you home!

Thank you, God, for your grace and your love and for being everything that we are, everything that we have, and everything that ever we hope to be. We love you!

HARSH WORLD

Then some began to spit at Him; they blindfolded Him, struck Him with their fists, and said, "Prophesy." And the guards took Him and beat Him.

Mark 14:65

Because of the nature of the fallen world, we as fleshly people apart from God can be incredibly cruel and hateful and prideful and selfish. Just when I think I have it bad and feel unloved in this world, I look here at what Jesus went through and the betrayal and loneliness that he must have felt, and then I realize that I haven't yet walked as he did and that I don't have it all that bad. He was God! He could have stopped this torment and abuse and ridicule at any time, and he could have wiped everyone out and proved that he was the Son of God, and yet he didn't. And the reason that he didn't had to do with his love for you and me. You see, he could have never redeemed us and reunited us with God the Father had he not gone through what he did to pay the penalty for our sin. Jesus Christ stayed the course and suffered greatly all because of his love for you and for me. And still yet, even today, many people selfishly say that they don't want to have anything to do with him by the way that they live their lives. Sure, they might go to church on Sunday and they might try to be a good person and put on a good act, but when it comes right down to the heart of the matter, they do not want to make any changes in their lives or sacrifice their time or their money or their small gods who they put in front of living their life for Christ every day. For some of us, we start out and try to be obedient, but as soon as we run into a little ridicule or peer pressure or resistance from friends or family, at that point we turn our backs and decide that the sacrifice is too great. One thing that you need to remember as a Christian is that we do live in a fallen world and that we are in the midst of a spiritual battle that goes much deeper than what you can see with your eyes. You do have an enemy that is fighting for control of your heart and mind, who wants nothing less than for you to give up the pursuit of God in your life and to live for yourself. The journey that you are on will not always be easy; in fact, it will take everything that you have at times to resist the enemy, to resist the calling of this world to live for yourself instead of being obedient to God. When this happens, do not lose heart. Remember that Jesus suffered much more and was much worse off than our lives could ever compare and that he did it all for you! There is much joy and fulfillment and love that awaits you on the other side. Surrender everything to him today.

GOD IS CONCERNED ABOUT THE HEART

Although most of the many people who came from Ephraim, Manasseh, Issachar and Zebulun had not purified themselves, yet they ate Passover, contrary to what was written. But Hezekiah prayed for them, saying, "May the Lord, who is good, pardon everyone who sets his heart on seeking God—the Lord, the God of his fathers—even if he is not clean according to the rules of the sanctuary." And the Lord heard Hezekiah and healed the people.

2 Chronicles 30:18–20

Back in the Old Testament, there was a written law called the old covenant that God's people were to follow. In the New Testament, after Jesus' sacrifice for our sins, He declared a new covenant, which replaced the written law of Moses. In the new covenant, the written law is no longer needed since Christ now can live inside of you, through the Holy Spirit, and convict you of sin and guide and direct you by being a part of your life. The significance of this verse here in the Old Testament is that even though at that time there was a written law to follow, God was not as concerned about his people obeying all of the rules and regulations of the written instructions, as he was about the condition of their hearts! Even more so today, God is not as concerned about you obeying a list of rules or performing physical acts of worship (works), as he is about you surrendering your whole heart to loving and having a relationship with him! What God wants from you and from me is to fall in love with him; he wants us to trust him with everything that matters in our lives; he wants us to be willing to do anything, to step out of our comfort zone, to feel a little inadequate, to take a risk—all because of our great love for him and what he has done for us.

POPULAR OPINION COMPARED TO
GODLY DECISIONS

Wanting to satisfy the crowd, Pilate released Barabbas to them. He had Jesus flogged and handed Him over to be crucified.

Mark 15:15

"Wanting to satisfy the crowd ..." How many times have you and I in our own lives crucified Jesus all over again because of our fleshly desire to blend in to the popular opinion of our day and compromise our own beliefs and morality in situations where the majority vote is not the right thing to do? The Christian life can be hard; that is why Jesus called it the "narrow road" in Matthew 7:13–14. Jesus calls us as Christian to step out and be different from the world. You will be in situations with other colleagues, other family members, friends, and even other Christians at times where you may have to say no despite the popular opinion of the group that you are in. It is these small decisions of obedience that will set you apart and allow God to work in your life and transform your heart and mind so that he can use you in an awesome way to reach other people for him. Today, please guard you heart from just blending into the crowd, and make a stand for Jesus. Don't compromise your beliefs in order to be comfortable; take a risk by stepping out in faith and doing the right thing because of the one who lives inside of you. If you do this then you will experience the love and power of God in your life like never before! Pilate had the Son of God crucified because he wanted to please the crowd—learn from his mistake and seek to please God today!

BE STRONG AND COURAGEOUS

Be strong and courageous. Do not be afraid or discouraged because the king of Assyria and the vast army with him, for there is a greater power with us than with him. With him is only the arm of flesh, but with us is the Lord our God to help us and to fight our battles.

2 Chronicles 32:7–8

Remember that the one who lives inside of you is much greater than any problem you will face! What a comforting reminder this is from King Hezekiah that the God of this universe, who now lives inside of us because of Jesus' sacrifice on the Cross, will fight our battles for us and will always be here to protect us, to comfort us, and to hold us in his arms as we rest and put our confidence in him. He is much greater than anything in the world and he will always be there for you, even in the midst of failure, as he loves you more than you can imagine and wants you to stand strong in him today.

GODLY GOALS IN LIFE

After the Lord Jesus had spoken to them, He was taken up into Heaven and He sat at the right hand of God. Then the Disciples went out and preached everywhere, and the Lord worked with them and confirmed His word by the signs that accompanied it.

Mark 16:19–20

The war is over—Christ has won! He now sits at the right hand of God the Father and there is eternal life and victory for all who accept his gift and put their faith in him. There is still much work to do here on earth, however, as we as Christians continue on with what the disciples started so many centuries ago. They were charged to spread God's Word everywhere, with his help and direction. They were charged to let Christ live in them and to be witnesses for the entire world to see. They were the hands and feet of God now as they spread the news about this new life that could be lived as a result of his sacrifice and love for us. And so it is with you! If you are a Christian, then you too have a job to do; you are here for a reason. God has chosen you to be his witness to all of the people that you encounter that do not know him in a personal way. God is calling you to let his Spirit live in and through your life to reach other people for him. He has given you talents and abilities and supernatural gifts to help you on your journey to become more like him and to reach others for him. Let's not forget, however, that you are being opposed and that there is an enemy that knows your weaknesses better than you do who will try to distract your attention away from God and from your purpose. In order to stay on the right path and keep a clear vision in life, it is important that you have written goals or life resolutions to keep you on the right track and pointed in a godly direction.

A folded piece of paper fell out of my Bible this morning with three life resolutions that I had written down many years ago. God knew how much I needed a reminder this morning of what is important in life and in what direction I am heading. I would challenge you today to write down three godly goals for yourself and to keep them close at hand, as you will need them in the heat of the battle. Here are my three that I have not yet attained but that I strive for as I continue on in this journey with Christ:

- I will not let Satan deceive me with his lies that the world and things of the world will bring me more joy and satisfaction than the joy that comes from resting in God's peace, grace, love, and direction and experiencing his power in and through my life in order to advance the cause of Christ and reach others for him.
- I will give willfully and freely of whatever resources, talents, time, and abilities God has blessed me with.
- I will always give 110% to: My job, working as if I am working for the Lord. My wife, loving her to the same magnitude that Christ loves me. To other brothers and sisters in Christ, encouraging them to be steadfast in their faith.

Many times God has used these three written goals to remind me of what is important in life and to point me back in a godly direction where he can use me for his glory. I would challenge you to prayerfully consider three goals of your own this morning and to write them down in order that you too will have a clear direction and purpose for your life. God can and will use you in a great way. Be proactive concerning your faith today!

SENT FROM GOD

There came a man who was sent from God; his name was John. He came as a witness to testify concerning that light, so that through him all men might believe. He himself was not the light; he came only as a witness to the light. The true Light that gives light to every man was coming into the world.

John 1:6–9

What a privilege and honor that it must have been to have been sent from God to be a witness to the entire world, testifying about the Son of God who was yet to come. Do you know that as a Christian, just as John the Baptist was sent from God, you too are sent from God to testify to the world about him? I would take this idea even deeper and say that you have more power and can have a much bigger impact on people than John the Baptist did since Christ now lives inside of you (if you have received him) after his death and Resurrection. Jesus tells us himself in Mark 16:15–16, just before he left this world to go sit at the right hand of God after reappearing to his disciples: "Go into all the world and preach the good news to all creation. Whoever believes and is baptized will be saved, but whoever does not believe will be condemned." God has a plan for you and for your life as a Christian to have an impact on people as they see him living inside of you. God has a plan for those of you who have not yet accepted him into your heart to do the same. He wants to restore your relationship with God and give you an abundant life in him as he uses you in a big way to love other people and show them through your very life that he is real, that he is alive, and that he can change and transform any heart and life to be like his. In him you will live forever with God, and although your problems here on earth will not disappear, you will be able to stand up under them and persevere because God will be holding you in his arms as you walk through this life together in him. Go now, son and daughter of the Most High, and start fulfilling the purpose that God has had for you all along. Surrender your heart and life completely to Jesus Christ and start living the abundant life that satisfies and fulfills your deepest desire to be loved and used by God!

A NEW PERSPECTIVE

He was in the world, and though the world was made through Him, the world did not recognize Him.

John 1:10

There is something about this world and sin and selfishness and our own flesh that blinds us from seeing God for who he really is, living among us in the lives of all the people that have accepted him into their hearts and lives. To be successful as a Christian is to live your life with a new perspective in which you are looking for God, staying connected to him in sorts by looking for his direction, providence, and presence in your work life, marriage, relationships, children, entertainment—in every area, in every thought, in everything that you say and do. The key is to be seeking him in everything. In Matthew 7:8 Jesus tells us: "Ask and it will be given unto you; seek and you will find; knock and the door will be opened to you." This takes a continual, proactive effort on our part—it does not just happen! Ask God to reveal himself to you every day; if you ask him, then he will. Maybe all of this is foreign to you; maybe you have never seen God in a very real way here on this earth. If this is the case, then I would challenge you to pray right now and ask God to reveal himself to you. Tell him that you want to know him in a personal way and invite him into your life. The God of this world will then not only show up but He will become a part of you and will never let you go!

SALVATION: THE GIFT OF GOD
BY GRACE ALONE

Yet to all who received Him, to those who believed in His name, He gave the right to become children of God—children born not of natural descent, nor of human decision or a husband's will, but born of God.

John 1:12–13

The footnote in my NIV Study Bible says this concerning this passage: "Membership in God's family is by grace alone—the gift of God. It is never a human achievement, as vs. 13 emphasizes; yet the imparting of the gift is dependent on man's reception of it, as the words 'received' and 'believed' make clear." This idea of God's grace has been a long, hard life lesson for me to understand in my journey of becoming more like Christ. As a young Christian, I had a perspective of God that was shaped as a child through my life experiences as a very judgmental God who would only accept a person into his family who performed perfectly up to his standards and lived a holy life. This perspective left no room for failure, and as a result my Christian walk was like a huge rollercoaster ride; after countless efforts of trying to measure up and failing, I would surrender to my flesh and live for myself, not wanting to misrepresent Christ and be a hypocrite. It has only been in the last five years at my church that God has changed my tainted perspective of him and has helped me to understand what a loving, faithful, and forgiving Father he is. God is not interested as much in my performance—my own efforts to try to attain righteousness by living a godly life as he is in my dependence on him to transform my heart and mind through his Spirit as I stay connected and walk with him every minute of every day. It has only been in the past five years that God has helped me understand how deeply he loves me and how deeply he wants a relationship with me, despite my failures. It has only been in the

past five years that God has helped me to understand how he can take the junk of my life and use it in a very awesome way for his glory. Ephesians 2:8–9 says this: "For it is by grace that you have been saved, through faith—and this is not from yourselves, it is the gift of God—not by works so that no one can boast." God loves you and I today more than you can ever imagine, despite your failures, despite your weaknesses, despite your own perspective of him that has been shaped by your own life experiences. Accept this free gift of God's grace today and start living the abundant life that is free in Christ and full of joy and purpose and love!

HUNGER FOR THE WORD

The Word became flesh and made His dwelling among us. We have seen His Glory, the Glory of the One and Only, who came from the Father, full of Grace and Truth.

John 1:14

The Word of God and Jesus are one in the same. Jesus came to earth to live out in the flesh the Word so that we could see a perfect example of what life in Christ is like. If this same Jesus—who died and then was resurrected in order that he could live inside the hearts of all who believed and accepted him—is a part of your life, then there is no doubt that you should have a hunger for his Word. It is with his Word that he teaches and instructs you in his ways in order to transform your mind and heart to become more like him. It is with his Word that he will protect you from the evil one and all of his schemes to distract your attention away from God. He will use his Word through you in order to reach other people for him. Hebrews 4:12 says it this way: "For the Word of God is living and active. Sharper than any double-edged sword, it penetrates even to dividing soul and spirit, joints and marrow; it judges the thoughts and attitudes of the heart." The Word of God is one of the main tools that Jesus will use in your journey toward developing a deeper relationship with him. Do you have a hunger for his Word? Are you involved in a small group where you study it and talk about how to apply it to your life? Are you spending time alone with God in his Word and in prayer in order for God to reenergize your Spirit and equip you with everything that you will need in order to make the right decisions in life? Ask Jesus today to fill your heart, to give you this hunger for his Word and then to help you interpret and understand it for yourself. Ask him to give you the desire for him to be a bigger part of your life. If you ask then he will come and your life will never be the same.

MORE THAN JUST OBEDIENCE

For the law was given through Moses; Grace and Truth came through Jesus Christ.

John 1:17

In the Old Testament, we read about the Ten Commandments that were given to Moses for God's people to follow. The written law was the guidebook back then for all of the people to follow in order to live their lives in accordance with God's will and in order to please him with their actions. Today, as a believer in Jesus Christ, you have much more than just the law. Today, we have Jesus, who wants to be a part of your life. He wants to come and live inside of you and change your heart and mind to be holy and righteous before our loving Father. He gives you his truth, written on your heart, in order that you can make the right choices in this life that will be pleasing to God. The amazing thing about the gift of Christ is that he also gives you his amazing grace. His gives his grace to cover your sins when you do not choose right as well as grace to wipe your slate clean from the original sin in order that when God looks at you, he only sees perfection and purity and a heart that is as white as snow because of the sacrifice that Jesus made on the Cross. So today, if you have accepted this grace and truth from our Lord and Savior Jesus, then live your life for him because of his great love for you. And today, if you have never accepted Jesus Christ to be a part of your life, then pray the following prayer and he will come in and be a part of your life forever as you spend the rest of eternity together with him:

> Jesus, thank you for the sacrifice that you made for me on the Cross. I accept your sacrifice as atonement for my sins and want to receive you into my heart and life. Please come into my heart and change me to become more like you. I love you and want to live my life for you from this day forth. Amen!

PERFECT EXAMPLE

No one has ever seen God, but God the One and only, who is at the Father's side, has made Him known.

John 1:18

To be a Christian means to be Christ-like. So how can you live your life like Jesus Christ? One way is to study the way that he lived his life in one of the four Gospels of the Bible (Matthew, Mark, Luke or John). We have the perfect example and the privilege of being able to see God—to see how he lived his life, to see how he related to other people, to see how he solved problems and handled controversy, to see how he loved people and what made him angry. It is all there in his Word that he left us as a guide in order to transform our hearts and minds to be more like his. If you want to know how to live your life pleasing to God, then I would challenge you to study the life of Christ and to read through the Gospels that he left us. How can you call yourself a Christian and claim to be like him? How can you claim to know him if you have never read about him in the Bible? The whole premise behind Christianity is to let God and his Spirit come into your heart and change and transform your mind and life to be like him. Start this process today of getting to know your Lord and Savior Jesus Christ by letting his example of how to live soak into your heart and mind. Spend some time in the Word today and your life will never be the same.

LAMB OF GOD

The next day John saw Jesus coming toward him and said, "Look, the Lamb of God, who takes away the sin of the world!"

John 1:29

Jesus is the Lamb of God, the Son of God that was sent from heaven in order to pay the price for both your sin and mine. If you accept him into your life, then your sins are forgiven and forgotten, both past and present. Psalm 103:12 says, "As far as the east is from the west, so far has He removed our transgressions from us." I don't understand it, I don't deserve it, but I humbly and gratefully accept this gift of grace with hands held high. Our lives as Christians are not going to be perfect. God does not expect perfection; if we were able to live a perfect life, then we wouldn't need a lamb, we wouldn't need Jesus. What Jesus does expect is for us as Christians to embrace his sacrifice by accepting him into our hearts and then to love him with our lives. All that he wants from us is an ongoing relationship where we persevere in our relationship with him by learning from our mistakes, seeking his forgiveness when we do make the wrong choices, and then seeking his direction for our lives once again. All that Jesus wants to hear from us in return for this amazing gift of forgiveness and salvation is that we love him and give our heart and lives to him to use as he wishes. Surrender is what he seeks and abundant life is what we get in return. Surrender to him today.

THE CALL OF GOD FOR A GREAT LIFE

Andrew, Simon Peter's brother, was one of the two who heard what John had said and who had followed Jesus. The first thing Andrew did was to find his brother Simon and tell him, "We have found the Messiah" (that is, the Christ). And he brought him to Jesus. Jesus looked at him and said, "You are Simon, son of John. You will be called Cephas" (which, when translated, is Peter).

John 1:40–42

In Greek, "Peter" is Petros and "rock" is Petra. In Matthew 16:18 Jesus says this of Peter: "And I tell you that you are Peter, and on this rock I will build my church." I love what the NIV study note says of this passage in John: "In the Gospels, Peter was anything but a rock; he was impulsive and unstable. In Acts, he was a pillar of the early church. Jesus named him not for what he was but for what, by God's grace, he would become." Sometimes in this life I can so relate to the early Peter—sometimes I feel a little unstable and too many times make impulsive decisions. The encouraging thing is that God does not call me to do his work because of the way that I am today; no, he calls me because he knows the plans he has for me and what I can become in him as a result of his grace! The same is true for you today! God has a plan to do things with your life that are unimaginable. He wants to use you in ways that you have never thought of. He wants you to do things that you would have never thought you would be doing. I would have never thought that I would for almost two years now have been writing a devotion each morning and sharing insights into God's Word with so many people. God wants to, by his grace, change you from the inside out. He wants to give your life purpose and meaning and abundance. He has a great life planned for you. He is waiting for you to take a risk and to start living your life for him. He will never ask you to do anything without giving you the tools and abilities to accomplish the task as you trust and obey his direction for your life and surrender your life into his loving arms. Seek him today with all of your heart and live your life for him.

TESTS AND TRIALS IN LIFE

The crucible for silver and the furnace for gold, but the Lord tests the heart.

Proverbs 17:3

Sometimes God will allow trials and temptations to happen to you in this life for one reason—so your heart will be refined and all of your impurities will be removed just like the crucible and the furnace had refined silver and gold. The Lord will test your heart because he knows the abundant life that you can have once he changes you to become more like him. James, the brother of Jesus, says it like this in James 1:2: "Consider it pure joy, my brothers, whenever you face trials of many kinds, because you know that the testing of your faith develops perseverance. Perseverance must finish its work so that you may be mature and complete, not lacking anything." So today, don't be discouraged because of challenges that may await you around the corner; in fact, accept them joyfully and with great anticipation, knowing that God Almighty is changing you to become more like him.

TRANSPARENCY IN CHRIST

This is the verdict: Light has come into the world, but men loved darkness instead of light because their deeds were evil. Everyone who does evil hates the light, and will not come into the light for fear that his deeds will be exposed. But whoever lives by the Truth comes into the light, so that it may be seen plainly that what he has done has been done through God.

John 3:19–21

Something happens to you when you become a Christian by genuinely surrendering your heart and life to the Lord Jesus Christ. What happens is that your life will be illuminated. Other people will begin to take notice of your actions and the way that you live your life—not because you are perfect, but because you are different from the rest of the world that is still living in darkness. You see, if you have made this decision, then you now have the King of kings and Lord of lords living inside of you. You now have the God of this world who is changing you from the inside out. He is changing your actions, your desires, your passions, your motives—everything about you is being molded and shaped to become more like him. This doesn't just happen, though. As the author of John tells us here, you have to "live by the truth." You have to choose to surrender you own will and submit to God's will.

Speaker and author Steven Covey calls this "the gap between stimulus and response" in his most recent book, entitled The 8th Habit. In this gap is where the Christian life is lived in my opinion. As you choose to obey God after some sort of prompting by either a thought or a suggestion by a friend or colleague, whatever the stimuli are, the response is the difference between those who are walking in the light and those who are not. Today you can choose to walk in the light, to be used by God, and for your life to be illuminated so that others will see and know that God is alive and living inside of you. Or you can choose to stay hidden in darkness where the enemy will hold you captive so that your true passions, desires, and purpose in this life will never be realized. How will you choose today? I for one will choose to obey Christ and for my life to have an impact on the world around me, knowing full well that I may fail at times, but also knowing full well that it is not me, but God in me that is making the difference. I challenge you to do the same.

CHRISTIAN THEME

He must become greater; I must become less.

John 3:30

John the Baptist here in this passage is speaking of his relationship with Jesus Christ. If the whole Christian life could be summed up into one sentence, it would be this sentence above. To be a Christian means to put Jesus Christ and your relationship with him above absolutely everything else—above your own passions and desires, above your job, your family, your hobbies, your appetite, and even above your own intelligence and logical thinking because your mind is but a minute fraction as compared to the mind of our Creator. The Christian life is about making decisions based on what pleases him and not on what pleases you and your own flesh.

To an outsider who has not experienced the abundant life in Christ, this idea of self-sacrifice must sound like a death sentence. It is, in fact, just the opposite. It is the secret and key to freedom in this life, freedom from the chains of bondage that we wrap ourselves up in when we selfishly live for ourselves and our own pleasures. You see, when you live your life for Christ, then he will give you so much more than you could ever hope or imagine. He will give you purpose in this life, he will give you a peace that passes understanding, he will give you a love that goes deeper than anything that you have ever felt before. Jesus, as you live and sacrifice your own desires for him, will give you an abundant life that is full of grace and forgiveness and love and joy that will last for the rest of eternity, but you have to be willing to let your own life go. Jesus tells us in Matthew 10:39: "Whoever finds his life will lose it, and whoever loses his life for my sake will find it." Make him the Lord of everything you do, every-thing you say, every decision you make, every thought you think, and enter in to a whole new world that is filled with the Love of God.

REAP AND SOW

Do you not say, "There are still four months and then comes the harvest"? Behold, I say to you, lift up your eyes and look at the fields, for they are already white for harvest! And he who reaps receives wages, and gathers fruit for eternal life, that both he who sows and he who reaps may rejoice together. For in this the saying is true: One sows and another reaps.

John 4:35–37 (NKJ)

To sow is to plant seeds into people's lives that do not know the Lord by letting his Spirit work in your own life in a way that God could have an impact on other people through you. The only way to do this is to live your life sold out to Jesus Christ, totally surrendered to his will and his principles and directions to live by—to stay connected to him through his Word and in prayer every minute throughout the day and to listen for his quiet voice in your mind, directing your thoughts and your actions as you seek to know him more and become more like him. Many times you might not even realize the impact that your life may be having on other people. You never know who may be watching you and whose decision to accept the gift of eternal life in Christ is resting on the example that your life has on them as far as what it means and what it looks like to be a Christ follower. To represent Christ in this lost world and to sow the seed of his love is a very high calling of extremely important measures and should not be taken lightly. Consider all of this as you make decisions today as to how you will live your life.

Lastly, let's not forget to be bold enough to reap—to direct a person to Christ whose seed has already been sown and who is ready to make the decision to follow Jesus. I recently heard a story of a Christ follower who was bold enough and who took the time to call a young man and lead him to Christ. One of our fellow church members had been praying for this coworker for several years, and the joy that she felt after hearing his story of how he had accepted Jesus is indescribable. She had sown the seed of God's love for several years and an acquaintance in the gym was bold enough to reap the harvest, and in the end yet another soul will live forever in perfect relationship with our Lord and Savior!

STOP LOOKING AND LISTEN

Then Jesus said to him, "Unless you people see signs and wonders, you will by no means believe."

John 4:48 (NKJ)

I remember early on as a young Christian many years ago that I was always waiting and looking for God to do big things around me. I was always looking for that divine appointment with another person that I knew was from God or for some radical changes to happen in my life or in the lives of others. I was intrigued and amazed at stories of miraculous things that have happened all across the world. I was looking and hoping for encounters with angels, quoting the Scripture from Hebrews that speaks about how many people have encountered angels and have not known about it. It has only been in the past years that God has taught me some very important truths about my journey with him. I have learned that the Christian life is not about dramatic events as much as it is about a genuine relationship with God where he whispers to me through his Word and through other people and in the quietness of my mind. It is about getting to know him so intimately that I long to be connected with him through his Spirit that lives inside of me each and every minute of every day. It is about listening and obeying and enjoying his presence in my life as well as anticipating how he may use me, even in the very smallest of ways, to make a dramatic impact on someone else's life.

Today, you may hear him calling you, whispering your name. You may feel supernaturally attracted to him, like you are uneasy and need to make a decision. This is not by accident but it is a divine appointment with God himself. He is calling you to accept him into your life so that he can change you also from the inside out and give you the abundant life that I speak so much about. If this is you today, then stop what you are doing right now and ask him into your life. Tell him how much you love him and that you accept his sacrifice that he made for you on the Cross. Surrender to Jesus and then listen for his voice as he quietly guides and directs you into this journey of becoming more like him!

CONSEQUENCES FOR SIN

Afterward Jesus found him in the temple, and said to him, "See, you have been made well. Sin no more, lest a worse thing come upon you."

John 5:14 (NKJ)

In this story a man had been inflicted with an infirmity for thirty-eight years prior to being healed by Jesus. Why this had happened to him or what he was inflicted with we do not know; however, by Jesus' response we could conclude that the sickness had to do with sin in this man's life. God puts boundaries and principles in place for us to follow as Christians because he loves us and does not want to see harm come our way. Make no mistake, we live in a fallen world and even though God's grace is big enough to cover any sins that we may make as his children, there still are consequences for sins that you commit. Now, don't get me wrong; sometimes the tragedies that we face in this life are just a result of our fallen, sinful world; however, there are other times when we create our own destiny by our obedience or disobedience to God's Word. God's plan is always the safest route that brings the most joy and satisfaction. He, after all, has a much broader perspective than us.

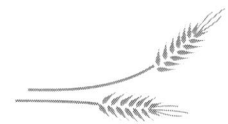

TROUBLE IN LIFE

He who digs a hole and scoops it out falls into the pit he has made.
The trouble he causes recoils on himself; his violence comes down on
his own head.

Psalm 7:15–16

Isn't it ironic that many times in this life, trouble that happens to you is a direct result of your own decisions and behavior? God has given you the power to choose. You have the power to choose to obey him and thus reap a life that is safe and full of purpose and fulfillment and abundance. You also have the power to choose to live for yourself and to satisfy your own fleshly desires, which will always lead to heartache and despair. You see, the emptiness that you feel inside, the thing that you are searching for to complete your life, will never be found outside of God's plan. His plan is the best plan for you since you were uniquely created to live in relationship with him, acting out your part. And if you play your part well, then you will find no trouble, as everything will work together for good. This is not to say that life will be easy or that you will not have trials to go through in order to help you grow and become more like Christ; the point is that God will be with you and in control and will see to it that you make it out on the other side if you include him in your decision making throughout your life. Easier said than done I know, but still true. Make a decision to follow God's plan today and see for yourself the reality of abundant life, walking side by side with your Creator.

GOD'S PROVISION COMES THROUGH FAITH

"When Jesus looked up and saw a great crowd coming toward Him, He said to Philip, "Where shall we buy bread for these people to eat?" He asked this only to test him, for He already had in mind what He was going to do. Philip answered him, "Eight months wages would not buy enough bread for each one to have a bite."

John 6:5–7

I think that it is interesting here in this passage how Jesus knew all along how he was going to provide food for the five thousand people that followed him to the Sea of Galilee; however, he still questioned his disciple Philip as to what they would do in order to test his faith. I love Philip's response also, since I can relate to his thought process as he is worried about the worldly means to gain the food; he is worried about having enough money. Here he is with the Son of God who has the ability to perform any miracle he wishes and Philip is caught up in the worldly fear of not having enough money. Later on in the story, Jesus feeds all five thousand people with five small barley loaves and two small fishes. Not a dime was spent and everyone there was satisfied. You know if you have accepted Jesus into your heart and life then this same God who performed this miracle more than 2,000 years ago is living inside of you today. And guess what? He hasn't lost any of his power to provide for your needs. He may be asking you today, just as he asked Philip, how you will make ends meet financially in your life or how you will pay off your debt or pay for that unexpected medical expense or how your church will pay for that land or building that it is about to acquire; he may be asking you one of these questions in order to hear your response, knowing all along that he can provide in a second whatever your need may be. Are you going to respond like Philip did initially, with worry and fear because you can't see past your present circumstances? Or are you going to remember that you serve the God of miracles who is much bigger than this world system and who wants more than anything to provide for your needs and desires if you would only have the faith that he can make it happen in your life? Live your life proactively, claiming the promise of Jesus to provide for the needs of his children, and watch the miracles unfold all around you today!

HUNGER AND THIRST NO MORE

Then Jesus declared, "I am the bread of life. He who comes to me will never go hungry, and he who believes in me will never be thirsty."

John 6:35

All of us have been born on this earth with a hunger and a thirst deep inside or our souls, not for physical food and drink—though, we have this as well. What Jesus is referring to here is a hunger and thirst for something more, something spiritual, something much deeper and much more fulfilling than food, something to fill the emptiness that we feel inside our heart of hearts. People try to fill this void in their lives with many things. Some people turn to money, some to drugs and alcohol, some to power and prestige, some to lust or houses or boats or their jobs, to other people and some even to religion that is shallow and empty and full of works that are void of any significant relationship with their Creator. I have tried many of these things throughout my life in order to feel fulfilled and complete and significant in this world, and although there are times in moments of weakness that I will revert back and believe the lie of the enemy that these worldly things will bring me joy and satisfaction, I have come to the conclusion after thirty-six years of searching that there is only one thing that is foolproof; I have come to the conclusion that there is only one thing that fills the emptiness in my life completely and has no negative side effects or disillusionment about it whatsoever. There is only one thing that will never let me down, that brings me much joy and fulfillment, that gives me purpose and meaning and peace and contentment. There is only one thing that has mercy for my weaknesses and is always there for me—even when I turn my back, it never goes away and is always patiently waiting for me to shift my focus and to align myself to the narrow way once again. That one thing is Jesus Christ.

He is indeed the Bread of Life. He, without a doubt, will fill the hunger and thirst inside your soul. He loves you more than you could ever imagine and accepts you right where you are today, no matter what you have done or where you have been or whatever you have tried to use to fill the gap in your heart that ultimately belongs to him. He wants to make you whole and complete today. He wants to fill you up with his love! Let him in.

ASSURANCE OF SALVATION

But as I told you, you have seen me and still you do not believe. All that the Father gives me will come to me, and whoever comes to me I will never drive away. For I have come down from heaven not to do my will but to do the will of Him who sent me. And this is the will of Him who sent me that I shall lose none of all that He has given me, but raise them up the last day. For my Father's will is that everyone who looks to the Son and believes in Him shall have eternal life, and I will raise him up the last day.

John 6:36–40

It is God that stirs in hearts of people through his Spirit in order that they would believe in his Son Jesus Christ and accept him into their hearts and lives in order to have eternal life. Once he has done this and a person genuinely believes and puts trust in him, the good news here today is that it can never be taken away from that person! God has promised to "raise you up on the last day" if you have indeed believed and put your faith in him. There are some of you, however, that Jesus is describing here at the beginning of the text that have felt the pull of his Spirit, have seen him at work in the lives of other people around you, and still you do not believe. For you the future is not good unless you take that step of faith and surrender your heart and life to Jesus. If you have already believed, then today and every day you can rest in the assurance of your salvation, knowing that whatever happens in your life from this point forward that God will indeed raise you up with him at your final hour so you can abide in his love for the rest of eternity. Thank you God for your love and faithfulness.

ARE YOU LISTENING?

It is written in the Prophets: "They will all be taught by God." Everyone who listens to the Father and learns from Him comes to me.

John 6:45

I drove back to Charlotte today from Nashville, TN through the mountains of Western North Carolina. As I gazed at the snowcaps on the mountaintops, at some point the music on the radio sounded like just noise to me, so I turned it off. I then quietly drove and enjoyed God's beauty in nature as I listened for his voice in the quietness of my mind. He had some comforting things to say to me as we drove together for the next few hours or so. Jesus is speaking here in the text above and is describing how the Spirit of God is the one that teaches all of us about him and about how to live our lives in relationship to God.

God speaks to us in many ways. He speaks to us first and foremost through his Word; that is why I have been convicted to read and write and share a few thoughts about his Word each day in order that all who read them will be encouraged and challenged in their personal walk with Christ. God also speaks to us through other people like our pastors and friends and relatives who know our Lord and are walking with him. Lastly, he speaks to us in the quietness of our minds as we pray and reflect on him and his creation. Take some time today to get away from the hustle and bustle of this world, and in a quiet place listen for God's voice. He has much to tell you and many new adventures to take you on. He is just waiting for you to listen!

LIVE BY THE SPIRIT

The Spirit gives life; the flesh counts for nothing. The words I have spoken to you are Spirit and they are Life.

John 6:63

The key to experiencing an abundant life on this earth, the key to overcoming sin and temptation in your life, the key to having joy and peace and fulfillment is to stay connected to the Spirit of God all throughout your day. Christianity is not about anything that we do physically with our bodies or what the Bible calls our "flesh." It is not about just going through the motions of religion—you know, going to church on Sunday, studying the Bible, trying to be good—sure, you do all of these things as a result of your renewed Spirit that is living inside of you, but they are not the source of that renewal or transformation in your life. The source of a transformed life is the Spirit of God, having control of your life and being the Lord of everything that you say and do. You might say, "How does this happen?" This happens through surrender. You surrender your own will and desires to God. You let him control and transform your heart and mind to become more like him, and you do this through a relationship with Jesus, where you daily communicate through prayer and listen as well as obey his instruction that he gives you through his Word and through other people and through your conscience. It all starts with a relationship with him, where your spirit man is healed and transformed by Almighty God. Ask God today to fill you with his Spirit; ask him to give you direction as to what he would have you do today and what the next steps are in order to know him more and become more like him, and then obey and surrender and you too will experience abundant life and peace and joy and fulfillment as you give your life away for Christ.

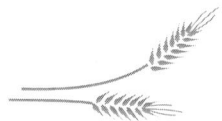

BACKSLIDING

For Jesus had known from the beginning which of them did not believe and who would betray Him. He went on to say, "This is why I told you that no one can come to me unless the Father has enabled him." From this time many of His disciples turned back and no longer followed Him.

John 6:65–66

If you have been a Christian for a long period of time, then there is a good possibility that you have gone through a period in your journey to become more like Christ when you have turned back to living for yourself. You very possibly might have given up on your pursuit of knowing God for all sorts of reasons. There was a time or two in my personal walk with the Lord that I had given up, mainly because of defeat in trying to live a holy life. You see, I had this whacked out idea that I had to obey and live a holy and righteous life, all within my own strength and that success in trying to achieve holiness was what the Christian life was all about. It was black or white, no gray area, and I didn't want to be a hypocrite. It was only later in life that I understood what Jesus is trying to explain here to his disciples in the book of John. You see, God is the one that enables you to know and have a relationship with him. It is God, living inside of you, and your relationship with him that matters. The Christian life has nothing to do with human achievement of salvation and everything to do with connecting in relationship with the God of this world and surrendering to his grace and his direction for your life as you rest in his peace and in his love during the journey. You see, you are not perfect; you are going to make mistakes along the way; if you were able to do it alone then you wouldn't need a Savior! The Christian life is about letting God's strength live through you as you surrender your will to his. As you do this, he will mold and transform and heal and change your broken heart to become more like his, but it is God that does the work. Maybe you are backsliding today in your faith. Maybe you have given up hope because of failure or unanswered prayer or some sort of hypocrisy from another believer. I would challenge you today to not look at your own flesh and weaknesses, to not look at the failures of others who are on their own journey as well, but to look to the only perfect one, the only one who can heal your broken heart and make you more like him. With hands lifted high, surrender yourself and your life once again to the God of this world who can and will transform your life back to its original glory and purpose in Christ.

WORLD AT WAR

For even his brothers didn't believe in him. Jesus replied, "Now is not the right time for me to go. But you can go anytime, and it will make no difference. The world can't hate you, but it does hate me because I accuse it of sin and evil." So Jesus remained in Galilee. But after his brothers had left for the festival, Jesus also went, though secretly, staying out of public view.

John 7:5–10

The Christian life diabolically opposes what the world stands for and what other people in the world stand for who do not know and have a relationship with Jesus. Sometimes even your own family, as Jesus demonstrates here in the book of John, will reject and try to deceive you and your efforts to live your life for Christ simply because they do not believe. Make no mistake; we live in a world that is at war for the devotion and direction of your heart. Even if you have accepted Jesus into your heart—well, even more so then— the enemy will consistently try to distract your attention away from your newfound faith onto selfish things of the world that will do nothing but separate you from God's abundance and blessing. The only way to guard your heart and protect yourself from the enemy's blows it to stay connected to your Savior in your mind and in your heart. Take some time today to connect to God through prayer and through reading his Word and then live your life today through his Spirit in order that you can be victorious in your journey to become more like him.

RELENTLESS OBEDIENCE

Stop judging by mere appearances, and make a right judgment.

John 7:24

This verse is Jesus' last word after rebuking the religious leaders for wanting to kill him because he had broken the law by healing a person on the Sabbath. Sometimes to be a Christ follower means to go against the grain of superficial religious tradition that has been handed down by earlier generations. Is it more important, for instance, to wear your best and finest clothes on Sunday morning or to genuinely welcome someone to church with a sincere heart that has never been and who might not have clothes as nice as you do? Is it more important to be reverent or real in the way that you worship? Is it better to pretend like everything with your life is okay or better to cry out to God for help in healing your broken heart? What Jesus was calling for and is still calling for today is true surrender and worship from deep in the heart that is very real. He doesn't care much about tradition or the superficial religious acts that look good on the outside but have no real effect on someone's life. Be real today concerning your faith. Step outside of your comfort zone today and love someone with the love of Christ. Step out of your comfort zone and confess your sin or ask for the help and prayer that you need in order to take the next step in your journey to become more like him. Don't worry about appearances or shallow observations—completely surrender to the Lord your God, open your life up so that it may be used by him in ways that you could have never imagined. God is seeking people to follow him with their whole heart. Answer his call today.

LIVING WATER

On the last and greatest day of the feast, Jesus stood and said in a loud voice, "If anyone is thirsty, let him come to me and drink. Whoever believes in me, as the scripture has said, streams of living water will flow from within him." By this He meant the Spirit, whom those who believed in Him were later to receive. Up to that time the Spirit had not been given, since Jesus had not yet been glorified.

John 7:37–39

My wife, Paula, and I have been blessed with the privilege of living next to a body of water called Lake Norman. On some days when the lake is very still it has a calming effect and offers much peace and tranquility as we gaze upon it in the evenings when I am home. On windy days, the waves splash up against the rocks along the edge and the lake offers a different kind of tranquility that suggests power and freedom that extends way beyond our human strength and constraints that we place upon ourselves and our lives. The lake reminds me of God's Spirit, which Jesus speaks of here in this analogy of living water that flows inside of every believer. God's Spirit offers a peace that passes all understanding, a power that extends way beyond our own mental capacity to comprehend, and a love and freedom that is indescribable and yet offers fulfillment, purpose, and direction for all of our lives who have accepted him! Is God's Spirit living inside of you today? If so then surrender today to the Spirit's direction for your life on your journey to become more like Jesus. If not then the good news is that you can have this wonderful gift as well—all you have to do is ask. Ask God today to come into your heart and life and start on this incredible journey and relationship with the God of this world that will last forever and will be perfected one day when you stand before him in paradise!

ACTION ON YOUR PART

In those days Hezekiah became ill and was at the point of death. He prayed to the Lord, who answered him and gave him a miraculous sign. But Hezekiah's heart was proud and he did not respond to the kindness shown to him; therefore the Lord's wrath was on him and on Judah and Jerusalem.

2 Chronicles 32:24–25

Here's the scenario: God allows some sort of tragedy in your life to get your attention—it may be a sickness in the family, a loss of a job, a loss of a loved one, a broken heart, a financial problem, a marriage problem, you name it; we live in a fallen world where all of these things can happen on any given day. So, you pray and God miraculously answers your prayer, he reveals to you the deeper issue that he was trying to point you toward in your life. Maybe this issue is that you need to surrender your life to him, accept his amazing gift of salvation, or feel his Spirit tugging on your heart and drawing you closer to the Lord. Maybe the deeper issue is not salvation as you have already accepted him in; maybe you need to confess a secret sin and then repent by turning the other direction; maybe it is a career change that he has been wanting you to do but you have avoided; maybe it is a change in focus or direction for your ministry—it could be a number of things, but at the end of the day the Lord is trying to get your attention and is desperately seeking a response from you.

The proper response for the person that God is enticing through his Spirit to enter into the Kingdom of God is to surrender to him first privately in your heart and in prayer and then publicly as a confession of your faith in Christ through getting baptized. The proper response for the person who has been hanging on to some sort of secret sin or selfish desire is to first confess it to God and then to confess it to another Christian in order that you may have some accountability and can receive some help in being free from that sin and being obedient in the future. The proper response for the others is to just do whatever it is that he is prompting you to do, even if you don't know how it is going to work or even if it seems like the most impossible situation that could never work. What God is looking for is for you to trust in him completely for the outcome and not to try to figure it out on your own. The only excuse for not responding to God's call is the sin of pride, which God wants no part of as we read here in the Old Testament book of 2 Chronicles. God wants for you to take action today, and the cool thing is that once you take that first step, you will never be alone, for he will be with you all the way to see you through! It's time for you to respond.

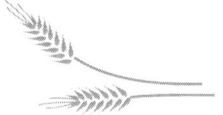

PRAYER POWER AND INFLUENCE

O Lord, let your ear be attentive to the prayer of this servant and to the prayer of your servants who delight in revering your name. Give your servant success today by granting him favor in the presence of this man. I was a cupbearer to the king.

Nehemiah 1:11

Do you know that God has a plan and purpose for your life to have a dramatic impact on this world for him and that if you are willing and if you ask him that he will carry out that plan no matter what your position or social status is today? Above is the last part of a prayer from Nehemiah, who was a cupbearer to King Artaxerxes, pleading to God to pave the way for him to carry out his purpose, which was to help rebuild the city of Jerusalem, which had been destroyed in the years past. Upon presenting the king with his cup of wine that day, Nehemiah makes his request known and is granted the privilege of returning to help build the city of Jerusalem. The coolest thing about Nehemiah is that he prayed earnestly before, during, and I am sure even after to give thanks at the end of his meeting with King Artaxerxes. God wants to hear from you today. He wants to hear your prayer. He has placed a desire deep down in your heart of hearts that can only be realized as you live out your purpose for him here on this earth. The key to living out this purpose is to have a relationship with Jesus where you pray continually, worshipping your God, making your requests known, and giving thanks for all that he has done for you. Take time today to talk with your Creator and Savior; tell him what is wearing on your heart and see for yourself how much he loves you and all that he can do with one of his children who takes time to pray.

SPIRITUAL FRIENDS

As iron sharpens iron, so one man sharpens another.

Proverbs 27:17

In my experience as a Christian over the past thirty years or so, I have learned that it is merely impossible to walk the narrow way, to stay on the path to becoming more like Christ, without the help, direction, encouragement, and even rebuke of close Christian friends. As I look back at times in my life when I have been the closest to God I can always remember a godly friendship that was there at that time in my life to help me along the way. Friends and mentors are blessings from God and should never be taken for granted. These kinds of relationships also take much courage and effort as you must be willing to be transparent in deep issues of the heart in order to make the most of the relationship by helping each other on your spiritual journey of knowing Jesus and becoming more like him. I remember the very first time that I ever spoke in a very real way to another person about my relationship with God. I was in the tenth grade and it was very awkward at the time. We were in the cafeteria of our high school and I will never forget the conversation, as it was the first step that I needed to take in order to start this incredible journey of making Jesus the Lord of my life. Maybe you need to take that step today. I can tell you from experience that it will be the best thing that you have ever done. Don't ever take your friends for granted. Tell someone else how much you love and appreciate him or her today.

A WOMAN'S GODLY COUNSEL

Then I prayed to the God of heaven and I answered the king, "If it pleases the King and if your servant has found favor in his sight, let him send me to the city in Judah where my fathers are buried so that I can rebuild it."

Then the king, with the queen sitting next to him, asked me, "How long will your journey take, and when will you get back?" It pleased the king to send me so I set a time.

Nehemiah 2:4–6

Now, the text here doesn't say that the queen of King Artaxerxes had any influence over his decision to let Nehemiah go to rebuild the city of Jerusalem; however, why else would the writer have mentioned that the queen was sitting next to him if her presence didn't have some influence over his decision? Men, your wife, who sits outside of your performance-driven, sometimes selfish world of trying to get ahead, many times offers an untainted perspective of the godly choice to make in any given situation. My wife often sees through my own hidden motives and selfish desires in order to guide and direct me on the unselfish, sacrificial, narrow way of life, from preventing needless spending to keeping a balance in my work and family life. I am blessed to have a woman beside me with a clear perspective on how to live an unselfish, fulfilling life. If you have been blessed like me with such a discerning wife, then I would encourage you to take heed of her advice today as she probably has the right answer to offer you on how you should live.

A SERMON LIVED

The teachers of the law and the Pharisees brought in a woman caught in adultery. They made her stand before the group and said to Jesus, "Teacher, this woman was caught in the act of adultery. In the law Moses commanded us to stone such a woman. Now what do you say? They were using this question as a trap, in order to have a basis for accusing Him. But Jesus bent down and started to write on the ground with His finger. When they kept on questioning Him, He straightened up and said to them, "If any one of you is without sin, let him be the first to throw the stone at her." Again, He stooped down and wrote on the ground. At this, those who heard began to go away one at a time, the older ones first, until only Jesus was left, with the woman standing there. Jesus straightened up and asked her, "Woman, where are they? Has no one condemned you?"

"No one sir," she said.

"Then neither do I condemn you," Jesus declared. "Go now and leave your life of sin."

John 8:3–11

I recently heard a quote: "I would rather see a sermon preached then hear one any day." What does it mean to live your life like Christ? What does it look like to represent him on this earth? It means that you love the unlovable. It means that you have compassion for people who struggle with things that turn your stomach and seem intolerable. It means that you don't ever judge other people but that you realize that they need Jesus and it may be that the only way that they will see and know that he is real is if they see him living through you. A popular song in the eighties by Steve Camp rang the words, "Don't tell them Jesus loves them until you are ready to love them too." Let your life be a sermon today to all who see the way that you live!

BEACON OF LIGHT

Jesus said to the people, "I am the light of the world. If you follow me, you won't be stumbling through the darkness, because you will have the light that leads to life."

John 8:12 (NLT)

Sometimes in the summer, Paula and I have the opportunity to go to dinner on the lake, and it is always a blast to get there by boat. Coming home after the sun has gone down is always quite challenging. For those of you that have not been on the water at night, it is very different than during that day, as you basically can't see anything because everything is pitch black, especially if the moon is not full. The only saving grace is what are called channel markers that have a beacon of light on top of them. They are red and green and as long as you keep the right color on the right side and stay between them, then you will most likely have a safe journey home on the lake.

I can't think of a better analogy to living the Christian life, as many times walking with God can be confusing and it is easy to lose your way in this fallen world; however, there is one way to ensure that you stay on the narrow road, and that is to keep your focus on Jesus as he lights the way for you in your journey. Jesus will light the way for you as you live out your purpose on this earth for him and not for yourself. He will light the way for you as you stay connected to him in prayer and through reading his Word and through being a servant to all for his name's sake. He will light the way for you as you humble yourself and surrender completely to the control of his Spirit who lives inside of you if you have indeed accepted him in. Walk in the light that leads to abundant, eternal life today—seek God with all of your heart and all of your soul and all of your mind and you will find peace and joy and great love on the journey of becoming more like him.

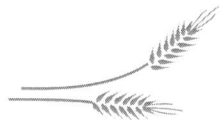

SAFETY PROVISION AND ABUNDANCE

I am the gate; whoever enters through me will be saved. He will come in and go out, and find pasture. The thief comes only to steal, kill and destroy; I have come that they may have life, and have it to the full.

John 10:9–10

There is no other way for you to live your life today! Life in Christ—obeying his commands, walking with him hand in hand as he keeps you safe—supplies all of your needs and then on top of all of that give you fullness, abundance, purpose, meaning, and fulfillment. The enemy would have you believe that what he has to offer you is better, but he is a liar and only comes to steal the joy and fulfillment that you can have with Jesus. Jesus loves you so much today. He has a whole new world to show you, a spiritual world where he is the center and where you play a huge part in spreading his love to others who don't know him yet like you do. Don't miss out on this incredible journey today by believing the enemy's lies. Cling to Christ, walk with him, and start living the abundant life that he offers to all who believe!

COLLECTIVE OBEDIENCE

So we rebuilt the wall till all of it reached half of its height, for the people worked with all of their heart.

Nehemiah 4:6

So we read here about the remnant of Jews that were left after the fall of Jerusalem and how they worked together, each one repairing his own section next to his house in order to rebuild the wall of Jerusalem, up against insurmountable odds and led by Nehemiah, a cupbearer to the king. During this process, they were ridiculed by the Persian government and their response was to stay the course and to pray to God for protection and guidance as each one obediently acted out his part of this huge effort of rebuilding the holy city. Now, if you were a Jew at that time with no support from the government as far as resources and no materials other than stones and rubble, it would be very hard to envision the completion of such a huge task as you worked diligently on your little piece of the wall. What struck me as I read through this story in the Old Testament book of Nehemiah is the strong faith and obedience that these people had even though the completion of the task seemed, in their limited human perspectives, very unlikely and hard to imagine.

We can parallel this story with the work today that you and I do for the Kingdom of God. The winning of souls, the building of God's Kingdom, changing hearts and lives to become more like Christ may all seem insurmountable at times, and it may even be hard to picture the realization of God's Spirit changing the lives of people from the perspective that you have today. It may even be hard to picture or imagine God changing your own heart as you have tried to be faithful and have failed time and time again. The message today is to be encouraged; there is a much broader perspective that only God can see, and he is working and he is in control and he will change you and many others to become more like him! Tasks can seem and often are much too big and much too important for just one person to carry the load. If each one of us does our part by staying faithful in prayer and obedience to our heavenly Father, if each one of us works with all of our heart to stay surrendered to the lordship of Jesus Christ and stays committed to serving others with humility and living out an example of Jesus for all to see, then we all will see—just as God's people did here in the Old Testament—a miracle of God performed in our midst. Let's stay collectively obedient to him today!

RELATIONSHIP PROBLEMS

Some time later Paul said to Barnabas, "Let us go back and visit the brothers in all the towns where we preached the word of the Lord and see how they are doing." Barnabus wanted to take John, also called Mark, with them, but Paul did not think it wise to take him, because he had deserted them in Pamphylia and had not continued with them in the work. They had such a sharp disagreement that they parted company. Barnabus took Mark and sailed for Cyprus, but Paul chose Silas and left, commended by the brothers to the grace of the Lord.

Acts 15:8–9

One of the coolest things about the Bible in my opinion is that it reflects humanity and reality and it doesn't hide struggles that believers have because of sin and pride and flesh. On the contrary, it reveals these struggles in order to encourage us all in the grace of God! Here we have Paul, one of the greatest of all saints in the New Testament, basically having such a horrible disagreement with another believer about one of their own that he separates himself from Barnabus and Mark for a time. It is interesting to know that later on, at the end of Paul's life, he thought so much of Mark that he requested him to come and be with him during his final days (2 Timothy 2:11). How encouraging is that? God has a way of healing broken relationships over time and using them to draw other people to himself. Even after being somewhat rejected by Paul, Mark goes on to write the second book of the New Testament and to become one of Paul's closest friends in prison at the end of his life. You never know how God is going to move in people's hearts and how he is going to change and transform lives and attitudes as we all grow to become more like him. Don't ever give up and don't ever stop loving people no matter what they do. Keep your eye on Jesus and you will see his plan unfold in front of you and you will never be the same!

LEADERSHIP

He came to Derbe and then to Lystra, where a disciple named Timothy lived, whose mother was a Jewess and a believer, but whose father was a Greek. The brothers at Lystra and Iconium spoke well of him. Paul wanted to take him along the journey, so he circumcised him because of the Jews who lived in that area, for they all knew that his father was a Greek. As they traveled from town to town, they delivered the decisions reached by the apostles and elders in Jerusalem for the people to obey. So the churches were strengthened in the faith and grew daily in numbers.

Acts 15:8–9

The text here is speaking of the Apostle Paul and a young convert, believed to be in his teens at this time, named Timothy. Paul's leadership and commitment to the development of this young man impresses me greatly! Here we see Paul, traveling from town to town preaching the Gospel and in many cases fearing for his life and instead of surrounding himself with seasoned veterans in the faith, Paul chooses Timothy, a young believer who was from a mixed marriage (highly frowned upon at that time) and whose mother was a believer, but his father was not. Paul was more concerned about mentoring and teaching young Timothy the things of God than he was about his own circumstances—or life, for that matter. A good friend of mine reminded me of a quote on leadership last week by the famous author Steven Covey, which says: "Leadership is communicating to other people so clearly their worth of potential that they start seeing it in themselves." How much better it is to communicate by living it out and experience firsthand what it means to be a disciple of Jesus by walking next to one of the great leaders of all time! Be concerned about others today; look for the good in them and what they can become in Christ and then communicate that to them in a way that they see it in themselves, and you too will take a giant step toward leadership.

LED BY THE SPIRIT

Paul and his companions traveled throughout the region of Phrygia and Galatia, having been kept by the Holy Spirit from preaching the Word in the province of Asia. Whey they came to the boarder of Mysia, they tried to enter Bithynia, but the Spirit of Jesus would not allow them to. So they passed to Mysia and went down to Troas. During the night Paul had a vision of a man of Macedonia standing and begging him, "Come over to Macedonia and help us." After Paul had seen the vision, we got ready at once to leave for Macedonia, concluding that God had called us to preach the Gospel to them.

Acts 16:6–10

The Holy Spirit kept the Apostle Paul and his crew from preaching the Word in Asia and Mysia and Bithynia. The Holy Spirit through a dream enlightened the apostles on where to go next in order to keep living the life and spreading the Gospel of Jesus Christ. This same Spirit lives today in you and in me if indeed you have accepted him into your heart and life and have committed to live your life for Jesus! This same Spirit will guide and direct you into the meaningful, purpose-driven life that God has planned all along for you if you would only take the time to listen to the Spirit's call on your life today and then do what you hear. The key to hearing is to stay connected to the Most High through prayer and through reading his Word and through spending time with other believers. Don't get distracted by the world today and get off track from the narrow way that God has for you—pray now that God would give you crystal clear vision as to how he would have you respond to him today and what you should do, and then obey and you will see and know how awesome it is to be led by the Spirit of God.

REWARDS AWAIT THE GODLY

Godliness helps people all through their life, while the evil are
destroyed by their wickedness.

Proverbs 13:6 (NLT)

A good friend of mine loves to say that "things just do not seem
to go right when I am not living my life in obedience to God and
keeping my heart and mind pure before the Lord." The reason that
God has rules for us to live by in his Word is not so that he can take
all of the fun out of our lives; it is indeed to help steer and guide
us into a life that is good and joyful and safe and free from the
bondages of sin that we can get so easily entangled in if we are not
careful to keep our eyes on him. On the contrary, if we try to make
our own way—if we follow our own fleshly passions that are apart
from God and his plan—this way will only lead to much heartache,
much pain, and eventually death and destruction. Keep your eyes
on him today. Pray now that his Spirit would guide and protect you
as you live your life for him!

OPENED HEART

One of those listening was a woman named Lydia, a dealer in purple cloth from the city of Thyatira, who was a worshiper of God. The Lord opened her heart to respond to Paul's message.

Proverbs 16:14 (NLT)

It is interesting how the text here describes Lydia as a worshiper of God, and yet, she had not yet until this point responded to the Gospel by taking that step toward Jesus and inviting him into her heart and life. She had not responded because she did not understand, and she did not understand because the Lord had not opened her heart and eyes to see and know what needed to be done on her part until that day. Many of you can probably relate to Lydia—you believe in God, however, you have never taken that step of inviting Jesus into your life and surrendering to him. God has even opened your eyes as you feel something going on inside of your heart each morning as you read these daily devotions or on Sunday morning as you sit in church and listen to the sermon. You may have sweaty palms or an anxiousness that you can't describe. What is happening is the Holy Spirit is opening your heart and encouraging you to respond to God by surrendering your life to him. See, God can only open your eyes so that you understand. He cannot respond for you, because if he did, then your love for him would not be genuine— that is why he left us all with the power of choice. So, God is calling you right now and it is up to you to respond to his call by accepting his Son Jesus into your heart and life in order that he can transform your life to be all that he has planned for you to be from the beginning. No one else can do this for you—only you can respond. If this is you, then lift your hands now high to heaven. Tell the Lord that you accept his sacrifice on the Cross and ask him for the forgiveness of your sins and to come into your heart and life to be your Lord and Savior. If you prayed this prayer, then tell someone else today, for God says in Romans 10:9, "If you confess with your mouth, 'Jesus is Lord,' and believe in your heart that God raised Him from the dead, you will be saved." Welcome to the family of God!

PRAYER PRAISE AND FALLEN CHAINS

About midnight Paul and Silas were praying and singing hymns to God, and the other prisoners were listening to them. Suddenly there was such a violent earthquake that the foundations of the prison were shaken. At once all the prison doors flew open, and everybody's chains came loose. The jailer woke up, and when he saw the prison doors open, he drew his sword and was about to kill himself because he thought the prisoners had escaped. But Paul shouted, "Don't harm yourself! We are all here!" The jailer called for lights, rushed in and fell trembling before Paul and Silas. He then brought them out and asked, "Sirs, what must I do to be saved?"

Acts 16:24–30

Paul and Silas had just been arrested, stripped and severely flogged, almost to the point of death, and here they were in prison at midnight worshipping the Lord by signing hymns and praying to their Lord whom they loved so deeply, even in the midst of their current circumstances. We see the result of such Faith in God when God responds by performing several miracles in their midst. Chains fall down; the jailer's life is saved and transformed as he accepts Christ as a result of what just happened. Don't you know today, that when you worship and when you pray that God moves? The bondages of sin that bind up your heart and life disappear in his midst as you confess them and worship him, and then a miracle happens in your midst as he uses your life to reach people around you so that they too can know the awesome God whom you serve! Praise him today no matter what is happening in your life and watch a miracle happen for you as well.

PURE MOTIVES

Once when we were going to the place of prayer, we were met by a slave girl who had a spirit by which she predicted the future. She earned a great deal of money for her owners by fortune telling. This girl followed Paul and the rest of us, shouting, "These men are servants of the Most High God, who are telling you the way to be saved." She kept this up for many days.

Finally, Paul became so troubled that he turned around and said to the spirit, "In the name of Jesus Christ I command you to come out of her!" At that moment the spirit left her. When the owners of the slave girl realized that their hope of making money was gone, they seized Paul and Silas and dragged them into the marketplace to face authorities.

Acts 16:16–19 (NLT)

At first in reading this story I didn't see the harm in what was happening here. I mean, after all, what this young slave girl was saying was true, Paul and Silas were indeed serving the Most High God and their purpose for being in Philippi was indeed to tell people the way to be saved. But then, as we read in verse 19, we see how the motives for this slave girl and her owners were corrupt in letting this evil spirit continue on to predict the future; they did this not because they loved Jesus or even knew him, but because they were in it to make money. The enemy can be very deceptive. Sometimes people and groups and even churches can have the appearance of godliness but in the end may be doing what they are doing for the wrong motives. What are your motives today? Why do you do what you do? Is it to make money or to have more power or influence or friends? Is it to be liked by others or to elevate yourself in the community? God only accepts one reason for the work that you and I do here on this earth. There is only one motive that can assure that he is glorified and that our acts of service are above the fray and not polluted by the selfishness and self-gratification of the world in which we live. That motive is because we love Jesus Christ so much that we are willing to sacrifice our very lives in service to him! Be sure that whatever you do today is done with pure motives out of love for God and he will bless your efforts as you live your life for him!

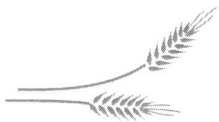

GOD'S WAY IS THE BEST WAY

The jailer brought them into his house and set a meal before them; he was filled with joy because he had come to believe in God—he and his whole family. When it was daylight, the magistrates sent their officers to the jailer with the order: "Release those men." The jailer told Paul, "The magistrates have ordered that you and Silas be released. Now you can leave. Go in peace.

Acts 16:34–36 (NLT)

Isn't it interesting that as a result of this jailer surrendering his life to the Lord that not only is his whole family brought into the family of God but as a bonus his job is secured and earthly life is spared? If you remember, when Peter was miraculously rescued from prison, the prison guards were executed by King Herod. Listen, good things happen when you make the right choices, and when you choose God's plan for your life you can be assured that you have chosen the very best path that will bring you the most joy, fulfillment, and satisfaction, not only in this life but in eternity! When the Spirit of the Lord comes knocking on the door of your heart, it may not be as obvious as the miraculous circumstances that surround this jailer's conversion. It may only be a still, small voice in your head or the encouragement of a friend or colleague or a sermon that gives you goose bumps as if the preacher was speaking directly to you. However it happens, be sure not to miss the opportunity to choose God, as it is the most important decision that you will ever make. And even after you have surrendered your heart and life to God, his Spirit will still guide you and call you as he convicts you of sin in your life and keeps you on the narrow road that will transform your heart and make you more like Jesus.

Recently I was discouraged by the actions of a good friend—the enemy uses times like these to pour thoughts of defeat and discouragement in my mind, and for a short period of time I even felt like giving up the race, because what is the use if people are going to act and respond like this friend did? Let me assure you that those thoughts and feelings are not of the Lord! No matter what happens to you today, no matter who lets you down or what problem or obstacle arises in your life, no matter what sin you committed yesterday or what seemingly hopeless situation that you may be in, keep your eyes on the Lord and his love will never let you down and never let you go. His way is always the best way!

MAKE A STAND FOR CHRIST

But Paul said to the officers: "They beat us publicly without a trial, even though we are Roman citizens, and threw us into prison. And now do they want to get rid of us quietly? No! Let them come and escort us out."

Acts 16:37 (NLT)

To flog a Roman citizen in public without a trial was unacceptable under Roman law and so, after learning that Paul and Silas were Roman citizens, the magistrates tried to release them quietly as to forego the public knowledge that what they did was wrong and that Paul and Silas had actually not committed any crimes. I love Paul's response here as he is concerned about the perception of the church in Phillipi and the future of its growth and ministry after witnessing two of its leaders humiliated and beaten so badly in public. To be a Christian does not mean that you give the green light to be walked on by the world and by those who oppose the cause of Christ. No, on the contrary, there are times when it is right to lovingly make a stand for Christ and for what you believe in. There is a time to "live dangerously in the hands of God," as the old Steve Camp song perfectly articulates. Don't compromise your faith and your beliefs in order to blend into society and be "safe" in your little comfort zone; no, be willing to step out of your comfort zone and live your life for Jesus. He will be there for you when you radically live your life for him. Make a stand for him today!

A HEART SURRENDERED

O Lord, the king rejoices in your strength,
how great is his joy in the victories you give!
You have granted him the desire of his heart,
and have not withheld the request of his lips.
You welcomed him with rich blessings,
and placed a crown of pure gold on his head.
He asked for life and you gave it to him—
length of days, for ever and ever.
Through the victories you gave, his glory is great;
you have bestowed on him splendor and majesty.
Surely you have granted him eternal blessings,
and made him glad with the joy of your presence.
For the King trusts in the Lord;
through the unfailing love of the Most High he will not be shaken.
Your hand will lay hold on all your enemies;
your right hand will seize your foes.
At the time of your appearing
you will make them like a fiery furnace.
In His wrath the Lord will swallow them up,
and His fire will consume them.
You will destroy their descendants from the earth,
their prosterity from mankind.
Though they plot evil against you and devise wicked schemes,
they cannot succeed;
For you will make them turn on their backs,
when you aim at them with drawn bow.
Be exalted O'Lord, in your strength;
we will sing and praise your might.

Psalm 21

What a beautiful description of the blessings and rewards of walking with God from David, whom God called "a man after his own heart." Joy, strength, blessing, love, peace, security, victory—they all await the man or woman that walks with Christ, obeys his Spirit and lives his or her life for him! Keep your eyes on the King today and reap the great rewards of his awesome love.

INTIMACY WITH GOD

The God who made the world and everything in it is the Lord of heaven and earth and does not live in temples built by hands. And He is not served by human hands, as if He needed anything, because He Himself gives all men life and breath and everything else. From one man He made every nation of men, that they should inhabit the whole earth; and he determined the times set for them and the exact places that they should live. God did this so that men would seek Him and perhaps reach out for Him and find Him, though He is not far from each one of us. For in Him we live and move and have our being. As some of your own poets have said, "We are His offspring."

Acts 17:24–28

Have you ever heard the term "spinning your wheels"? I am embarrassed to say that this is exactly how I feel I have been living here recently. It was just yesterday through a sermon and today though this passage from the book of Acts that God has given me an understanding of what I have been missing here recently in my relationship with him. I have been doing my job and doing church and doing ministry and working on my marriage and struggling with my finances and struggling with sin and struggling with relationships and wondering where I fit in, and at the same time in all of this activity, I have been moving farther and farther away from what God really wants for me in this life. You see, God is God! He doesn't need our best efforts in service or our schedules to be so full doing his work that we miss the reason that we are doing it in the first place. He doesn't need our money, he doesn't need our talents or our abilities or even our best efforts to recruit other believers into the family. What God needs and what God wants and what God desires more than anything else is our attention and for us to have an intimate relationship with him where we are truly surrendered to his will. A relationship where our significance is not found in productivity or results from our own fleshly work here on earth, but a sacred connection where our significance is found only in the fact that we know him and that he loves us unconditionally with a love that is greater than any love that we have ever known before. He wants to be our God. He wants for us to surrender and to obey and to love him back as a son loves a father and to look to him for guidance and for protection and to fill the emptiness in our hearts that can only be filled by him! Spend some time alone with God today! He is waiting for you to put aside the busyness of this life and to begin to know him in a way that you have never known him before. Give it all to God—let our heavenly Father take the stresses of your life and mold and shape them into a beautiful masterpiece as you surrender your life to him.

IDOL WORSHIP

Therefore since we are God's offspring, we should not think that the divine being is like gold or silver or stone—an image made by man's design and skill. In the past, God overlooked such ignorance, but now He commands all people everywhere to repent. For He has set a day when He will judge the world with justice by the man He has appointed. He has given proof to this to all men by raising Him from the dead.

Acts 16:37 (NLT)

Paul, speaking here to the people in Athens, is pleading with them to repent of idol worship and to follow the one true God, Jesus Christ. I never really understood idol worship; I mean, what good can there come from worshipping an object that is dead and lifeless and that can't really interact with your life at all in any way? I say that, but then as I think this through, I believe that there is much more idol worship going on all around us today than we realize. To many people, Christianity and religion has nothing to do with a relationship with the God of this world who lives inside of them and interacts with them on a daily basis as they look to him for guidance and direction; no, to many people, their idea of Christianity has to do with a building that they go to on Sunday mornings and then they put it out of their minds until the next week when they go to this building again in hopes of some sort of cleansing or forgiveness from the life that they lived throughout the week. Many people today worship the almighty dollar, they live and breathe, and their thought life is constantly centered on their financial situation and making more money. Many people today worship another human being, maybe a movie star, another famous person of some sort, or maybe even their significant other or spouse—their entire thought life is consumed with thoughts of another human being.

Many people are consumed with the worship of drugs or alcohol or pornography or even infidelity. All of these things, every one of them, is a form of idol worship.

What God wants more than anything is for us to worship him—he wants to consume our thought life so that our minds are renewed by his Spirit in order that our thoughts are pure and holy, and he wants to direct our lives into a deeper relationship with him. He wants to control our actions so that his love is seen by others who don't know him yet and need him just as much as you and I do. He wants us to live out our lives as he designed them, using our gifts and talents and skills in order to be the unique reflection of God's love and glory in the perfect way that he had planned all along. You see, Christianity is much more than a building or a Sunday morning exercise to get holy from living an unholy life throughout the week. Christianity is a minute-by-minute and day-by-day personal relationship with the God of this world who, if you have invited him in, will live inside of you and transform your heart and mind from the inside out in order that you can be all that he created you to be and that you can live eternally together with him! Put aside the idols and start worshipping the one true God today. Surrender your heart and life to Jesus. Invite him in, yield to his Spirit's prompting on your heart, and start living your life for him. Do this and you will never be the same!

FOOLISHNESS APART FROM CHRIST

As a dog returns to its vomit, so a fool repeats his folly.

Proverbs 26:11

The book of proverbs describes a "fool" as someone who lives his life apart from the safety and direction and wisdom that is found in a life that is surrendered to the lordship of Jesus Christ. Whatever vice you have; whatever sin there is that haunts your soul and keeps you captive to its luring pull on your heart, apart from Christ you will indeed keep returning and keep living a life that will eventually lead to ruin and ultimately to death. God wants to show you a way that is better! God wants to heal your scars and bring you to a place that offers peace and joy and fulfillment. God wants to offer you purpose and meaning for your life that can only be found in him. Don't start your day today without spending some time with the Creator of the world! Jump into his arms. Surrender to his will, and live your life for him! There is no other way.

MINISTRY AT WORK

After this, Paul left Athens and went to Corinth. There he met a Jew named Aquila, a native of Pontus, who had recently come from Italy with his wife Priscilla, because Claudius had ordered all the Jews to leave Rome. Paul went to see them, and because he was a tentmaker as they were, he stayed and worked with them. Every Sabbath he reasoned in the synagogue, trying to persuade Jews and Greeks.

Acts 18:1–4

I think it is so cool to read here how Paul worked in the marketplace, just as you and I do, and to read how his ministry was not just traveling to remote countries to spread the Gospel, but how God used him at his job as a tentmaker to reach out to, encourage, and befriend Aquila and Priscilla. God can use you today right where you are today in your company to be a light for him. As you work as if you are working for the Lord, in your attitude, in the way that you treat people, in your work ethic, in the very job that you do—all of these things God can use for his glory and to show others that he is real and is living inside of you! Always remember that God has a master plan for your life and it could be that you are right where he wants you to be in order to reach out to your colleagues that do not know him, or even to encourage colleagues that do know him in their journey to become more like Christ! Let your light shine in the workplace today.

BELIEVE AND BE BAPTIZED

Crispus, the synagogue ruler, and his entire household believed in the Lord; and many of the Corinthians who heard him believed and were baptized.

Acts 18:8

It's all over the New Testament—people believing in Jesus Christ, and then immediately following their decision to accept him into their heart and life they are baptized. Baptism is an outward expression of your faith in God. It is a public act that you do after you make this most important decision of your life in order that the world would see and know of the decision that you made. Your parents can't make that decision for you, like when you were possibly sprinkled as an infant—baptism is completely separate from a baby dedication that is more for your parents' commitment to raise you up in the faith than it is for you. Adult baptism, though, is an act of worship; it is between you and your Creator and only you can willingly take that step of faith in obedience. Maybe you have accepted Christ into your heart and life but have never publicly expressed that decision by being baptized. I would encourage you to step our of your comfort zone—to be obedient to God and to respond with your request to celebrate publicly the commitment that you have made to Jesus Christ by being baptized! This will be the first step that you take into the abundant life that comes with surrender and obedience as you start your journey to becoming more like him.

ON GOD'S SIDE

One night the Lord spoke to Paul in a vision: "Do not be afraid; keep on speaking, do not be silent. For I am with you, and no one is going to attack and harm you, because I have many people in this city." So Paul stayed for a year and a half, teaching them the word of God.

Acts 18:9–11

It is so refreshing to hear a reminder from God's Word today that he is on our side! If your heart is sold out to the Lord; if you have pure motives for doing whatever it is that you are scheduled to do today, then you are on God's side and nothing can stop the work that he is doing in and through your life! Because of some childhood experiences, I tend to often look to others for approval, appreciation, and affirmation and sometimes get discourage when that doesn't happen. The cool thing about God is that he loves us so much more than we could ever understand and he appreciates us just as we are, right where we are—even considering all of our faults. His love encompasses everyone who looks to him as Lord and Savior. Our God is so good and his love is so great. What an honor it is to be one of his children that is surrounded by his indescribable love and protection! Press on today, knowing that you are on God's side.

THE TASK AT HAND

However, I consider my life worth nothing to me, if only I may finish the race and complete the task the Lord Jesus has given me—the task of testifying to the gospel of God's grace.

Acts 20:24

If only there were more Christians today with a focus and a determination and a mind-set like the Apostle Paul. Too many Christians today, myself included, get so easily wrapped up in our own appetites and get distracted so easily by this world that sometimes we forget why we are even still here and why God saved us and brought us into his family in the first place. This life has nothing to do with us and everything to do with spreading the love of Christ to everyone around us so that people who don't know him will see him living inside of us and believe! This world is but a second in eternity and we have a job to do in the short period of time that we are here. Run the race today with perseverance and focus and do not waiver to the left or to the right but keep your eyes on Jesus as you live your life for him.

THE LORD STANDS NEAR

The following night, the Lord stood near Paul and said, "Take courage! As you have testified about me in Jerusalem, so you must also testify in Rome."

Acts 23: 11

Now, I don't know about you, but it gives me incredible encouragement to know that our God who is on the throne stands near us today! Our God, who is all Sovereign and in control of everything, stands near us in times of crises, in times when we need strength and encouragement, in times when we lay it all on the line for him! One of my favorite versus in the Old Testament is 2 Chronicles 16:9: "For the eyes of the Lord range throughout the earth to strengthen those whose hearts are fully committed to Him." My brothers and sisters in Christ, the Lord stands near you today to strengthen you as you live your life for him.

TURN

Go to this people and say, "You will be ever hearing but never understanding;

   you will be ever seeing but never perceiving." For this people's heart has become calloused; they hardly hear with their ears, and they have closed their eyes. Otherwise they might see with their eyes, hear with their ears, understand with their hearts and turn, and I would heal them.

Acts 28:26–27

The Apostle Paul, repeating the words of the prophet Isaiah, has relevance today in your heart and mine. God is the Master Healer! God can make all things new, he can dramatically change your life for the better; he can heal you from addictions, from bitterness, from bad choices that you have made and are now suffering the consequences for in your life. He can break the chains that bind your heart; he can free you and give you peace and joy and fulfill-ment and purpose in this life. He wants to do this for you more than anything because he loves you; he died for you so that he can come into your heart and life and bring healing and restoration. He wants to have a genuine relationship with you and is waiting for you to first seek him by letting him know that you want that too and then turning from your old selfish, self-fulfilling ways of this world to a new life that is guided and directed by our awesome God who gave his life to make this all possible. Turn to him today and find healing and love and life.

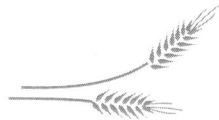

BOLDLY AND WITHOUT HINDRANCE

For two whole years Paul stayed there in his own rented house and welcomed all who came to see him. Boldly and without hindrance he preached the Kingdom of God and taught about the Lord Jesus Christ.

Acts 28:30–31

The dictionary defines "hindrance" as "something immaterial that interferes with action or progress." Boldly and without hindrance! How many of us can say that we testify to others about our relationship with Jesus Christ in this way? It is a high calling indeed. God is calling us as Christians to be bold and to tell others about him and about how he has changed our lives for the better, without being distracted by immaterial things of this world. It is far too easy to get wrapped up in the false sense of safety and security and short-lived pleasure that comes from immaterial things. God is calling for his children to boldly approach the Throne of Grace—to live our lives for him no matter what the sacrifice or what the perception of others might be. What is hindering your testimony today? Could it be pride or stubbornness? Or maybe you are wrapped up so deep in your selfish passions and desires that you feel like you are drowning and there is no hope for you in this life. I have good news for you today! The God of this world can break those chains that are binding your heart in the blink of an eye. All you have to do is fall down before him and ask him to heal your scars and to come into your life and make you whole. Start afresh in your relationship with Jesus today. Spend some time with the Master Healer and then go and live a godly example of his love—boldly and without hindrance—so that others will see and know that Jesus lives and that they too could receive this awesome gift of eternal life in him.

HOLY AND SANCTIFIED IN CHRIST

To the church of God in Corinth, to those sanctified in Christ Jesus and called to be holy, together with all those everywhere who call on the name of our Lord Jesus Christ—their Lord and ours: Grace and peace to you from God our Father and the Lord Jesus Christ.

Acts 1:2

The Apostle Paul is greeting the church in Corinth here who are Christians, just like you and I, and the words that he uses to describe our brothers and sisters in Christ are true and relevant to Christians of our time as well. To be sanctified means to be set apart for the Lord and can also mean made Holy. As Christians, we are made holy by the work of the Spirit in our life as a result of Christ's atoning death on the Cross. God said that when he enters into our hearts and lives that he will make all things new! He restores us back to our original glory and relationship with him prior to original sin. You see, the only way that you can change your past; the only way that you can be made clean from bad decisions that were made apart from Christ, is to enter in to a relationship with God where you invite him into your heart in order to restore you back to the perfection that only comes in a relationship with Jesus. I have talked with many friends, some of whom claim to be Christians, who are trying to clean up their lives a bit before they get serious about their relationship with God. The thing that they don't realize is that they can never do anything that would make them acceptable for service and relationship to a holy God. No, if they could do that then we wouldn't have needed Jesus to die on a cross in order to bridge the gap between us and God. You see, the work is done! When you accept Jesus into your heart, he sanctifies you with his Spirit, and it is because of him that you are holy and acceptable to the Lord. He accepts you right where you are, regardless of anything that you have done in your past. He can use you today to make a difference in this world—you don't have to clean anything up in your life, Jesus will do that for you as you surrender to his will and his purpose and his Spirit, who is living inside of you. In John 15:5, Jesus says: "Apart from Me you can do nothing." It is only in Christ that you are sanctified and it is only in him that your heart can be cleansed and grace and peace can be granted. God loves you right where you are today! He wants to use you in extraordinary ways in this world to be a witness for him and to love other people with his love. Don't wait any longer—stop trying to do the work yourself and fall into his loving arms today as you live your life for him.

FOOLISHNESS TO MANY

For the message of the cross is foolishness to those who are perishing, but to us who are being saved it is the power of God. For it is written: "I will destroy the wisdom of the wise; the intelligence of the intelligent I will frustrate."

1 Corinthians 1:18–19

Don't be discouraged when those around you think that your faith in Christ is foolish and only for the uneducated or naive of this age. As we read here, God will reveal his power in your life! He will make sense and purpose and do a great work out of a life that seems to be just foolishness to those who don't know Jesus. The power of God lives inside of you today. Rest in the power and live your life for him.

MIND OF CHRIST

The Spirit searches all things, even the deep things of God. For who among men knows the thoughts of a man except the man's spirit within him? In the same way, no one knows the thoughts of God except the Spirit of God. We have not received the spirit of the world but the Spirit who is from God, that we may understand what God has freely given us. This is what we speak, not in words taught us by human wisdom but in words taught by the Spirit, expressing spiritual truths in spiritual words. The man without the Spirit does not accept the things that come from the Spirit of God, for they are foolishness to him, and he cannot understand them, because they are spiritually discerned. The spiritual man makes judgments about all things, but he himself is not subject to any man's judgment: "For who has known the mind of the Lord that he may instruct him?" But we have the mind of Christ.

1 Corinthians 2:10–16

Spiritual discernment happens when you have received Jesus Christ into your heart and have accepted his Spirit into your life in order to live by faith in the Spirit's prompting and direction for how you should live. If the things of God seem confusing to you, if the Scriptures that I write about seem foolish or just don't seem to make sense, then I would suggest that you do not have the Spirit of God living inside of you. You see, as the text describes here, it is the Spirit of God that enables you to discern his Word, and it is the Spirit of God that helps you to understand what God is trying to tell you through the Scriptures. The encouraging thing about all of this is that if you have not accepted Jesus Christ into your heart and life in a genuine way, then there is an easy fix. See, God is pounding on your heart's door, begging you to let him inside in order that he can bridge the gap between you and God for eternity. He wants to make the best of your life right now, right where you are—he wants to forgive your sins and restore your life to an abundant union with your Lord and Savior that will last forever. He is waiting for you to get on your knees and ask him in! Receive today the mind of Christ by accepting his Spirit into your heart, and then hang on for dear life, as you will never be the same.

SECRET AMBITION

For where you have envy and selfish ambition, there you will
find disorder and every evil practice.

James 3:16

Wow, this is a pretty harsh verse, huh? The dictionary defines ambition as "an eager or strong desire to achieve something such as fame or power." In climbing the corporate ladder the past seventeen years, selfish ambition has been my driving force! In worldly performance reviews and interviews, ambition has been consistently defined as a clear strength in the worldview of positive attributes. We are asked to boast about ambition in interviews, and people that are not as ambitious are not seen in the same positive light as those who are. This is really completely opposite from what the Bible says of "selfish ambition" in this verse. For many years of my life, I have been ambitious for worldly recognition as a successful businessman. No wonder there has been some unbalance and inconsistency in my walk with the Lord. It is really embarrassing and silly when you look at it for what it really is! Through God's Word I have learned that recognition for being a successful businessman is so shallow compared to the recognition for being a man of God who loves people and puts other people's needs and desires above his own. A man who is unshakable in his convictions to live a godly life, who lives within the boundaries that God has established for him, never compromises to "fit in" to the crowd, but with unwavering faith clings to Christ with all of his strength; he is a man whose life overflows with love, humility, understanding, patience, kindness, and gentleness. He is an example for others to see God for who he really is here on this earth—a real life example in the flesh by God's Spirit controlling his every move! That is what this life is about, and that is the godly ambition that will satisfy and fulfill you completely and eternally.

What is your driving force today? Pray that God will fill you with a godly ambition that will change the hearts and minds of people around you!

TEAMWORK

I planted the seed, Apollos watered it, but God made it grow.

1 Corinthians 3:6

As Christians, each of us has different gifts; each of us has different strengths and different weaknesses and struggles and a different part to play in this new Kingdom that God is creating for eternity. Some of us encourage, some of us teach, some of us spread the Good News of Jesus Christ to those who have never heard, some of us counsel and pray and serve, and some of us are experts in creating beautiful music for worship. We all have a huge part to play and we all need each other, despite our differences. That is why we belong to a group of believers that we call a Church. It is in Church that God molds all of our unique gifts and talents together in order that we could as one body reflect his image of love and grace to the world around us! If you have not done so already, get connected today to a body of believers in order that God's Spirit could use your life for the purpose that it was originally created—to be united as one to God and God's family for the rest of eternity!

FAITHFUL IN GOD'S EYES

So then, men ought to regard us as servants of Christ and as those entrusted with the secret things of God. Now it is required that those who have been given a trust must prove faithful. I care very little if I am judged by you or by any human court; indeed, I do not even judge myself. My conscience is clear, but that does not make me innocent. It is the Lord who judges me. Therefore judge nothing before the appointed time; wait till the Lord comes. He will bring to light what is hidden in darkness and will expose the motives of men's hearts. At that time each will receive his praise from God.

1 Corinthians 4:1–5

As a Christian, you have a whole new world that is hidden inside of your heart. You have a divine purpose and meaning and have heavenly gifts and talents that have been assigned to you and you alone to use in order to help further the Kingdom of God! There are people that you will come into contact with today that will not happen by accident—they are divine appointments from God and you are part of God's plan for those people to see and know that Jesus is real by seeing his love reflected from your life to theirs. You have secret things of God inside your heart that are waiting to be revealed, waiting to be shared with this lost and hurting generation that is all around us. What will you do with this burning passion that is inside of your heart? Will you be found faithful? It is God who judges and only God who knows the true motives of your heart. Stay focused today on what matters! Keep your eye on the ball. Be willing to be used by God in a great way and start experiencing this abundant life that Jesus wants you to have more than anything. If you take your eye off of the ball, then you may miss an opportunity today to make a huge difference in another person's life; you may miss the awesome joy and fulfillment that comes when your spirit is aligned with God and is working together to fulfill his purpose in your life. Prove faithful in God's eyes today.

CLEAN HANDS AND A PURE HEART

Who may ascend the hill of the Lord? Who may stand in His Holy place?

He who has clean hands and a pure heart,
who does not swear to an idol or swear by what is false.

He will receive blessing from the Lord and vindication from God his Savior!

Psalm 24:3–5

Clean hands and a pure heart are something that we all strive for and something that only Jesus can provide as we keep our eyes on him and cling to the direction of his Spirit who lives inside of us. Thanks be to God for his all-encompassing grace that covers us when we fail and for his unconditional love that picks us up and guides us on that narrow road again when we have lost our focus and lost our way. Don't miss God's blessing today! Cling to Christ with everything that you have and he will guide and direct you into a very real and very fulfilling relationship with your Creator who will never let you go!

ONE FAITH, ONE BODY, ONE CHURCH

So then, no more boasting about men! All things are yours, whether Paul or Apollos or Cephas or the world or life or death or the present or the future—all are yours, and you are of Christ and Christ is of God.

1 Corinthians 3:21–23

The Corinthian church was arguing and divided about which apostle they were going to follow. I relate this to the different denominations that we have in the Church today. What the Apostle Paul is telling them here in his letter is that they are missing the point. He speaks a lot about wisdom and of how the wisdom of this world is foolishness in the eyes of God. Things that we may think are important like the way that we worship or where we worship or how we dress or which demographic we are trying to reach are irrelevant when compared to the indescribable divine wisdom that comes from the Holy Spirit through a genuine relationship with Jesus Christ. It really frustrates me when you ask someone about his faith in God or Christianity and he responds by telling you what denomination of the Church he belongs to: "I am a Baptist," or "I am a Catholic," or I am Methodist." These people are missing the point as well, just like the church here in Corinth. Christianity has nothing to do with what denomination you belong to and everything to do with surrendering your heart and life and mind to the authority of Jesus Christ and inviting his Spirit to come inside and restore your relationship with the God of this world. If you have never done this then I would highly recommend that you ask Jesus to come into your heart today. Do this and your life will never be the same.

PREMEDITATED IMMORAL SIN

It is actually reported that there is sexual immorality among you, and of a kind that does not even occur among pagans: A man has his father's wife. And you are proud! Shouldn't you rather have been filled with grief and have put out of your fellowship the man who did this? Even though I am not physically present, I am with you in Spirit. And I have already passed judgment on the one who did this, just as if I were present. When you are assembled in the name of our Lord Jesus and I am with you in Spirit, and the power of our Lord Jesus is present, hand this man over to Satan, so that the sinful nature may be destroyed and his spirit saved on the day of the Lord.

1 Corinthians 5:1–5

The Apostle Paul, speaking here to the church in Corinth, makes it very clear that unconfessed, unrepented, premeditated immoral sin has no place in the Church of Jesus Christ! The church in Corinth is not unlike some churches that exist even today that tolerate and even seem to condone immoral living using the façade of "love." Love sometimes involves just blatant honesty and calling sin what it is and exposing the darkness in one's life in order that he may be free from the chains of this dark world that bind up his heart when he gives into fleshly desires without any regard for God's Spirit who lives inside of him.

All of this is not to say that we as Christians should or will by any means live a perfect life, as we are all broken and scarred, and in need of healing by our Father's hand; however, what it does mean is that each one of us should be daily confessing our sins and turning from them and slowly but surely should be growing to be more like Jesus through our faithfulness of being committed to live our lives under the control of his Spirit who lives inside of us! To knowingly live an immoral lifestyle using the excuse of the fallen world and our brokenness as a result is unacceptable in God's eyes, and tolerating such behavior will do nothing to encourage repentance, as God has placed the power of his Spirit within us all to live a holy life that is acceptable and good. If this is you, then return today to God! Repent of your sin and burn the bridges that will lead back to ungodly living. God loves you no matter where you are or what you struggle with, but in order to experience his healing and transforming power in your life you will need to come to him on bended knee and agree to move in his direction by denying yourself and living your life for him. He died on a cross to set you free. He gave his life so that your sins could be wiped clean and so that you could live a joyful, fulfilling life that is holy and acceptable in his eyes. Start walking in this great love today and experience the freedom that comes from a life that is surrendered to our Lord and Savior Jesus Christ.

SINCERITY AND TRUTH

Get rid of the old yeast that you may be a new batch without yeast— as you really are. For Christ, our Passover Lamb had been sacrificed. Therefore, let us keep the festival, not with old yeast, the yeast of malice and wickedness, but with the bread without yeast, the bread of sincerity and Truth.

1 Corinthians 5:1–5

Yeast is defined as an agent of ferment or agitation. What the Apostle Paul is describing here in this analogy is the disharmony that the sexual sin and immorality causes in the life of a believer as well as in the body of a church family. You see, in Christ, as a result of his death and Resurrection, you are a new creation. He has restored your relationship to God the Father and his Spirit is alive and well inside of your heart. What happens when you allow immorality as a part of your newfound relationship with Jesus is that it acts as a deterrent, an agitation to the new purity that you now have as a result of Jesus Christ living inside of your heart. It confuses the truth of your new life in Christ and causes you to live in a lie of deceit and wickedness and malice that is not a part of your new abundant life with Christ. What Paul is encouraging the church in Corinth here to do is instead of muddying up their souls with such destruction and distraction, to fill them with the truth of who they are now in Christ—to fill their hearts and lives with God's Word and with his Spirit and his love so that he may overflow out of their lives and touch those around them with God's love in order that they too may be changed! Be filled with God's Spirit today and maintain the simplistic harmony of your new life in Christ. Don't let the enemy distract your attention away from the new abundant life that you now have as one of God's disciples. Flee from sexual immorality and any kind of sin that would distract your attention away from your Lord and Savior Jesus Christ. His way is always the best way and he alone can make you whole and complete in him.

FREEDOM FROM THE CHAINS

Do you not know that the wicked will not inherit the Kingdom of God? Do not be deceived: Neither the sexually immoral nor idolaters nor adulterers nor male prostitutes nor homosexual offenders not thieves nor greedy nor drunkards nor slanderers nor swindlers will inherit the Kingdom of God. And that is what some of you were. But you were washed, you were sanctified, you were justified in the name of the Lord Jesus Christ and by the Spirit of our God.

1 Corinthians 6:9–11

We all have struggles; we all have scars and wounds from our past for which we are in need of healing by the Master Healer's gentle touch on our life. The good news today is that in Christ you are a new creation! You have been washed and sanctified and have freedom from these horrible chains of sin that will bind your heart and keep you from experiencing God's best for your life. The key is to fill your life with his Spirit and let his love and grace and healing take place inside of your heart as you worship and study and pray and live a life of obedience to our Lord. In him, you have freedom from these chains that bind up your heart and do nothing but destroy. Let your life be filled with his Spirit today and start living the abundant life that the God of this world who is so wildly in love with you would want you to live. And if you have never crossed that path of entering into a relationship with God, then I would encourage you to make that giant leap of faith today. It is the only way that you can be free and you can have peace and the only way that you can live forever in him.

BOUGHT AT A PRICE

Do you not know that your body is a Temple of the Holy Spirit, who is in you, whom you have received from God? You are not your own; you were bought at a price. Therefore honor God with your body.

1 Corinthians 6:19–20

And what a huge price it was indeed! Jesus Christ, the Son of God died a horrible death on a cross in order that you could be free from the unbearable consequences that sin in this world causes in your life! The God of this world lives inside of you and wants you to be filled with his Spirit and full of his love in order that he could use you to make a difference in this fallen world for him. He has a plan and a purpose for your life today. Don't miss the great things that he has for you today by stepping outside of his will and sinning against your own body. Whatever that sin may be, the short-lived joy that it may bring you is not at all worth the consequences that the sin will cause, as you will miss the fullness of God's blessing and lordship on your life today. God loves you more than you could ever imagine! He is so wild about you and he has such great plans to use your very life in order that other people on this earth would know that he is real and believe in him as well. Keep your body consecrated unto him today. Stay focused on the Spirit's prompting on your heart and just see how awesome it is to stay pure and holy before the One who lives inside of your heart of hearts! God will use you above and beyond anything that you could have ever dreamed of or imagined if you would just honor him with your body and keep your perspective and focus on him today.

DELIVERANCE

O Lord my God, in You I put my trust: save me from all those who persecute me; and deliver me.

Psalm 7:1 (NKJ)

We live in a world at war! Even this morning as my plane is delayed in trying to get back to Charlotte for a lunch outreach event, I am more than ever aware of the spiritual warfare that is happening all around us. Only in Christ can we be victorious. Only in him can we truly live the abundant life. Only Jesus can deliver us from the evil that lurks all around, and he is the only One that can do anything good with your life or mine. None of your own efforts or abilities outside of God's Spirit working through you can do you any good here on this earth as far as God's purpose goes for your life. So, knowing all of this, be sure to spend some time with your Maker today. Let his Spirit fill your heart and mind so that you are prepared for the great things that he has for you today. Rest in knowing that he is your Deliverer and that he is in control and that he has an awesome plan to use your life today in a big way. Cling to Jesus with everything that you have and let him do the work in your life as you surrender to His Lordship and are carried by his amazing Grace and unconditional love!

SEX IN MARRIAGE

Now for the matters you wrote about: It is good for a man not to marry. But since there is so much immorality, each man should have his own wife, and each woman her own husband. The husband should fulfill his marital duty to his wife, and likewise the wife to her husband. The wife's body does not belong to her alone but also to her husband. In the same way, the husband's body does not belong to him alone but also to his wife. Do not deprive each other except by mutual consent and for a time, so that you may devote yourselves to prayer. Then come together again so that Satan will not tempt you because of your lack of self-control. I say this as a concession, not as a command. I wish that all men were as I am. But each man has his own gift from God; one has this gift, another has that.

1 Corinthians 7:1–7

Paul was a single man all of his life and was completely content in being single since his heart and devotion and attention and focus was completely on Jesus Christ, who lived inside of him, and on his ministry to spread the Gospel to as many people as he could. What he is saying here is that some people have the gift of being single and other people are supposed to be married so that they will not be taken out by the sexual temptations that are all around us in this fallen world. What is important to take away here from this text are three major points: (1) It is okay and even encouraged to be single if you have the ability to stay morally pure in the process. (2) Sex is meant to stay within the realm of marriage and even the thought of it outside of sacred wedding vows is sin that causes separation from God. (3) Sex must not be used as a negotiating tool in marriage; your body belongs to your spouse and vice versa, and you must not deprive each other, as one of Satan's strongest temptations is to separate families by using sexual immorality. This concept applies not only to the act itself, but also to your thought life, what you think about, what you view with your eyes, and staying pure in your thought life. That is why God calls us as Christians to renew our minds, to think pure thoughts, and to fill our minds with his Word and his Spirit in prayer. The divorce rate among Christians is horrible. Start submitting to each other and to God today in this area of sexual purity and guard your heart and your life in order that you can be used by God and experience his best in this life as well as the eternal life to come.

DIVORCE

To the married I give this command (not I but the Lord): A wife must not separate from her husband. But if she does, she must remain unmarried or else be reconciled to her husband. And a husband must not divorce his wife.

1 Corinthians 7:10–11

First and foremost, let me just say that I am not sharing this Scripture to judge or condemn anyone who has already been through the horrible tragedy of divorce, as the statistics say that most likely more than 50% of married people who are reading this devotion have had this experience of divorce for one reason or another. I know that God's unconditional grace and amazing love is more than enough to cover and forgive and heal anyone that has had the unfortunate life experience of being separated from his or her spouse. I feel like this is important to share with those who have not yet married as well as those who are in a difficult marriage and are considering a divorce. The world would tell you that everyone gets divorced and that it is just part of life. What God would tell you is that he has a much better plan and a much more fulfilling way to reconcile your differences with your spouse. I can only speak from my own personal experience when I say that God's way is without a doubt the best way!

Paula and I have been through some tough times in the years past and we could have chosen to take the easy way out as the world would suggest and even to a point encourage on a daily basis. We, however, took the narrow road and found in each other a love and friend and amazing blessing from God that we enjoy and are so thankful for today! As we look back on the tough times that we have had in our marriage, we both agree that we would do it all over again. If we didn't go through those times, then indeed we wouldn't be as close to one another as we are today. This closeness is a result of our relationship with God and is a consequence of how he has changed each of us to be more like him and in the process has created an unconditional love and respect and trust for each other that is indescribable and very fulfilling and just the greatest thing on this earth outside of our own personal relationships with Jesus Christ.

Marriage is not easy as two people who are being molded together to become one; the two will experience some pain in the process; however, the end result is a miracle and blessing from God that you will definitely not want to miss! Submit to God and to each other and stay married. God has a plan for both of you and his way is always the best way!

MINISTRY: RIGHT WHERE YOU ARE

Brothers, each man, as responsible to God, should remain in the situation God called him to.

1 Corinthians 7:24

Don't you know that to be used by God in a very radical way you do not have to quit your job and travel to the ends of the earth? No, God wants to use you right where you are today! It very well could be that he called you and wooed you into the family of God in order to make a difference in your current work and life situation. It's hard to imagine what God's plan is, and many Christians have some illusion of grandeur that their life somehow would be much better served in a third-world country than reaching out to the lost people in the same old job or the same old neighborhood or community that they have been in all of their lives. Listen, God wants to use you today, right where you are. God wants you to be a witness and his representative to your family—to the boss that really gets on your nerves, to your neighbors who play their music too loud, to your in-laws. Wherever you are in this life, wherever God has found you, that is exactly the place where he wants his love to overflow out of your life in order to reach other people for him! Make a difference in this world for Jesus today.

SPIRITUAL TRAINING AND ENDURANCE

Do you not know that in a race all the runners run, but only one gets the prize? Run in such a way to get the prize. Everyone who competes in the games goes into strict training. They do it to get a crown that will not last; but we do it to get a crown that will last forever. Therefore I do not run like a man running aimlessly; I do not fight like a man beating the air. No, I beat my body and make it my slave so that after I have preached to others, I myself will not be disqualified for the prize.

1 Corinthians 9:24–27

Do you want to know why Tiger Woods is by far the best pro golfer in the game of golf today? It has less to do with the natural ability to golf and much more to do with the commitment that Tiger has made from a very young age to training each and every day in order that he can play his best and be the strongest player on the tour. The race that you and I run as Christians is much more important than any contest that we are exposed to here on this earth, as the race that we run involves not only spiritual crowns and blessings that will last for eternity but also the saving of souls. It involves helping others that are perishing and hurting and empty and have lost all hope to know and have the abundant life that you and I have in Christ Jesus! How have you trained for the spiritual race that you will run today? Are you prepared for the battle? Do you have a plan for times today when you know that you will be tempted? Have you spent time alone with God in order to be tuned in to the direction of his Spirit in order that he could use you in a radical way to share his love to those around you? Have you connected with other believers who know your weaknesses and are committed to hold you accountable in your pursuit of holiness today? The Christian life that you live and God's purpose for your life is much more serious and much more important than any other thing that you will encounter in the world today. Make sure you are prepared and well trained for the race that leads to abundant life and ends with our Father in heaven!

BE SENSITIVE TOWARD OTHERS' WEAKNESSES

Do not cause anyone to stumble, whether Jews, Greeks or the church of God—even as I try to please everybody in every way. For I am not seeking my own good but the good of many, so that they may be saved. Follow my example, as I follow the example of Christ.

1 Corinthians 10:32–11:1

It is good as you live your life of freedom in Christ to always be sensitive to the Spirit's prompting on your heart of who you are near and what their perception may be of your choices and actions. Paul is very clear here in his letter to the Corinthians that even though an action or choice that you make about something may not be a sin in your own personal relationship with Jesus, it may be a sin for someone else who thinks differently or may have different struggles than you; so in this case where you know that your actions may cause another one to be discouraged and to sin, it would be a sin for you to act out whatever it is in front of them.

This concept can be a little confusing so let me give you an example. It may be Okay for you to have a glass of wine with dinner if you do not struggle with drinking wine or alcohol in excess, and yet you may be dining with someone who has struggled with alcoholism in the past and so taking just one drink of wine would be detrimental to him and his relationship with God. In this case, your having the glass of wine in front of this person may be a sin, if indeed your actions cause this brother or sister in Christ to have one as well and to stumble back in to alcoholism. This is an extreme example of sorts; however, the idea is to be sensitive to your audience and to always be thinking of the impact that your actions are going to have on others and if your decisions are going to encourage or discourage them in their own personal relationship with God. After all, as Christ followers, we are all here to love and serve and to be a true reflection of God's love to other people in order that they too may see and believe.

OUR GOD IS GOOD

Shout for joy to the Lord, all the earth. Worship the Lord with gladness;
    come kneel before Him with joyful songs.
    Know that the Lord is God. It is He who made us, and we are His;
    we are His people, the sheep of His pasture.
    Enter His gates with thanksgiving and his courts with praise;
    give thanks to Him and praise His name.
    For the Lord is good and His love endures forever;
    His faithfulness continues through all generations.

Psalm 100

It is so refreshing for me to be reminded of how faithful our God is, how much he loves us, and how he is in control of all of his creation! Know that whatever meetings you have today, whatever work that you need to get done or chance encounters that you may have in your travels, that the Lord your God is holding you in his loving arms and that his will will be done in your life if you continue to seek his face and surrender to his lordship. God loves you today more than you can imagine! He wants to use your very life in a huge way to reach a lost world for him. He wants his love to overflow out of your very life as you love him and love others. He can and will change the world with just one faithful heart that willingly accepts his gift of love and then unselfishly surrenders his will to him. He has a plan and a purpose for each of his children; he wants to change the world through you today! Take time to worship him today. Give thanks for the life that he has given you through his Spirit, and then remember to keep your eyes on him wherever you go and whatever you do today, and you will see and experience the miracle of his love having an impact on the world in which you live!

YOUR ROLE TO PLAY

Now the body is not made up of one part but many. If the foot should say, "Because I am not a hand, I do not belong to the body," it would not for that reason cease to be a part of the body. And if the eye should say, "Because I am not an eye, I do not belong to the body," it would not for that reason cease to be part of the body. If the whole body were an eye, where would the sense of hearing be? If the whole body were and ear, where would the sense of smell be? But in fact, God has arranged the parts in the body, every one of them, just as He wanted them to be. If they were all one part, where would the body be? As it is, there are many parts, but one body.

1 Corinthians 12:14–20

As a member of Christ's body, you have a unique gift and a unique role to play—a role that you were created for and one that only you can do! The Master Creator will take your gift and will unite it with all of the other diverse gifts and talents of his people in order to accomplish the unified purpose of knowing him and bridging the gap in your relationship with your Creator. Listen, as cool as it is to have a unique gift and as cool as it is to be used by God, this life is not about that; it is really about the end result of knowing God and having a genuine relationship with him! Use your gifts and talents today and play your role well in order that you and many others may be reconciled to God and experience this abundant life in Christ.

MOST EXCELLENT WAY

And now I will show you the most excellent way. If I speak in tongues of men and of angels, but have not love, I am only a resounding gong or clanging cymbal. If I have the gift of prophecy and can fathom all mysteries and all knowledge, and if I have a faith that can move mountains, but have not love, I am nothing. If I give all I possess to the poor and surrender my body to the flames, but have not love, I gain nothing. Love is patient, love is kind. It does not envy, it does not boast, it is not proud. It is not rude, it is not self-seeking, it is not easily angered, it keeps no record or wrongs. Love does not delight in evil but rejoices with the truth. It always protects, always trusts, always hopes, always perseveres. Love never fails.

1 Corinthians 12:31–13:8

Being a type A personality with a huge desire for approval and recognition, I tend to do a lot and to fill my time up to the limit, believing the lie that the more I do and the more I accomplish, the more I will be accepted by God and by others. The problem with this approach to life is that sometimes—no, many times—the most important attribute in God's eyes gets lost somewhere in the chaos of all that service that seems the right thing to do at the time but is missing the most important ingredient of God's love! You see, God cares much less about our efforts and accomplishments and much more about our hearts! God wants us to take time to spend with him, to be filled with his love in order that it may overflow in our lives to other people. My best efforts for ministry, for success, and even for many other good things in this life mean nothing unless they are fueled by God's love that is overflowing from deep inside of me as a result of me, spending time alone with Jesus and letting his Spirit fill me with this indescribable, perfect love that only comes from above! Many of you are running on empty. Choose the most excellent way today and take some time to be filled by God so that His love may overflow out of your life and change the world.

BAD COMPANY

Do not be misled: Bad company corrupts good character. Come back to your senses as you ought, and stop sinning; for there are some who are ignorant of God—I say this to your shame.

1 Corinthians 15:33–34

The church in Corinth was hanging out and believing in a few folks that were teaching false doctrine, saying that there was no resurrection from the dead. Sometimes in this world it is easy to get wrapped up in a lie. See, the enemy is very clever and is always trying to confuse the Truth of the Gospel. Paula and I attended a secular concert recently, and as I watched the crowd cheering for this famous musician of whose name I won't reveal, I was dumbfounded as to the control that this man who stood for nothing good had over the thousands upon thousands of people who had come to listen to the music. When this musician spoke, the crowd was hanging on every word, not because there was Truth in anything that he was saying but because he wrote and performed popular songs more than thirty years ago. Now, I don't think that there is anything wrong with going to a rock concert, but I do think that there are many influential people in the world that can cloud your focus and lead you astray. Be careful as to what and whom you believe and always examine God's Word for yourself and let God make up your mind about him and his plan for your life. There is Truth and power and love in the Word of God—always be sure that it is the only thing that you build the foundation of your life on and you will be sure to maintain "good character" and rock on forever in him.

NEW BODY IN CHRIST

So it will be with the resurrection of the dead. The body that is sown is perishable, it is raised imperishable; it is sown in dishonor, it is raised in glory; it is sown in weakness, it is raised in power; it is sown a natural body, it is raised a spiritual body.

1 Corinthians 15:42–44

One of the benefits of surrendering your life to Jesus Christ and making him the Lord of your life while you are here on this earth is indeed the fact that when he returns we all will be resurrected into a new body that is our own and one that is perfect and imperishable, glorious and powerful, one that is fit to live eternally with God forever! No more sickness, no more hair loss, no more aches or pains or aging or cancer or diabetes or anything else that we see today as a result of original sin, but a completely new body in Christ that will be fit for eternal service and worship of our Lord of lords and King of kings forever! Oh how I long for that day when we will all be made perfect in him.

SPIRITUAL MAN

If there is a natural body, there is also a spiritual body. So it is written: "The first man, Adam, became a living being, the last Adam a life-giving spirit. The spiritual did not come first, but the natural, and after that the spiritual. The first man was of dust of the earth, the second man from Heaven."

1 Corinthians 15:44b - 47

Remember that song by Kansas that said, "All we are is dust in the wind"? Well, this song was only partly true. Part of us is made from dust of the earth and will one day return; however, another part of us is spiritual and will live forever somewhere, either in heaven or hell. Most people spend quite a bit of time developing their physical bodies, which will one day pass away, and very little time developing their spiritual man, that part of them which will live on forever, either with God or apart from him for the rest of eternity. What have you done lately to develop your spiritual being that is deep inside each and every one of us? Have you passed over the line from death to life by accepting Jesus Christ into your heart and life? Are you growing to become more like Christ by spending time alone with God in his Word and through prayer and surrender and humility and self-control? Is your spiritual man overflowing with love from the inside out, so much so that other people can see that you are different? The physical is dying and decaying and will soon pass away. You never know when your time will be up; however, the spiritual will live on forever. Make sure that you are taking time today to work on your spiritual man, for your spiritual man will never pass away!

COURAGEOUS BUT GUARDED LIFE OF LOVE

Be on your guard; stand firm in the faith; be men of courage; be strong.
Do everything in love.

1 Corinthians 16:13

God wants you to live a life today that is sold out to him, courageously opposing the way in which the world would want you to live today and lovingly sharing the Gospel to everyone you meet through your actions. Even still, don't ever forget that you are being opposed and that you do have an enemy that does not want you to experience God's best in your life. Knowing this, stand guarded, ever so careful to only take steps that are directed by the Holy Spirit, who is living inside of you. Keep your mind on God and on his love and his purpose and his providence so that you won't miss his awesome power in your life and how he would want to use you today to reach a lost world for him!

BE ENCOURAGERS IN THE FAITH

I was glad when Stephanas, Fortunatus and Achaicus arrived, because they have supplied what was lacking from you. For they refreshed my spirit and yours also. Such men deserve recognition.

1 Corinthians 16:17–18

It is easy in this day and age to argue and complain and to grumble, as there are very few absolutes in the world's eyes, and one can dispute just about anything in this life and have a following of sorts. It is much harder to communicate directly and to lovingly question another person directly, bringing every decision under the lens of the Holy Spirit and God's providence in your life. I would challenge you today not to grumble and complain and create controversy secretly, but to boldly and lovingly bring any area of concern directly to the source as honest communication will always be blessed by your Father in heaven and an encouragement to those around you. Heed Stephanas' family's example here and have the tough and uncomfortable conversations, as you will be rewarded because they are for your integrity and transparency in this life.

LOVE THE LORD YOUR GOD

If anyone does not love the Lord—a curse be on him. Come, O Lord!

1 Corinthians 16:22

The Apostle Paul is being very firm here about those who declare themselves unbelievers and have a lack of love and obedience to our Lord and Savior Jesus Christ. After all, how could anyone who has heard the story of the Gospel of Jesus Christ and how could anyone who has heard about his saving grace and unconditional love not want to give his life away in love to him as a thank you for all that he has done? The Bible also tells us that the greatest command in Scripture is to: love the Lord your God with all of your heart and all of your soul and with all of your mind (Matthew 22:37). One day soon he is coming back to take all of those who love him and who have accepted his Spirit into their hearts back to an incredible place called heaven, where our minds cannot even comprehend the awesome joy that will be found there by all of God's people. Are you ready to go? Have you accepted his love into your life so much so that you can't help but to love him back? Today, don't worry about your failures or your weaknesses or your struggles or where you have fallen short, for God loves you today, right where you are, and he is waiting for you to love him in return.

ACCOUNTABILITY

My brothers, if one of you should wander from the truth and someone should bring him back, remember this: Whoever turns a sinner from the error of his way will save him from death and cover a multitude of sins.

James 5:19–20

I recently received an e-mail from an old friend of more than seventeen years ago. After catching up on happenings with work, family, etc., he shared with me that he has been praying for an accountability partner to meet with once a week. He shared with me that he is a hard guy to get to know and that God has not answered his prayer as of yet. My heart really softened as I remembered the kind of relationship that my friend and I had many years ago. I mean we knew each other so well that we could just look at each other and know what the other person's spiritual state of mind was! It sounds weird, I know, but I am telling you that God put us together as friends for a reason since we struggled with some of the same worldly sins and could hold each other accountable. These types of friendships are a blessing from God! I have heard people say that their relationship with the Lord is personal and that it is nobody's business but their own. After reading the verse here, I would have to disagree with that statement. We cannot live this life on our own! We need accountability and we need other Christian friends to encourage us and sharpen us in our faith. And yes, sometimes we need that person to help pull us out of a ditch of sin that we have dug for ourselves.

What about you? Have you shared your struggles and challenges in the faith with another person? Confessing your sins to another believer brings not only accountability, but also freedom from the bondage that your sins create. It is hard at first, but as you really get to know another believer at that deepest level, you will crave that kind of relationship that holds you accountable, encourages you in your faith, and is there to catch you when you fall!

Pray today that God will put this kind of friend in your life.

HEART CHECK

The Lord does not look at the things man looks at. Man looks at the outward appearance, but the Lord looks at the heart.

1 Samuel 16:7

What is the condition of your heart today? You see, we may be able to fool other people around us; however, we can't fool God! God knows us at the very deepest level of our hearts. He knows our innermost desires that flow out of our hearts—both good and bad. The interesting thing about our hearts is that we cannot change a thing ourselves concerning our hearts. We can change our outward appearance. We can change the way that we act. But only God can change our hearts. He does it through his Word and through his Spirit in order to make our hearts more like him.

Have you asked God to come into your heart? If not, this is the first step to real change in your life that will fulfill you at the very deepest level! If you have already asked God into your heart, then are you spending time with him each day reading his Word and in prayer so that he can begin the process of creating a clean and godly heart within you? God is the master surgeon, but we have to be willing to let him in to all areas of our hearts so that he can begin his work in our lives.

Pray now that God would begin to change your heart. All you have to do is ask and then hold on for dear life! You will begin to experience a heart and life change that will complete you, fulfill you, and give you a most awesome joy and peace like nothing that you have ever experienced before!

PEACE THAT PASSES UNDERSTANDING

I will lie down and sleep in peace, for you alone, O Lord, make me dwell in safety.

Psalm 4:8

In this world that we live in there are so many things for us to be anxious about when we retire for the evening or wake up in the morning. Many of us worry about our finances, jobs, future, family, friends, clothes, food, church, etc., and the list goes on and on. As the writer of this psalm points out so eloquently, isn't it nice to be reminded that we don't have to go to bed with all of these worries on our mind, but to the contrary we can sleep in peace knowing that the Lord our God is in complete control of everything in our lives and that he wants the very best for us? For there is a peace that passes all understanding that is felt by the person that has surrendered 100% of his heart to Jesus Christ. In fact, one of my favorite verses in the New Testament is a verse in Matthew where Jesus himself says,"Come to me all you who are weary and burdened, and I will give you rest" Matthew 11:28. Wow. To be able to rest in the arms of the creator of the universe—not having to have everything all figured out, but knowing that he is control, knowing that he is about to do something so amazing with your life that you can't even begin to imagine, and experiencing the joy, peace, and fulfillment of his Spirit on a daily basis! Now that is living! Below is a poem that I wrote early on in my Christian walk about this very life in Christ:

Wouldn't it be great
To have a place to run;
When you feel alone and hurt,
When the world has lost its fun.
A place where you can be yourself,

Accepted for who you are;
A place where you can feel at peace,
Your worries and troubles afar.
A place where you are deeply loved,
Despite your sin and shame;
A place where you're forgiven,
And all are treated the same.
I have found a place
Where all of this is true;
And you're invited to go there,
It's solely up to you.
A relationship with Jesus Christ,
That's what you're searching for;
Surrender you heart and life to him,
And search for love no more.

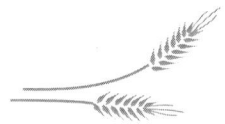

FAITH IN ACTION

Was not our ancestor Abraham considered righteous for what he did when he offered his son Isaac on the altar?

James 2:21

What a role model for us as Christians today is the life of Abraham in the Old Testament! What a godly man who was obedient even to the point of being willing to sacrifice the one thing in this life that was most precious to him—his very own son! What would happen in this world if we had more people that were as obedient to God and his calling as Abraham was? As Americans, we grumble and complain over missing a meal, having to work, having to listen to our wives, at the other driver who cut us off, being single, being bored, and numerous other petty little things that can't even begin to compare to the sacrifice that Abraham was willing to make for his God whom he loved and trusted completely. That is faith in action, and it would do us good to follow his example.

I don't know what you are going through today, but please remember that God loves you more than you can begin to comprehend! All he wants from us if for us to love him back and to trust that he knows what's best for our lives. We can't see the big picture; we don't know the ramifications of what God may be asking us to do today. We don't know who might be watching our reaction to see if what we say about God and our faith is real or not! So today, I ask that you remember Abraham when you start to question why God may be leading you in a certain direction and press on to act out your faith by being obedient! The blessings that will come as a result of your faithfulness are above and beyond anything that you could ever dream or imagine! The chapter in James goes on to say, "Abraham believed God, and it was credited to him as righteousness, and he was called God's friend" (James 2:23).

Go in faith. Be strong and courageous. Be a friend of God today by being obedient to his calling!

BELIEF OR RELATIONSHIP

You believe that there is one God. Good! Even the demons believe that—and shudder.

James 2:9

Do you just believe in God, similar to the demons, or do you have a personal relationship with Jesus Christ? Does God control your actions? Are you digging into his Word each day, developing a genuine love for his Word and getting to know him better? Is he changing your heart and mind so that your actions and priorities are different? Do you love him more than anything in the world including your spouse, job, or material possessions? Do you worry constantly about issues within your life, or do you give them over to your loving Father and rest, knowing that he is ultimately in control and wants only the best for you? Are you different from the rest of the world that you see all around you, or do you blend into the crowd, no one noticing anything at all that is different about the way that you live your life? It is not enough just to believe in God! Jesus says it himself in Matthew 7:22–23: "Many will say to me on that day, 'Lord, Lord, did we not prophesy in your name and in your name drive out demons and perform many miracles?' Then I will tell them plainly, I never knew you. Away from me you evildoers!" God wants you to know him in a personal way. He wants to come into your heart and begin to change it to become more like his. He wants you to be the man or woman that he designed you to be from the very start. He wants to give you a peace and love that will consume all of your entire being so that people around you can't help but notice that there is something different about you. He wants to be your friend and to use you in a powerful way to make an impact for him in the world around you. He died a terrible death on the

Cross to make all of this possible for you! All you have to do is make that first step toward him.

It's not too late—seek him now with all of your heart and you will enter into a life worth living that is far greater than anything you could ever dream or imagine!

DISCERNMENT

And this is my prayer: that your love may abound more and more in knowledge and depth of insight, so that you may be able to discern what is best and may be pure and blameless until the day of Christ, filled the fruit of righteousness that comes through Jesus Christ—to the glory and praise of God.

Philippians 1:9–11

Every day we make hundreds of decisions about our life. We decide what we are going to do with our time, what we are going to eat and drink, who we are going to spend our time with, where we are going to spend our time, what we are going to spend the resources that God has blessed us with, etc. God gives us the freedom to make these choices in our lives and in any given situation there may quite possibly be several good choices that we could make. For instance, I can give you an example from my own life this morning. It is a good choice for me to stay in bed and get some much-needed rest; however, it is a better choice and probably the best choice for me to take a shower and attend the men's morning Bible study this morning since my wife will probably sleep until late in the morning anyway. What the Apostle Paul is telling us here in the book of Philippians is that in order for us to grow in our Christian faith, we should always discern what the best decision is that we can make in relation to our relationship with Jesus Christ. If we always discern what is best, then, as he says in the text, we will be pure and blameless and filled with the fruit of righteousness!

If you want God to use you to make a difference in this world and you want to grow to be more like him, then you must filter all of your decisions through him, no matter how small. This will enable you to decide what the best choice is for you to make in any given situation. God's Spirit will help you, and if you live your life this way, then you will experience God in a most awesome and powerful way. You life will be filled with his power, grace, and love, and you will be a vessel that he can use for his glory!

Make a difference in your world today. Pray that God will help you always make the best choices as they relate to your faith in Jesus Christ!

POWER OF PRAISE

I will praise you, O Lord, with all of my heart; I will tell of all your wonders. I will be glad and rejoice in you; I will sing praise to your name, O Most High.

Psalm 9:1–2

There is truly power in a life that praises God Almighty with all of his heart! A heart that praises God and shares with others all of the great things that he has done in his life has a peace and an overwhelming joy that can't help but be passed along to other people. In this world of paranoia, pessimism, and the tireless race for worldly success, how sweet it is for a life to be filled with an inexpressible joy and peace that is truly foreign to those around us! We deserved death, but instead received an abundant life in Christ because of his most precious sacrifice on the Cross! How could we not be filled with praise when we remember God's gift to us and when we see this gift alive in our life and the lives of our brothers and sisters in Christ?

Others are watching. They don't understand our joy and peace, although they would love to have it for themselves and for the emptiness of their heart to be filled! Praise God today for what he has done in your life to those around you. You never know who he might touch or how he might use you to make a difference in other people's lives. You have the opportunity today to help change someone's heart for eternity!

Be Glad and rejoice in Him!

GOD IS OUR REFUGE AND FUTURE HOPE

The Lord is a refuge for the oppressed, a stronghold in times of trouble. Those who know your name will trust in you, for you, Lord, have never forsaken those who seek you.

Psalm 9:9–19

Do you know the Lord? Are you trusting him with all of your heart? If this is true, then there is nothing that the world can dish out that can harm or discourage you! You see, our refuge is God Almighty! Who can protect us better than he? He will always meet all of our needs and, as the verse says, he will never forsake us! Where I go wrong is when I trust in myself or my job or my finances, etc. As silly as this sounds, sometimes it is so easy to do. Yesterday I was feeling a little discouraged because of a seemingly missed opportunity with my job. You see, my hope was in the wrong thing. God has a better plan for me—far better than my limited human mind can even begin to comprehend. He promises to never forsake me. All that he asks us to do is to trust in him to meet our needs, trust in him to protect us, and trust in him for all of our future hopes and dreams! God is in control and wants the very best for those who seek him with all their hearts. Who am I to think that my plan is better than his? He is God—all-powerful, all-knowing, Almighty God! What a privilege it is to be his son and under his care and direction! I will trust and hope in him, for he is the reason that I live!

What about you? Seek him today with all of your heart and replace your worries and anxieties in this life with an incomprehensible peace and joy that will fulfill you completely and eternally!

ETERNAL JOY

For to me, to live is Christ and to die is gain.

Philippians 2:10

We can learn much here from Paul's example in Philippians. Here is a guy who is in prison because of his relationship with Christ, and yet his joy becomes even greater behind the prison bars. You see, Paul's single most important possession and ultimate concern in life was his faith in Christ. Not even death could steal his joy since death meant that he would be with Christ forevermore, completely, without any worldly or fleshly distractions; united with him in one Spirit—purely and completely fulfilled. Nothing could separate him from God and the love and joy that he received from this most precious relationship: "For I am convinced that neither death nor life, neither angels nor demons, neither the present nor the future, nor any powers, neither height nor depth, nor anything else in all creation, will be able to separate us from the love of God that is in Christ Jesus our Lord" (Romans 8:28).

How refreshing it is to know no matter what we encounter today in this world, those of us that have committed our lives to Christ have a joy that nothing or no one can take away. Indeed, he is the very reason that we live and ultimately when we die we will be made perfect in him. Seek him today with all of your heart! You will find that when you do this, even in the midst of troubles, your heart will be overflowing with joy because of your future hope and present reality in him!

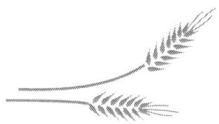

ALIENS AND STRANGERS

You adulterous people, don't you know that friendship with the world is hatred toward God? Anyone who chooses to be a friend of the world becomes an enemy of God.

James 4:4

What does it mean to be a "friend of the world"? A friend of the world is someone who is driven by the pleasures of this world in lieu of being driven by his love for Jesus Christ! Let's take a simple test to determine where your loyalty lies. What do you think about the most throughout your day? If you answer this question honestly, then it won't take you long to discover whether you are a friend of the world or a person that is 100% sold out for Jesus Christ and totally surrendered to the work of God in your life. You see, this is not our home. If you have truly surrendered your life to Christ and God's Spirit lives inside of you, then you should not be blending into the crowd here in this world. God calls us to be different in the short time that we are on this earth so that others may see him in our lives and believe. He says in 1 Peter 2:11: "Dear friends, I urge you, as aliens and strangers in the world, to abstain from sinful desires, which war against your soul." We are "aliens and strangers" here on this earth. Our priorities and morals should be so different from other people that we encounter in this world that we can't help but be a living example of God's love and righteousness on this earth! Are people around you blown away by your humility, unselfishness, love, and commitment to live for Jesus Christ? Or do you just blend into the crowd, seemingly becoming a friend of the world?

Because of our sinful nature and our fleshly bodies, there are times when all of us become "friends of the world." Don't be discouraged; God's grace covers us all when we fail, as long as we confess and then turn back to run the race toward him! The key is to be actively seeking the Lord and letting his Spirit continually change our hearts and minds, attitudes and desires to be more like his! Don't be a friend of the world today. Make a stand for Jesus Christ! Seek him with all of your heart and he will come into your life and fill you with a peace and joy that is so incredibly different than anything you have ever experienced before! You won't regret it.

Step out and be different; live your life for him.

PRESENCE OF GOD IN YOUR LIFE

Lord, who may dwell in your sanctuary?
Who may live on your holy hill?
He whose walk is blameless and who does what is righteous,
who speaks the truth from his heart
and has no slander on his tongue,
who does his neighbor no wrong,
and casts no slur on his fellowman,
who despises a vile man,
but honors those who fear the Lord,
who keeps his oath,
even when it hurts,
who lends money without usury
and does not accept a bribe against the innocent.
He who does these things
will never be shaken.

Psalm 15

In the Old Testament days there was only one person that could experience the presence of God. This person was the high priest who would enter the most holy place in the temple at certain times of the year. There was a linen curtain embroidered with cherubim that separated this most holy place from the rest of the temple and no other person besides the high priest was permitted to enter to meet God. A miraculous thing happened the moment that Jesus Christ was crucified on the Cross for our sins. The curtain that separated the most holy place from the rest of the temple was literally torn in two—this was a physical representation of the relationship that all people could now have with God. Because of Jesus' sacrifice on the Cross, each one of us can now experience the presence of God in our lives! After we have accepted Christ into our hearts and then begin to obey his commands, it is then that we can commune with him and experience his perfect peace, omnipotent power, and indescribable joy in our lives. You see, for those of us that are Christians, the temple of God now is our body. His Spirit lives and moves inside of us—if indeed we are obedient. Let's not miss this important piece of the message described here in the book of Psalms. For God's Spirit to be fully active in our lives, and for us to experience the power of God in our lives, we must obey his commands to live a righteous life! Where sin is present, God cannot be. In fact, the definition of sin is separation from God. Yes of course Jesus died for our sins and paid the price for them; however, we must continually confess and accept his forgiveness and turn 180 degrees from them back to God.

Living a "blameless" life, speaking the truth in love, having no slander on our tongue, keeping our oath even when it hurts—these are challenging principles for us to live by for sure. The great thing is that God gives us the power to do all of this, the power to choose him over the pleasures of this world! What sin is it in your life that is keeping you from experiencing God? Whatever it is, let me assure you that it is not worth it. Confess it to God right now and then turn back to him with all of your heart. Give God everything and you will experience him in a mighty way! Your life will be filled with a power, joy, and love like no other! You will finally find what you have been looking for to fill the gap in your life and make you complete in him. What an awesome feeling it is to never be shaken, trusting in God Almighty as your rock and foundation, resting in his presence, knowing that he wants only the very best for you and promises to be with you for all eternity.

Don't waste any more time: enter into the most fulfilling relationship that you could ever have today—a relationship with Jesus Christ.

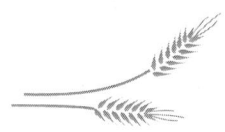

SERVANT OF ALL

Do nothing out of selfish ambition or vain conceit, but in humility consider others better than yourselves. Each of you should look not only to your own interests, but also to the interests of others.

Philippians 2:3–4

I heard a worship song years ago that really explained what this verse is talking about. The chorus of the song said, "If you want to be great in God's Kingdom, learn to be a servant of all." The secret to experiencing God in a big way in your life is found in this verse here in Philippians. As Americans, we are brought up to look out for number one—ourselves. We are taught at an early age to: be ambitious, be all you can be, enjoy life, shoot for the top, control your own destiny, etc. For many Americans, their whole life is spent climbing the proverbial corporate ladder so that they can have more money to spend on pleasures for themselves. Our icons as kids are movie stars and famous people who have achieved greatness in our minds because of their bank accounts. Because of this upbringing, we have a self-centered focus on life that really seems natural and right.

The problem with this worldview, as we read here in Philippians, is that it is totally contradictory to what the focus of a Christian should be. No wonder we see such lukewarm faith, failure, and deadness in many churches today. Imagine what can happen to us as a Church if we begin to focus, not on ourselves, but on how we can make other people's days! To have the attitude on Sunday morning of "How am I going to minister to someone else today," rather than, "What am I going to get out of the message this morning"; to go to work with a plan to help encourage that colleague who continually rubs you the wrong way; to become a friend to those neighbors across the street and try to help them through their problems even though you disagree with their current lifestyle; to smile and get to know the clerk at the grocery store, rather than always being in a hurry, rushing through life as if you are running a marathon—these are examples of what it means to be a servant of all, to always be looking out for the interests of others considering them better than ourselves. When we start doing these things as a Church and when you start doing these things as a man or woman of God, then hold on for dear life. You will begin to see God move in a dramatic way in and through your life and through the Church. You will experience his presence and have a joy and a motivation in this life that far outweighs the selfish ambition that the world is used to seeing!

Be a vessel that God can use for his glory today! Experience his power, be captivated by his love, and be filled with a joy that is incomparable to anything that the world has to offer. Pray now that God will give you the strength and desire to be a servant of all!

HOW GREAT THOU ART!

How great you are, O Sovereign Lord! There is no one like you, and there is no God but you, as we have heard with our own ears.

2 Samuel 7:22

What a beautiful prayer that was prayed by David just after God had spoken to him saying that he was about to make David's name great, like the names of the greatest men of the earth, and not only that but also that David's throne would be forever established and that God would never take his love away from him. The interesting thing about the depth of God's love that is so foreign to anything that we can understand with our fleshly minds is that God blessed David like no one before him, knowing that he was about to commit murder and adultery later on during his reign as king. God knew that and yet he poured out his love and blessings on David just the same! God is so great! He has a love for us that we can't even begin to comprehend. There is indeed no one like him! What a privilege it is to be his servant and have his Spirit living inside of me! God makes his home inside of us and pours out his love and blessings, knowing that our flesh is weak and that we as humans can't even begin to measure up to his standards. All of this is possible because of Jesus' sacrifice on the Cross. It is his grace that covers us and allows us to have this kind of relationship with an amazing God who is full of love and understanding beyond our comprehension.

God doesn't care what kind of man or woman that you have been. He doesn't care what sins you have committed. God's love goes much deeper than anything that we could do here on this earth! He loves you more than you could imagine and wants a relationship with you. He wants to meet you right where you are and begin to heal your scars, change your heart and mind, and fill you with his love. His Son died to make this possible! There is nothing that you can do that will be able to separate you from this love once you have accepted him into your life. So draw near to him today. Forget about your past, forget about the sins that you have committed, and rest in him! He is a great God, full of love, understanding, peace, and joy! Turn back to him today with all of your heart and you will have a life like no other!

ATTITUDE

Your attitude should be the same as that of Christ Jesus, who, being in the very nature of God, did not consider equality with God something to be grasped, but made himself nothing, taking the very nature of a servant, being made in human likeness. And being found in the appearance as a man, he humbled himself and became obedient to death—even death on a cross!

Philippians 2:5–8

In biblical times, dying on a cross was the most degrading kind of execution that could be inflicted on a person—only people that were thought to be cursed were put through the humiliation of being put to death on a cross for everyone to see. What a humble attitude that was taken by our Lord and Savior who at any time could have snapped his fingers and made it all stop! He went through all that humiliation and mockery for you and me so that we could spend eternity with him! After reading such a humbling example of Christ's attitude, how could we complain about anything that we will encounter in our lives today? We may go through a little discomfort, humiliation, failure, pain, you name it, but absolutely nothing will even begin to compare with the horror that Jesus experienced for us. And he went through it all with the utmost, excellent of attitudes, knowing that in the end he was rescuing us from death!

As Charles Swindol points out in his most famous quote concerning attitudes, there is only one thing that you can have 100% control over in this life, and that is your attitude! People are watching you to see how you respond to the trials and tests that you encounter in this life. Is your faith real? Is this Christian thing that you profess a farce, or do you really have the power of God in your life? They are watching you to answer these questions for themselves. You have the power to make a difference in someone's life today—maybe even to determine where someone will spend eternity, just by showing him or her the attitude of Christ in whatever situation that you find yourself in today. Pray now that God would instill his attitude into your heart so that others may see and believe!

ABUNDANT LIFE IN CHRIST

You have made known to me the path of life;
you will fill me with joy in your presence,
with eternal pleasures at your right hand.

Psalm 16:11

The path of life is made known to us by our most awesome God and Father! As Christians we are always filled with joy in the presence of the Almighty, not only here on earth, but for all eternity. What's even more awesome than that is to know that our joy will actually increase when we go to be with him, since at that time we will be made perfect in him. What a great God it is that we serve! Jesus said this in John 10:10, "I have come that they might have life and that they might have it more abundantly" (KJV). For those of us that have truly surrendered our hearts to Jesus Christ, we have been given eternal pleasures that are beyond belief! There is no greater joy than the joy that comes from communing with God each day and seeing him work in and through your life to not only change your heart to be more like his, but also to see him use you to help change and encourage other people.

Do you know this joy? Are you experiencing the presence of God in your life? Do you have an abundant life in him? If not, then it is easy enough to attain. All that needs to be done is for you to take that step toward him by accepting the sacrifice that he made for you on the Cross! Ask him into your heart and be willing to let his Spirit change your heart and mind. The cool thing is that it is God that does the work; all you have to do is to first believe and then to choose him by surrendering your heart and life to his control. God will then fill you with a joy and a purpose in this life that is like nothing else that you have ever experienced before! He is waiting for you to surrender completely to him. Don't waste any more time. Take that step of faith today!

SHINE LIKE STARS

Do everything without complaining or arguing, so that you may become blameless and pure, children of God without fault in a crooked and depraved generation, in which you shine like stars in the universe as you hold out the word of life.

Philippians 2:14–16

Stars are bright lights and the only things to be seen in the midst of an empty, black, and cold night sky. Paul uses a great analogy here to express how our lives should be seen in the empty, dark, and "depraved" world that we live in. It amazes me that such a simple thing—"to not complain or argue"—would cause us to stick out so much in a crowd. Some may say that because it is so common to complain or argue in the society in which we live that it must be okay to blend in to those around us by doing the same. But God says that it is not okay; in fact, he says that he wants to use us as an example for all to see—his children, blameless and pure, living godly lives, more than content with what we have, filled with a joy and a unwavering faith that can't help but stand out in a crowd!

Is your light shining today? There is something much bigger going on than the many little irritations that you will encounter in the world today—something so great that the enemy is throwing these irritations and distractions your way in hopes that you will be sidelined by them and, in a sense, your light dimmed or even snuffed out completely. Don't let the enemy steal your joy and light today. Keep your focus on Christ, look to these distractions as the enemy's ploy, and counter his efforts by shining your light even brighter in this dark world! Live your life for Christ without complaining or arguing and let the whole world see that you are filled with an amazing joy, an unspeakable love, and a genuine faith in God that does indeed cause him to be noticed and seen in this crooked and depraved generation in which we live!

Let your light shine!

PRESS ON

Forgetting what is behind and straining toward what is ahead, I press on toward the goal to win the prize for which God has called me heavenward in Christ Jesus.

Philippians 3:13–14

There are so many things that this world and the enemy can dish out to discourage and distract us in our walk with the Lord. There will be other people, many of whom are Christians, who are going to let us down in a big way. There are financial pressures, work pressures, time pressures, family problems, spiritual failures, and many other things that can and are going to happen in our lives here on this earth. Do not let these things sidetrack you from your primary reason for being here on this earth! Keep you focus on Christ, continue to trust in him, and he promises not only to get you through all of these battles of life but, even more, to fill you with his love and his grace both now and forevermore!

Press on, my brothers and sisters, for the glory of God today! Pray now that God will give you the strength, peace, and power to overcome whatever battle it is that you are facing today!

ROCK OF MY SALVATION

I love you, O Lord, my strength. The Lord is my rock, my fortress, and my deliverer; my God is my rock, in whom I take refuge.

He is my shield and the horn of my salvation, my stronghold.

I call to the Lord, who is worthy of praise,

and I am saved from my enemies.

Psalm 18:1–3

Webster's dictionary defines refuge as: "That which shelters or protects from danger, or from distress or calamity; a stronghold which protects by its strength, or a sanctuary which secures safety by its sacredness; a place inaccessible to an enemy." What an awesome reminder it is for us to know that no matter what we are facing in this world today that we can take refuge in our Lord and Savior! We can let our guard down and rest, all the while letting our loving Father comfort us, restore and renew our spirit, and fight the battles for us! The writer of this psalm calls to the Lord, and as a result he is saved from his enemies.

God allows things to happen in our lives so that we continually learn that we need to "call to the Lord" for help. We cannot do anything in and of ourselves. The enemy tries to make us believe that we can, and so we wallow in self-pity and just dig for ourselves a deeper hole, when at the end of the day all that we really needed to do was to call to the Lord for help and trust in him to carry us through the trials and temptations in this fallen world. The only reason that we are here is to learn to love him more and to share this love with other people. There is no way that we can even begin to accomplish this goal if we are not connected to the Father and taking refuge in him!

Thank you, God, for being our strength and fortress. Thank you that we can rest in you today, knowing that you are our protector and our comforter who wants only the very best for our lives here on this earth! We call to you for help today. What an awesome God you are! We love you!

RIVER OF GOD

There is a river whose streams make glad the city of God, the holy place where the Most High dwells.

Psalm 46:4

Early this morning I walked along a river in my hometown of Ohio, just like I had done many times before early on in my Christian walk, many years ago. I noticed a few things about this amazing river with the strong gushing waters and almost hypnotic sound and view that commands one's focus and attention. Although there had been many changes in the land that surrounded the river, the river itself had not changed a bit. It was the same river that it had been more than seventeen years ago, offering the same peace and serenity, joy and hope that it offered up to a teenage boy many times in years past—a great metaphor, like the one used in the book of psalms here to describe the sustaining and refreshing blessings of God that pour out of the river of his Spirit that lives within us. Like the river, God's love never changes. His glory always commands our attention and offers us peace, hope, and joy forever! For those of us that have accepted God's most amazing gift of his Son into our hearts, we have this river of love inside of us that continues to bless and shape our lives, making us more like him! Isn't it nice to know that in this ever-changing world we have such an amazing gift inside of us that will never change, will always fulfill us completely, and that nothing or no one can ever take away? Thanks be to God for his never-changing love and faithfulness.

Some of you maybe can't relate to this metaphor since you have never experienced this river of love in your life. God is calling you today. The river is drawing you in. Accept God's most precious gift of love, and surrender your heart and life to him today! I promise that it will be the best decision that you have ever made!

SUPERNATURAL JOY AND PEACE

Rejoice in the Lord always. I will say it again: Rejoice! Let your gentleness be evident to all. The Lord is near. Do not be anxious about anything, but in everything by prayer and petition, with thanksgiving, present your requests to God. And the peace of God, which transcends all understanding, will guard your hearts and minds in Christ Jesus.

Philippians 4:4–7

Rejoice, be gentle, do not be anxious about anything but have patience. I am not sure about you, but to me all of these things seem just a little bit out of reach at times. In this fast-paced world, keeping our minds occupied with our next strategic move for success has been a key ingredient for achieving success. The truth is, though, that this kind of success is what the Bible calls worldly success, and to clutter our minds with this kind of thinking does nothing but separate us from true joy and peace that can be found in "taking every thought captive" and resting in the arms of our Lord and Savior Jesus Christ. God's Spirit can help us to supernaturally renew our minds so that our thoughts mirror the thoughts of our Creator. When this happens, we indeed have a peace and a joy that is indescribable, supernatural, and truly what we have been searching for all of our lives! The key is that we as Christians need to stay connected to God in order for this to happen. God's Spirit cannot dwell in the same place where sin is present. We need to daily confess our sins, renew our minds through the study of his Word and refresh our spirits through prayer and worship in a quiet time with him. Oh how sweet it is to spend time with God each morning and then to pass along his thoughts to you through these daily devotions! My heart and mind are renewed, my focus is sharpened, and my spirit is ready to be used by him to be a gentle light, filled with joy and peace, in this dark, hectic world in which we live.

A high calling? Yes indeed. The good news is that it is his power that works within us to make this happen! It is nothing that we do in and of ourselves. You too can experience this joy and peace in your life today. Seek God now with all of your heart and mind. Give to him your worries in this life to bear so that you can be a light to those around you who desperately need to see God for who he really is!

SEEK HIS FACE

The earth is the Lord's, and everything in it, the world, and all who live in it; for he founded it upon the seas and established it upon the waters.

Who may ascend the hill of the Lord? Who may stand in His holy place?

He who has clean hands and a pure heart,
who does not lift up his soul to an idol
or swear by what is false.
He will receive blessings from the God his Savior.
Such is the generation of those who seek Him,
who seek your face, O God of Jacob.

Psalm 24:1–6

The world and everything in it belongs to God. We are just a microscopic piece of his beautiful creation and yet our accessibility to him and his love and blessings that he bestows upon each one of our lives is limitless! But as the psalmist says here, how do we have clean hands (guiltless actions) and pure hearts (right attitudes and motives) so that we can stand in the presence of God Almighty and experience his power in our lives? There is only one way, and it is found in the last phrase of this text: he cleanses and purifies those of us that seek his face, so that we may be holy and blameless before God. It is God himself that does the cleansing in our lives as we make that step toward him and seek him with all of our hearts!

Several months ago I was sharing what God was doing in my life at the time with a dear friend and colleague. As the conversation went on, this friend described to me his desire to really seek the Lord and live his life for him. His next sentence, however, was that he needed to clean up a few things in his life first before he would feel right about deepening his relationship with Jesus Christ.

My friend was missing the whole point. There is no way that we, in and of ourselves, can even begin to cleanse our own lives. The Bible says that "all our righteous acts are like filthy rags" (Isaiah 64:6). It is only when we seek God by coming just as we are and letting his Spirit have control of our lives that we can truly be transformed to be more like him! God makes us holy as we seek his face and bring all of our sin and shame and lay it before his holy throne.

So don't delay. Stop making excuses! Seek God today with all of your heart. Come to him just as you are and he will begin to change you and give you life like no other!

ALL THINGS THROUGH CHRIST

I know what it is to be in need, and I know what it is to have plenty. I have learned the secret of being content in any and every situation, whether well fed or hungry, whether living in plenty or in want. I can do everything through Him who gives me strength.

Philippians 4:12–13

Content in any situation—in today's world, this seems a little hard to digest. With horrible tragedies happening all around us, we sometimes wonder where God is in this world and why he would let such bad things happen to good people. The thing is, our lives are just a very small piece of a huge undertaking by God to save a whole human race from a fallen world of sin. We can only see one small part of this extraordinary movement of God's Spirit, and our small minds can't even begin to understand or comprehend the mysteries of God. One thing that I know for sure is that God is in control and that if you have given your life to him then his Spirit lives inside of you and he will indeed carry you through absolutely anything that you encounter in this life on earth! We are not going to understand everything about this life until we get to heaven. The good news is that we don't need to! We are not God and we do not call the shots. Our life is just a very small piece of clay in an awesome sculpture that God is designing to last for all eternity.

So whatever it is that you are facing today, be encouraged! If God is at the helm, then you can indeed do all things through him! I don't know what your situation is, but I do know that if you trust in him with all of your heart, then he will pass along to you a peace that passes all understanding and a joy and strength that will carry you through everything that you encounter in this short time that we have here on this earth. Remember it is his strength, not ours, his power and direction in our lives that moves us forward. Maybe today you just need to rest in the palm of his hand and let the Almighty God comfort and protect you with his indescribable love!

GODLY LIVING

Only let us live up to what we have already attained.

Philippians 3:16

Hear this: God's Word does you absolutely no good unless you put into action the lessons that are learned while diving into this most awesome instruction book for life! God speaks of his Word in the book of Hebrews, saying: "For the word of God is living and active. Sharper than any double-edged sword, it penetrates even to dividing soul and spirit, joints and marrow; it judges the thoughts and attitudes of the heart" (Hebrews 4:12). God's Word can change your heart and mind back to how God meant them to be from the start before they were tainted by this world of sin. There is no better feeling than having your heart, mind, and spirit in sync with God's Spirit, really living and experiencing God's best for your life! This, however, will never happen unless you choose to let God change you through his Word by obeying what he says! As Michael W. Smith says in his book and song, "Live the life"! Don't put if off any longer! The enemy will deceive you by letting you think that there will be plenty of time to live your life for the Lord. Don't believe his lies, he is just trying to keep you from really experiencing a great and fulfilling life on this earth. Take that step of faith today and put into action what God is teaching you through his Word. Trust me that when you do this, you will see the power of God revealed in your life and you will be overcome with joy, fulfillment, peace, and love like nothing that you have ever experienced before!

Don't procrastinate any longer—start the journey of godly living today.

GODLY ROLE MODELS

Join with others in following my example, brothers, and take note of those who live according to the pattern we gave you. For, as I have often told you before and now say again even with tears, many live as enemies of the cross of Christ. Their destiny is destruction, their God is their stomach, and their glory is in their shame. Their mind is on earthly things. But our citizenship is in heaven. And we eagerly await a Savior from there, the Lord Jesus Christ, who, by the power that enables him to bring everything under his control, will transform our lowly bodies so that they will be like his glorious body.

Philippians 4:17–21

In this world of multi-million-dollar athletes, entertainers, and businessmen, who do you take note of? Are you looking to godly men and women to be your mentor and role model, or do you secretly admire those whose appetites are consuming their lives? Are you looking up to men and women of strong character and righteousness or men and women that are heading for death and destruction? Don't be fooled, there is a spiritual war that is taking place all around us, and as Paul describes here in the text, even today there are many that live as enemies to the Cross of Christ. The attitude of "just have fun" and "if it feels good, do it" prevails in our world today. The self-centered idealism of looking out for number one (self) and living this life with the freedom to do as you wish is indeed the "glory" of many worldly role models today. The problem with our world is that there are not that many committed Christians that are "living the life," walking with Christ, empowered by his Spirit and relentlessly pressing on to be transformed by the same power that raised Jesus Christ from the dead. Or, if there are, we rarely see or hear of them since speaking of such people is not popular press in our fallen world of sin. Each one of us should be looking for a godly role model to teach and mentor us in our walk with the Lord. Then, ultimately, we should be striving to return the blessing and to be a man or woman of God that others can take note of and look up to and strive to be like. Although there is only one perfect role model—Jesus Christ—today, people need to see that same Jesus living in and through our very lives, being a servant, teaching, loving, and giving to all around us that are in need!

Pray today that God will provide for you a godly role model that can be a teacher and mentor to you in this life on earth. Pray also that God will begin to transform your life so that indeed you can be an example for others to look up to in the coming years.

RESTING IN GOD'S PROVISION

Unless the Lord builds the house,
its builders labor in vain.
Unless the Lord watches over the city,
the watchmen stand guard in vain.
In vain you rise early
and stay up late,
toiling for food to eat—for He grants sleep to those he loves.

Psalm 127:1–2

It saddens my heart to see so many people in America wasting their lives away to attain worldly riches that do nothing to satisfy the emptiness of their lives. All that God asks us to do here on this earth is to work reasonable hours that are prayerfully committed to the work that he wants to accomplish in and through our lives. If we work as if we are working for him, then we can truly rest in the midst of that work and not have to worry about the resulting pay, since he promises to provide all of our needs. Jesus himself says in the book of Matthew 6:31–33: "So do not worry, saying, what shall we eat? or what shall we wear? For the pagans run after all of these things, and your heavenly Father knows that you need them. But seek first His Kingdom and His righteousness, and all these things will be given to you as well." There are many people who work their entire lives and miss out on the many blessing that God would have for them if they would just have committed their lives and worked for him first! God loves you more than you can imagine and he wants to bless your life in ways that are indescribable and unfathomable! All that he asks in return is that you rest in his provision for your life, committing all that you do to him, for his glory. Seek the Lord today with all of your heart, and your life will be filled with blessings from above that are much more valuable than anything that you could ever attain on your own. You will have a peace that passes all understanding and will truly be able to rest in the arms of our loving Father!

Thank you, God, that we can rest in you today, knowing that you will provide our every need if indeed we seek you first above everything else!

HOLY LIVING WITHOUT DISCOURAGEMENT

Therefore, prepare your minds for action; be self-controlled; set your hope fully on the grace to be given you when Jesus Christ is revealed. As obedient children, do not conform to the evil desires you had when you lived in ignorance. But just as he who called you is holy, so be holy in all you do; for it is written: "Be holy, because I am holy."

1 Peter 1:13–16

Earlier in this first chapter of Peter, Peter talks of suffering grief and going through all kinds of trials here on this earth so that our faith in Jesus Christ may be proved genuine. Some of these trials we may pass through with flying colors and others may distract us just a bit from this race of faith that we are running here in our short time on this earth. After reading this text I am convinced that there is only one way that we as Christians can continually pick ourselves up, brush off the dust, and press on to live a life that is holy and pleasing to God. As Peter says so eloquently here in the text, that way is to "set your hope fully on the grace to be given you when Jesus Christ is revealed." We must only trust in one thing, and that is the power of God that is given to us through his most amazing sacrifice on the Cross and the grace that covers us because of this sacrifice. We must not trust in our own abilities, talents, knowledge, wisdom, strength, finances, friends, job, etc. There is truly only one thing that can give us the confidence to continue on and grow in our walk with the Lord, and that is this living hope that one day we will indeed be perfected in him and the promise that up until then, his grace covers us when we fail. That battle for holy living starts in the mind! Peter tells us here to prepare our minds for action. The good news is that there is nothing that can separate us from the faith that we have been given! We are sealed with the blood of Jesus Christ, eternally secure; there is nothing that we can do to lose this most awesome gift of salvation that God has given us! So the battle is already won—we already have victory over sin in this life. With that knowledge, it is much easier to strive each and every day to live a holy life that is pleasing to the Lord since ultimately we cannot fail! Yes, because of our fleshly nature we may lose various battles and suffer the consequences for our sin; however, we have already been given everything that we need in order to live a life that is holy and blameless before our heavenly Father.

So today be encouraged! Forget you past failures and set your minds on him. Hope in him. Let his Spirit control your actions and give you the power to live a holy life, full of joy and love, ready to be used by the God of this universe to make a difference in this world today—all for the glory of God!

PEER PRESSURE

Therefore, since Christ suffered in his body, arm yourselves also with the same attitude, because he who has suffered in his body is done with sin. As a result, he does not live the rest of his earthly life for evil human desires, but rather for the will of God. For you have spent enough time in the past doing what pagans choose to do—living in debauchery, lust, drunkenness, orgies, carousing and detestable idolatry. They think it strange that you do not plunge with them into the same flood of dissipation, and they heap abuse on you. But they will have to give account to him who is ready to judge the living and the dead. For this is the reason the gospel was preached even to those who are now dead, so that they might be judged according to men in regard to the body, but live according to God in regard to the spirit.

1 Peter 4:1–6

If you are a Christian and are trying to live a godly life, there will be other people that will ridicule and not accept you because you are living your life for God. Do not be surprised or discouraged when this happens. Be ready and prepared for this kind of ridicule in the world. There is a spiritual battle happening all around us and Satan wants more than anything else to shame you into going back to living your life "for evil human desires rather than for the will of God." Be encouraged when this ridicule comes, as you must be making a difference for Christ since people are noticing the change in your life! One day all of us will indeed have to give an account to God for our own actions on this earth. We are all responsible for our own actions; there is no peer pressure defense in the court of God's judgment. When all is said and done, be sure that you can lift up your clean hands to our heavenly Father and profess that you gave him your life, lived by his Spirit, denied yourself daily, and let God control your actions and influence your decisions rather than other people on this earth!

Nobody is perfect, and we all will fail at times. All that God asks of us is that we ask his forgiveness when we do fail and then turn back to him with all of our hearts and let his Spirit be in control of our lives once more. Don't be afraid of other people; live your life today for our heavenly Father and he will comfort, protect, and fill your life with an indescribable peace, joy, and love!

SPIRITUAL MILK

Like newborn babies, crave pure spiritual milk, so that by it you may grow up in your salvation, now that you have tasted that the Lord is good.

1 Peter 2:2–3

Over the years I have met several people that claim to be Christians and to know our Lord and Savior Jesus Christ; however, they say that they are not involved in a local church fellowship or do not read the Bible regularly. They have no apparent craving for the spiritual milk of God's Word and fellowship with other believers. One would have to wonder after meeting such a person if that person had indeed "tasted that the Lord is good—if, indeed, that person had surrendered his heart to God and experienced his most awesome power, grace, and love in his life. I have had the privilege of tasting what it is like to experience God here on this earth, and I don't know how someone could have truly tasted his presence in his life and not crave for more!

From the very core of our souls, this relationship with God is what we have been seeking our entire lives! Like a newborn baby desperately crying for milk in order to survive, there are people in this world that are desperately crying from the emptiness of their hearts and trying to fill that void in their lives with other things that will never satisfy, fulfill, or give them life! It is only God that can truly satisfy our cravings through a relationship with his Son Jesus Christ. When you have truly tasted this, you will have a craving, hunger, and a burning desire for more of him in your life—a desire to read more of his Word, a desire to fellowship with more of his people, and a desire to share this newly found life with other people who are lost.

Do you have this craving? Have you tasted that the Lord is good? If not then you need to truly surrender your heart and life to him today. Pray a prayer right now and seek his forgiveness for your sins, accept him into your heart and life, and you will see that this relationship with Jesus Christ is really what you have been searching for your entire life!

ROYAL PRIESTHOOD

But you are a chosen people, a royal priesthood, a holy nation, a people belonging to God, that you may declare the praises of him who called you out of darkness into his wonderful light. Once you were not a people, but now you are the people of God; once you had not received mercy, but now you have received mercy.

1 Peter 2:9–10

Back in the Old Testament times, it was through a priest that God would communicate and make amends to all of his followers. When Jesus Christ died on the Cross for our sins and then rose again on the third day, a miraculous thing happened—God's Spirit could now enter the lives of all the people that accept this sacrifice, making us all a royal priesthood, since God communicates and works in and through our lives directly. If you have accepted Jesus Christ into your heat, then you have not only been forgiven and have eternal life, but Jesus himself is living inside of you and wants to communicate and reach other people through your very life! Knowing this should make a dramatic difference in how you live your life today! In 1 Corinthians 3:16, Paul says this: "Don't you know that yourselves are God's temple and that God's Spirit lives in you?" Your body is the holy temple of God's Spirit, and you have been chosen to represent God to other people on this earth who don't believe or know or have a relationship with our amazing Savior. Knowing that, how will you live your life today? Will you wallow in self-pity and defeat, complaining and arguing with your fellow coworkers and friends, or will you tap into the power that God has already given you by his Spirit and reach out lovingly with a servant's heart to those around you, being well aware that they need to know this most amazing God who is living inside of you? God is calling you to make a difference in this world. He has chosen you and set you apart to be his instrument to use right where you are, right now, today! Will you answer his call?

Pray now that God would give you the strength to deny yourself and live for him today, declaring his praises indeed to those around you!

Go now in his power and make a difference in your world for him!

BEAUTY FROM WITHIN

Wives, in the same way, be submissive to your husbands so that, if any of them do not believe the word, they may be won over without words by the behavior of their wives, when they see the purity and reverence of your lives. You beauty should not come from outward adornment, such as braided hair and the wearing of gold jewelry and fine clothes. Instead, it should be that of your inner-self, the unfading beauty of a gentle and quiet spirit, which is of great worth in God's sight. For this is the way the holy women of the past who put their hope in God used to make themselves beautiful. They were submissive to their own husbands, like Sarah, who obeyed Abraham and called him her master. You are her daughters if you do what is right and do not give way to fear.

1 Peter 3:1–6

To understand this passage we need to look back just for a minute at the end of chapter 2. At the end of chapter 2, Peter is describing Jesus' obedience and sacrifice on the Cross. He says in verse 22–23, "He committed no sin, and no deceit was found in His mouth. When they hurled insults at him, he did not retaliate; when he suffered, he made no threats. Instead He entrusted Himself to Him who judges justly." How beautiful is that? God himself in the flesh, being beaten, ridiculed, spit on, and eventually dying the most humiliating death on a cross, all of this because of his love for us! He did not have to take any of that; at any time he could have proved to everyone that he was God and wiped out all of those that were hurling insults and mocking him, but he didn't. He didn't say a word because he knew what needed to be done in order for us to live together with him in eternity!

We live in a world that teaches us that if you have enough money, you too can be beautiful. Our world is running rampant with huge money being spent on fashion, plastic surgery, reality shows of the rich and famous—all of this, and the divorce rate is the highest it is has ever been. People today are spending all of their time, money, and energy on external beauty and in the end they are even less beautiful than when they began since true beauty, as Peter describes here in this controversial text, comes flowing outward from your heart. "The unfading beauty of a gentle and quiet spirit"—there is nothing more beautiful than seeing the love of a godly woman who has surrendered her whole heart to God Almighty and is living her life for him, reflecting his love to all of those around her!

Pray now that God would continue to mold and shape you to become more like him in order that your inner beauty of his Spirit would continue to shine brightly to those that you love.

RIGHTEOUS LIVING

Finally, all of you, live in harmony with one another; be sympathetic, love as brothers, be compassionate and humble. Do not repay evil with evil or insult with insult, but with blessing, because to this you were called so that you may inherit a blessing. For whoever would love life and see good days must keep his tongue from evil and his lips from deceitful speech. He must turn from evil and do good; he must seek peace and pursue it. For the eyes of the Lord are on the righteous and his ears are attentive to their prayer, but the face of the Lord is against those who do evil.

1 Peter 3:8–12

Just imagine what our world would be like, what your family or relationships would be like, what your church would be like, if we could really bless and love those who insult us and not gossip about them or want to cause them any harm! In my lifetime, I have seen bitterness and gossip toward others actually tear apart family relationships that have yet to be restored. It saddens my heart to see the face of the Lord against people, many of whom profess to be Christians who do not live righteous lives because of pride. The bitterness that is in their hearts eventually eats away at them and they live miserable lives all because of their refusal to surrender to God with all of their hearts by loving others unconditionally with his love, no matter what they have done!

Just look at our world today—we have Christians killing other people in the name of God, and giving abortions. We have siblings that do not talk to each other, parents that do not communicate with their children, close friends that are torn apart to be enemies, political parties that distort and confuse world catastrophes just to create even more of an uproar in the world than was caused by the catastrophe itself. Should not our focus as Christians be on God and our energy spent on loving people with his love no matter what they have done, hoping that as a result of our obedience they too would know our Lord and Savior Jesus Christ? God answers the prayers of those of us who obey him and do his will. Those people who pursue peace and live in harmony, are compassionate and humble; it is these people that God blesses in this life beyond belief!

You have a choice today to live for God and love people unconditionally or to give in to your own pride and try to repay others for what they have done to you. If you choose the first, then God will hear your prayers and give you peace and blessings in this life that are beyond belief. If you choose the latter, God's face will be against you, and you will reap the bitterness and strife of your own actions. Others are watching how you will respond today. What will they see? Will they see God's Spirit alive in your life by witnessing the unimaginable act of unconditional love and finally believe in him, or will they see just another person blending into this sinful, fallen world in which we live?

Be an example for God. Let others see him for who he really is by the unconditional love that you show to others!

GOOD THINGS COME FROM GOD

Keep me safe, O God, for in you I take refuge.
I said to the Lord, "You are my Lord; apart from you I have
no good thing."
As for the saints who are in the land,
they are the glorious ones in whom is all my delight.
The sorrows of those will increase
who run after other Gods.

Psalm 16:1–4

For those of us that take refuge in him, God keeps us safe and gives us many good things here on this earth, such as peace and joy, love and fulfillment; good things such as relationships with other believers in whom we can truly delight. Unless you have had such a relationship, you will not be able to understand the joy that comes from them; in fact, it may seem weird to outsiders looking in. When you have really sold your heart out to Jesus Christ, and then you have trusted another believer enough to partner with you in this commitment, it is like the two spirits connect and there is bond and a love that is genuine and real like nothing else on this earth! To take refuge in the Lord means to stay connected to him in our minds and in our hearts through his Word and through our relationships and fellowship with other believers. As much as Satan wants you to believe that all this God stuff is a farce and that it is things of this world that will truly fulfill you and make you happy, as we see in this verse here, the reality is that those things will only increase your sorrow and emptiness that you feel. As Christians, we need to stay connected with God by spending time with him each day through reading his Word and through prayer, and then by focusing our minds and hearts continually on him and his principles throughout the day. Secondly, we need to stay connected to his people through regular fellowship and transparent relationships that help us grow together in him. Apart from these two things, in this life is no good thing, just worldly things that are really other gods after whom we run, bringing us more sorrow and disappointment in this life!

Have you surrendered your heart completely to God? Are you taking refuge in him each day by reading his Word? Do you have relationships with other believers that are real, in which you can discuss things of the Lord—other people of God who encourage you in your faith with him and help you grow? When your faith is tested, will it prove to be real and genuine? Let me tell you from personal experience that there is nothing in this world that can fulfill you more, bring you more joy, or bring you more good things than having a heart that is truly sold out to Jesus Christ!

Live you life for him today!

GOD'S TIMING, NOT OURS

I am still confident of this:
I will see the goodness of the Lord in the land of the living.
Wait for the Lord;
be strong and take heart and wait for the Lord.

Psalm 27:13–14

Coming from a broken home and having to make my own way in life at an early age gave me a self-starter attitude toward life. "Wait" does not seem to be a word in my vocabulary; it ranks right up there with "patience" in my fleshly attitudes and perspectives on the way that one should live. Being a salesman with a type A personality does not help matters either. America teaches phrases at an early age like: "You are in control of your own destiny," and "You can do anything that you put your mind to." It is no wonder that many of us have a problem trusting God to do the work in our lives and in other people's lives and waiting on his perfect timing and providence. There are people that are very close to me that I want to see have the same relationship with God that I have been blessed with. I want them more than anything to experience the fulfillment, joy, peace, and love that Christ gives so freely. I want to be sure that they will be with me in eternity when we will do nothing but enjoy God's blessings and provisions together forever! Because of this desire, there are times when I try to control the situation with my own flesh. When this happens it almost always does nothing to help other people develop a deeper relationship with God, but on the contrary, it drives them farther from it, leaving a bad taste in their mouths toward Christianity.

Maybe, just maybe, God is working on my heart in the midst of these seemingly unanswered prayers. Maybe he is teaching me to love unconditionally, just as he has loved me all of these years.

Maybe God is teaching me to trust completely in him for everything in this life and not to depend on my own talents and abilities. Ultimately, it is God that is in control! He is the painter of this masterpiece of his Kingdom that he is painting and knows how and when all of the colors will fit together to form the most beautiful picture for all to enjoy at the end of this world, when all of his people are joined together in his glory for ever and ever!

Remember one thing today: it is only God that can change a heart! Trust in him today; wait on him to do the work in your life and through you life to make a difference in the world for him.

ABOVE ALL, LOVE DEEPLY

The end of all things is near. Therefore be clear minded and self-controlled so that you can pray. Above all, love each other deeply, because love covers over a multitude of sins.

1 Peter 7–8

If Christ were to return today, would he be pleased with your attitudes, actions, and relationships? Peter is warning us here that Christ could come back at any time and that we should live our lives just as if he is coming back today! The signs of the end times are all around us. There has been disaster after disaster, talk of one world government, rebuilding of the temple, you name it—the Bible prophesies of the end of the world seem to be happening all around us. Knowing this, what do we do? Do we go and hide? No! We should surrender to God our whole heart and mind and pray for people that we know are not saved that God would rescue them from eternal damnation. We should flee from sin and keep ourselves clean so that God can indeed hear our prayers. And above all else, as Peter says here, we should love each other deeply! Other people should see God's love in our lives as we love each other with an unconditional love that brings joy and comfort to everyone that we encounter. When God's love is present in your life, there is no bitterness, no hatred, and no self-serving attitude. There is a servanthood type of attitude that loves people unconditionally, no matter what they have done to you or how bad they have hurt you. It is a love that is all powerful and pierces deep to the soul of all that experience it. It has the power to bring healing and forgiveness; the power to mend broken relationships of the past that you thought would never be healed.

This is the love that God has given you and that He is calling you to pass on to others. It is time to stop thinking of your self and to enter in to God's way of living while you still have time. God needs you to be a vessel that He can use to reach others for Him! God wants to give you a life that is fulfilling and full of joy and excitement like you have never experienced before! In order to receive this love and experience this abundant life in him, you need to give up your own fleshly desires that are keeping you in the self-serving pit of despair that you are in. Pray now and give everything to God. Ask him to fill you with his love. Live you life today as if it is your last and you are going to stand before Almighty God tomorrow and give an account for how you treated this amazing love that he entrusted to you. Give it away today. Let others see God for who he really is in your life that they may believe and be saved!

BEWARE OF THE ENEMY

Be self-controlled and alert. Your enemy the devil prowls around like a roaring lion looking for someone to devour. Resist him, standing firm in the faith, because you know that your brothers throughout the world are undergoing the same kind of sufferings.

1 Peter 8–9

Make no mistake, Satan is real and there is a spiritual realm of angels and demons all around us that are fighting for our hearts and minds! Those of us that have accepted Christ have already won the war and are eternally secure; however, Satan wants more than anything to steal our joy and to put us on the injured reserve list in our efforts to make a difference in the world for Jesus Christ. As a Christian who has spent many years in the past consumed in my own fleshly desires, I can tell you that whatever sin he is enticing you with (and he knows the one that will make you fall), whatever that is, the satisfaction that it brings does not even come close to comparing to the fulfilling and abundant life that comes from living a holy life that is pleasing to God! The battle starts in the mind, so beware of the thoughts and images that you feed your heart. The Bible tells us to take every thought captive and to fill our minds with the Word of God so that we will have weapons to fight off the enemy and resist him. God promises not to tempt us beyond what we can bare, but at the end of the day we still have the freedom to choose. We have the freedom to choose to deny ourselves and stand strong in him or to take the bait that Satan is waving in front of our face and to fall back to our old ways. I ask you today to be strong and to choose life! Choose life in him that is full of peace and joy, love and power. Do not let the enemy get a foothold and render you useless for the work of the Lord. Resist him and he will flee! Be attentive to his trickery and run the other direction! There is something much bigger going on in this world that we can see with our eyes. There is a story playing out in which you are one of the main characters that God wants to use in a mighty way! Remain in him—resist the devil, and God will use you in this story to do amazing things in this fallen world for him!

PROACTIVE CHRISTIANITY

For this reason, make every effort to add to your faith goodness; and to goodness, knowledge; and to knowledge, self-control; and to self-control, perseverance; and to perseverance, Godliness; and to Godliness, brotherly kindness; and to brotherly kindness, love. For if you possess these qualities in increasing measure, they will keep you from being ineffective and unproductive in your knowledge of our Lord Jesus Christ.

2 Peter 1:5–8

Do you want to be used by God? Do you want to experience his divine power in your life? Do you want to be filled with his amazing peace and joy and rest in his most precious unconditional love and comfort? No problem! If you have accepted Jesus Christ as your personal Savior, then God has given you everything that you need to be complete in him and experience all of these great things in this present life! The key to godly living is to be proactive and intentional concerning your faith. Peter describes here in his second book the actions that we need to take as Christians to fully experience God in our lives! He says that we first need to practice goodness, which the footnotes of the NIV Study Bible describe as "excellence expressed in deeds—virtue in action." This means acting out the faith that you have through acts of kindness and virtue. Next, add to these good deeds the knowledge of God. How do you attain knowledge? By going to church, reading your Bible, listening to godly teaching programs, and learning from Christian friends and mentors. This knowledge will teach you about the spiritual war that you are in and how desperately important it is for you to be self-controlled and to persevere by denying your old sinful desires and choosing to let God control your mind, life, and actions. Godliness is the next step and, as the footnotes describe, is a "genuine reverence toward God that governs one's attitude toward every aspect of life." Make God the very essence of why you get out of bed in the morning and why you do everything that you do throughout the day. Next is having "warmhearted affection toward all in the family of faith." And finally is the call to love, which is the ultimate self-sacrifice of your own needs and desires for the good of others. The cool thing is that because of God's Spirit living inside of us, we have the power to experience all of this in our lives and even more! It is your choice to live the abundant life that Christ has freely given you by taking action to grow and become more like him or to do nothing and continue to live a powerless, ineffective, and unproductive life here on this earth.

Pray now that God would give you the opportunity today to be intentional about your faith and open a door for you to walk through, finally taking action to grow and become more like him!

SLAVE OF RIGHTEOUSNESS

They promise them freedom, while they themselves are slaves of depravity—for a man is a slave to whatever has mastered him.

2 Peter 2:19

In his second book here, Peter is giving us a warning concerning false teachers that will be present in the end times. He is describing their teaching of how moral depravity is okay and how they will be teaching that one can attain freedom from moral discipline and God's law. His point is that because these godless people are consumed in their own fleshly, sinful desires, there is indeed no freedom, but only slavery to those very desires. They are slaves to their own guilt and unhealthy consequences of their sinful ways. They are and will be mastered by the sin that has consumed their lives.

Doesn't it sound much better to be a slave of righteousness? To have your life consumed by God's Spirit, acting out his purpose for your life, filled with the joy, peace, and love that comes with surrendering your whole heart to God? Now that is my kind of slavery! This sounds much better than having your life consumed by sin and carrying around the burden of guilt and shame and living with the deadly consequences. You see, the only reason that God has laws for us to obey here on this earth is because he wants to protect us from ourselves, from our own fleshly desires, and from this fallen world of sin. He wants us to live an abundant life here on this earth! He wants to give you a joy and peace, love and purpose that are like nothing else that you have ever experienced before! The only way to really experience all that he has to offer is to let him be the Lord of your life and the master of everything that you do. He died to make it all possible.

What are you a slave to? What have you allowed to master your life? What do you think about the most throughout your day? Isn't it time for you to truly surrender your whole heart to God and start living this abundant life in him that finally satisfies and completely fulfills what your heart has been searching for all this time? Pray now and ask God to be the Lord of your life; commit everything that you are, everything that you have, and everything that you hope to be to him today and don't look back. This will be the best decision that you have ever made.

BETTER DAYS AHEAD

But the day of the Lord will come like a thief. The heavens will disappear with a roar; the elements will be destroyed by fire, and the earth and everything in it will be laid bare. Since everything will be destroyed in this way, what kind of people ought you to be? You ought to live holy and godly lives as you look forward to the day of God and speed its coming. That day will bring about the destruction of the heavens by fire, and the elements will melt in the heat. But in keeping with His promise we are looking forward to a new heaven and a new earth, the home of righteousness.

2 Peter 3:10–13

As I sat at the funeral of an awesome man of God recently and saw the pain and suffering of his loved ones, I couldn't help but stir with anger with this fallen world of sin. As the pastor at the funeral said, "This is not how this world is supposed to be." He is so right. Some days the only comfort that we have to hold on to as we live our lives here on this earth is the hope of better days ahead—the hope and promise of a new heaven and a new earth when we will finally be at perfect communion with our Lord and Savior Jesus Christ and we will once again be united with the entire family of God to fellowship and worship together, enjoying God's presence and love for the rest of eternity! The good news is that this day could come at any time! It could happen today, tomorrow, the next day—nobody knows that exact date when this earth and everything in it will be destroyed and we will stand before God Almighty and give an account for how we lived our lives here on this earth. Are you ready? Will you be able to stand before God like our good friend Mario did just days ago and tell him that you had accepted his sacrifice that he freely gave to you by making him the Lord of your life and that you lived your life for him and are therefore are sealed by his blood for the rest of eternity? Or will you stand before the God of this world and hear him say the words, "I never knew you, away from me you evil doers"? (Matthew 7:23).

Be ready for the better days ahead! If you don't have a relationship with Jesus Christ, then start one today before it is too late! Ask him into your heart, accept his forgiveness for your sins, and then start living your life for him!

LIGHTHOUSE OF FAITH

To Him who is able to keep you from falling and to present you before His glorious presence without fault and with great joy—to the only God our savior be glory, majesty, power and authority, through Jesus Christ our Lord, before all ages, now and forevermore! Amen.

Jude 24–25

What a beautiful picture of the only true goal, focus, prize, reward, whatever you would like to call it, the never-changing and magnificent guidepost for us that is always there to direct our paths in this life. A doxology to the one and only Savior who protects us from this evil world of sin and will carry us through to the very end when he will present us before God in all of his glory with joy and purity, all as a result of the sacrifice that he made for us that we gladly accepted! The picture of a lighthouse directing a boat to the shore is indeed a great analogy of what our focus should be like on this earth as we focus on Jesus Christ, the only true light that can direct our paths and keep us from falling! This doxology comes at the end of the book of Jude, which warns believers to be aware of false teachers and ungodly men that chase after their own evil desires in the last days. There is really only one way to be sure to not be deceived, and that is to keep your focus on Jesus Christ and let him and his Spirit direct your path in this life. He is alive! He is real! He wants the very best for you in this life and wants you to be with him forever, eternally. He wants to have a relationship with you, be your best friend, and fill you with great joy, satisfaction, and love like you have never experienced before!

Focus on him today. Give him your heart and your life!

NO FEAR

Since the children have flesh and blood, he too shared in their humanity so that by his death he might destroy him who holds the power of
death—that is, the devil—and free those who all their lives were held
in slavery by their fear of death.

Hebrews 2:14–15

There is no need to fear today, for God is victorious, the battle is
won, Satan is defeated, and if you have given your heart to Jesus
Christ then you too will live on forever in eternity with him! God
became a man—just like us, our own flesh and blood—and then he
sacrificed himself and died a terrible, most humiliating death on
a cross all because he loved you and me so much and wants to be
with us forever. The key to living a joyful, fulfilling life today is to
let Jesus Christ, who is alive and well, consume your very soul and
be the reason that you live your life today. He wants the very best
for you and me. He wants to be the focus of your attention and love,
the direction and motivation for living today. Don't be deceived by
the enemy today—although he can tempt you and grab your attention away from God at weaker moments in your life, he has lost the
war for your heart! The enemy's goal is to trick you into wasting
your life here on this earth and not experiencing God's best that is
here for the taking. Do not believe him! What he has to offer does
not even compare to the greatness of living your life for Jesus Christ
and resting in his unconditional love and peace! After all of that
pain, suffering, and humiliation just so that he could be a part of
our lives forever, doesn't he deserve our utmost attention and devotion today? Give it a try. Surrender your heart. Live for him today
and you will have no fear; you will have a reason for living and a
friendship that will last for all eternity!

HEARTS OF CLAY

See to it, brothers, that none of you has a sinful, unbelieving heart that turns away from the living God. But encourage one another daily, as long as it is called today, so that none of you may be hardened by sin's deceitfulness. We have come to share in Christ if we hold firmly till the end the confidence we had at first.

Hebrews 3:12–14

I am not schooled on the art of pottery; however, I would assume that as long as the clay is being worked by the sculptor, then it will stay soft and be able to be shaped into whatever the artist has planned. I would think that once the clay is not being worked on, then it would eventually become hard and unworkable. Daily, as we confess our sins to the living God and commit our way to him, we can feel the softening of our hearts that allows God's unfailing love to enter our lives and continue to shape our hearts into the masterpiece of righteousness that he is creating in our very lives. And when we confess our weaknesses to other believers in Christ, our hearts are softened even more, making them like fresh clay that is workable and shapeable for our Lord. God is not asking us to be perfect in this Scripture here. He is just asking us to admit our failures, learn from our mistakes, and then to press on in this race toward holiness. For it is when we give up and turn completely the other direction from God that our hearts are hardened and deemed unworkable and unshapeable by the Creator. So today, confess your sins and start afresh this awesome life we are called to live! Let our Redeemer's sacrifice make you whole and let his grace and unfailing love give you the peace and confidence to once again live your life for him and make a difference in this world in which we live!

SUPERNATURAL LIFE CHANGE

He said to them, "Go into all the world and preach the good news to all creation. Whoever believes and is baptized will be saved, but whoever does not believe will be condemned. And these signs will accompany those who believe: In my name they will drive out demons; they will speak in new tongues; they will pick up snakes with their hands; and when they drink deadly poison, it will not hurt them at all; they will place their hands on sick people, and they will get well."

Mark 16:15–18

Well, I am not sure that some of these activities are very relevant in today's culture, but whatever you believe about this passage, one thing that I know for sure is that when you have accepted Jesus Christ as your personal Savior, you will have a life change. If your commitment to Christ was real, then there should be evidence of him living inside of you by the way that you live your life. Your actions should be different from those around you that do not know Christ. He will begin to change you from the inside out. Your priorities will change, the things that make you happy will change, your purpose for living will change—the core of who you are will be supernaturally changed back to what God had originally planned for you from the beginning before sin entered the world. Jesus will make you more like hm in order that other people will see hs Spirit living inside of you and believe.

Is this supernatural life change happening in your life? Have you made the decision to accept Christ into your life and let him mold and shape you for the better? Are you making decisions now based on your faith in God rather than what other people think or what the popular opinion of the day is? Can the world see evidence of Jesus living inside of you? If not, then it is not too late to make that commitment and to enter a whole new world of life with Christ that will last for all eternity. Accept this awesome gift of Jesus into your heart. Pray to God right now in the quietness of your own heart and ask him in. Start living out the real meaning of life today!

LONELY HOLIDAY

At the sixth hour darkness came over the whole land until the ninth hour. And at the ninth hour Jesus cried out in a loud voice, "Eloi, Eloi, lama sabachthani?" —Which means, "My God, my God, why have you forsaken me?"

Mark 15:33–34

The studies show that during the Christmas holiday there are more people that struggle with loneliness than at any other time throughout the year. There are many people who feel like they have been forsaken by God because of a loss of a loved one or loss of a friend or job or hope for the future. There are many people that feel lonely or forsaken because they have no one to share the holiday with. For many, the holiday may bring back memories of an abusive parent or spouse or may be a reminder of a love they once had but lost. The Christmas holiday awakens the senses, it seems, since people switch gears, if only for one day, and think of others instead of themselves. Therein lies the problem for some of you who may feel like you have no one to share the holiday with.

My wife is especially sensitive around this time of year since our family is 500 miles away and we rarely have the opportunity to celebrate the holiday with them. Maybe the same is true for you. Well, let me encourage you today by reminding you that you are not alone! In fact, there is one who suffered much more than you could ever imagine and who experienced loneliness in its rawest form as God the Father did indeed look away from him as he suffered and died on the Cross, paying the penalty for my sin and your sin all by himself. I know that you are not alone because this same man is alive today in the hearts of his people, and you too can experience this awesome companionship and relationship with the Son of God all because of his willingness to suffer for you. His name is

Jesus Christ and he is the reason that we celebrate this Christmas holiday, and he will bring you great joy and comfort, even in the midst of your loneliness, if you would just look to him today for healing and comfort and companionship and love. For that is the only reason that he was born on Christmas day and that he gave his life many years later—all because of his desire to have a relationship with you and to fill your empty heart for the rest of eternity. Seek him today and let your lonely heart be filled with love!

HIDDEN TREASURE FROM GOD

When the angels had left them and gone into heaven, the shepherds said to one another, "Let's go to Bethlehem and see this thing that has happened, which the Lord has told us about." So they hurried off and found Mary and Joseph, and the baby, who was lying in the manger. When they had seen him, they spread the word concerning what had been told about this child, and all who heard it were amazed at what the shepherds said to them. But Mary treasured up all these things and pondered them in her heart.

Luke 2:15–19

When Mary was first told about what was about to happen to her life and how she was going to be used by God, she must have been terrified and a little uncertain as to the narrow road that she was about to take. I am sure that she suffered much ridicule and humiliation since being pregnant out of marriage in those days was more than frowned upon than it is in our day; it was a major infraction and one who did such a thing was considered an outcast to society. But look here at the end result: she has been blessed tremendously by God as a result of her obedience to him. Her joy and satisfaction for giving birth to the King of kings and Lord of lords is like a hidden treasure that is found deep within her heart; it is a treasure that no one can ever take away and a treasure that completes a person's soul and gives him a reason for living and a joy and fulfillment in this life that will last for all eternity!

What is God asking you to do today that may seem a little frightening to you? What is he asking you to do that may cause you a little discomfort or may cause you to totally trust in him for the outcome? Whatever it is, know that there is a hidden treasure at the end of your journey that is a blessing from God. This blessing will be well worth your obedience to him in that it is what you have been searching for your whole life. You will have joy and fulfillment, love and peace; you will be transformed even more to the likeness of your Creator and will have a purpose and meaning in this life if only you would set aside your fears and trust and obey God Almighty today. Don't miss out on God's best for your life. Seek him today with all of your heart and all of your mind—take that step of faith toward him and find the hidden treasure of life that is only found in total surrender to Jesus Christ!

GOD'S GIFT: NEW LIFE IN CHRIST

In Him was life, and that life was the light of men.

John 1:4

Before creation, before sin entered the world, before the world was even created, there was God the Father, God the Son, and God the Holy Spirit—the Trinity where there existed perfect unity, perfect relationship, and perfect life with God. And then, God created man in his image and the perfect relationship continued, life was found in the Father, and the relationship between man and God was illuminating and pure and excellent.

And then sin entered the world and that perfect relationship was destroyed. So, what we celebrate at Christmas is the solution to the separation from God that was caused by sin. What we celebrate is God's gift of his Son to us to take our place and pay the penalty for our sin so that our relationship with God could be restored, once and for all, to perfect unity once more. And so that is the miracle of Christmas—the gift of Jesus Christ whom you and I can now accept into our lives and as a result experience a new life with Christ that will be made perfect and complete when we leave this earth and live forever with him in heaven.

But even now, even here as we learn to live with him on earth in the midst of this fallen world, we can have a small taste of what this perfect relationship with God is like. We can have a small taste of the peace and joy that it brings, the power and love that comes with being reunited with our Creator who loves us ever so much. We can experience this because if you believe in him and ask him into your heart and life, he will come and live inside of you and change you from the inside out. He will give you "new life" and a taste of what heaven will be like when we will be made perfect in relationship with God once again. So don't miss this great gift. Choose today to accept Jesus and then to live in him through the help of his Spirit. It will be by far the best gift that you have ever been given, and it is one that is expected to be regifted to others as you live your life for him!

STAY CONNECTED TO THE LIGHT

The light shines through the darkness, and the darkness can never extinguish it.

1 John 1:5 (NLT)

The past month or so for me has been a time of growing in my understanding of this light or life that we have in Christ. I have had feelings of insignificance and low self-esteem and have felt like a failure for the most part. As I reflect on this now, outside of a few minor failures in my daily struggle to live a godly life, there really wasn't any significant reason for me to feel the way that I felt. My business life in the end was a success this year, my family has been incredibly blessed and is all healthy, and we've even been getting along, which is a feat in itself considering the "Italian" history of my family and conflict. God has used my wife, Paula, and me in new, exciting ways that he never has in the past, and the future of what he is doing in our lives is exciting and forthcoming! It was only yesterday that God revealed to me what was really going on in the past weeks. You see, as Christians we are being opposed! We have a real enemy here on this earth, and he will try to distract your attention, discourage you, and do anything he can to make you feel insignificant and stifle your work in the Kingdom of God. The encouraging thing that we read in the book of John is that no matter what the enemy does, if you and I as Christians stay connected to the light—that is, if we stay in relationship and communication with our Lord Jesus Christ—then there is nothing that the world can throw at us that will extinguish our light; there is nothing that the world can throw at us that will interfere with God's image shining through you and I to reach others for him! The enemy is a liar and you will have thoughts of timidity and uselessness and even failure if you are being effective for the work of the Lord. Let me encourage you today to disregard those thoughts as attempts by your enemy to discourage you in your journey to become more like Christ. Keep on striving for the goal; keep on pushing and scratching and fighting to stay connected to Christ and to live your life for him, for God is using you in a big way and has big plans for your life. The more effective that you are in reflecting his image, the more attacks that you will have on your efforts to become more like him. Always remember that Christ is King, that he has won, and the he will never let you go!

CONTACT THE AUTHOR

If this book has encouraged or challenged or inspired you at all in your journey to becoming more like Christ, please drop me a line. I would love to hear how God has used this book for his glory:

Matt Livigni
mattlivigni@bellsouth.net
www.journeybread.org